COMPUTER ARCHITECTURE:
A STRUCTURED APPROACH

A.P.I.C. Studies in Data Processing

General Editor: Fraser Duncan

A.P.I.C. Studies in Data Processing
No. 15

COMPUTER ARCHITECTURE:

A

STRUCTURED APPROACH

R. W. DORAN

Senior Computer Architect,
Amdahl Corporation,
Sunnyvale, California, USA

1979

ACADEMIC PRESS

LONDON   NEW YORK   SAN FRANCISCO

A Subsidiary of Harcourt Brace Jovanovich, Publishers

ACADEMIC PRESS INC. (LONDON) LTD.
24/28 Oval Road
London NW1

United States Edition published by
ACADEMIC PRESS INC.
111 Fifth Avenue
New York, New York 10003

British Library Cataloguing in Publication Data

Doran, R W
    Computer architecture. – (Brighton College
of Technology. *Automatic Programming Information
Centre.* Studies in data processing).
    1. Data processing
    I. Title   II. Series
    001.6′4   QA76   78–73879
    ISBN 0–12–220850–1

Printed in Great Britain by
Fletcher and Son Ltd, Norwich

Preface

This book originated from notes to accompany a course on Computer Architecture given at Massey University. At the time, the only texts available to be used for such a course were collections of papers describing many different computers or delving deeply into the logical design of one particular machine. Computer Architecture courses tend to be case studies looking at various machines at a not-too-deep level in order to find the best illustration for each topic of discussion. Such an approach is unfortunate because the student does not get to see how a computer architecture integrates the facilities it requires to accomplish a variety of purposes. However, the opposite approach of working through the complete description, usually the machine manual, of one computer leaves the student with detailed knowledge of one architecture but with no understanding of its rationale, its adequacy or the alternatives. One resolution of these two extremes is the approach taken here of discussing the principles behind computer architecture and at the same time developing a description of one example in detail.

In order to really understand a computer's architecture in detail, if you did not actually design it, you need to have access to field engineering descriptions, even logic diagrams, to make up for the lack of detail in programmer-oriented machine reference manuals—the low level documents are also a great source of clues as to the designer's real intentions. Having the computer available for student use makes the course more real and provides exercises such as examining the code produced by compilers. The choice of example computer was thus limited to those at hand, and, of those available, the largest and most modern was the Burroughs B6700.

The availability of the B6700 as an example was extremely fortunate because, at the time, it was the only general purpose computer about which one could say that it was clearly designed with its applications in mind. The B6700 is an extremely interesting, though complex, machine and, truth to tell, there would not be much point in writing a book of this nature without a machine like the B6700 to describe. The B6700 can serve as an example of one solution to many architectural problems but there are, of course, other alternative solutions. Where the alternatives are significant the approach taken here is to mention them but to not, usually, discuss them in detail and instead refer the reader to other sources. Note that the B6700 available for study was a small uniprocessor; details of the larger "reconfiguration systems" and the B7700 have been extracted solely from their reference manuals.

Every computer architecture is the concrete realization of a conceptual model of the computational process. Different computers embody quite different models which are not always easy to relate, especially in the case of the more complex, higher level computers. The main challenge when describing computers in a more general fashion than a case study is to "build" up a model that subsumes the examples being described so that they can be compared fairly and their inadequacies and strong points brought to light. In this book the first part of each chapter and section is spent in building a general model in terms of which the B6700 is then described. The model developed is definitely not that underlying the B6700 although very much based on the B6700's model (the B6700 model is described in the early papers on the machine and in Organick's monograph). One danger in developing a general model is that integration and generalization of the concepts behind different computers soon develops into research and speculation. An attempt has been made here to not go too far into the unknown although, admittedly, the model at times goes beyond what is widely accepted.

The level of this book reflects the particular mix of courses to which our students had previously been subjected. Most had looked at the detailed organization of a small computer and were also familiar with both high and low level programming. The text consequently assumes a reasonably high level of knowledge; however, there has been no hesitation in going right back to basics in order to clarify a principle. Although the level is mixed, the text should be of use to all computer professionals interested in computer architecture. The emphasis on details of the B6700/B7700 should make the book of particular interest to the users of such systems and to others who are intrigued by Burroughs' mysteries.

The Burroughs B6700/7700 has already been the subject of one monograph, that of E. I. Organick entitled "Computer System Architecture". It should be made clear that this book and Organick's are quite different in their scope. Organick's book is oriented towards the operating system of the B6700 whereas here it is the hardware architecture which is the main topic. Of course there is some overlap where the hardware which supports the operating system is described, but even then the approach taken here is one of the B6700 illustrating more general principles rather than being described solely for its own sake.

I would like to thank those who, directly or indirectly, assisted in this book's development. In particular; the students at Massey University who suffered through the courses where the book's material was gradually made intelligible; colleagues in the Computer Science Department, especially Mr L. K. Thomas; the Massey University Computer Unit, Professor G. Tate director, for providing access to their B6700; Burroughs Corporation (New Zealand) for allowing me to peruse detailed B6700 documentation; for assistance in reviewing—Dr H. C. Johnston, Professor C. A. R. Hoare and Mr R. D. Merrell; Mrs Verna Mullin for a sterling job of typing; finally, my wife and family for their patience and encouragement.

Palo Alto   R. W. DORAN
January 1979

Contents

I. The General Purpose Computer

Modern general purpose computer systems have become so complex that they are beyond the understanding of any one person. Although overall comprehension is impractical, it is still possible to come to grips with a computer at its architectural level. A computer's architecture is the interface between the designers of its hardware and software and is, after all, specifically intended to be fully understood by both teams of engineers. Unfortunately, the documentation provided with most systems does not facilitate understanding because, while it is exhaustive in detail, it is purely descriptive and lacking in rationale. It is the intention here to take one particular example computer and to set the matter to rights by describing it in such a manner that the reader can reach an understanding of what the computer's architecture is and why it is like it is.

As each successive aspect of the computer is described, we need, at the same time, to develop a model of what any general purpose computer is trying to accomplish in such circumstances. Before we can begin, we need, then, to have a feeling for what a computer is doing overall; indeed, to understand just what a computer *is*. In this introduction we will set the context for the later description by discussing just what "general purpose computer" means nowadays.

The epithet "general purpose" applied to computers has become so common that it is almost used automatically. However, here it is used with purpose and with a meaning which will be precisely defined. In fact, "general purpose" means different things to different people, but its imprecision appears slight when compared to the meanings associated with "computer" itself.

The most widely held concept of what a computer is has not remained constant but has changed over the years. Sometimes a change of viewpoint has come suddenly, as with the celebrated erratum for a computer manual in 1957—"Wherever the term 'computer' or 'digital computer' appears throughout the text, replace it by the term 'Data Processor'." [1]. Usually, however, the changes are gradual and concepts merge into one another, it being quite reasonable to consider computers from more than one viewpoint at the same time. However, when changes of viewpoint do occur there is a significant resulting impact on computer architecture itself. This is because a new aspect of the computer system assumes dominance and a major alteration to the system in order to make it fit in with the new view does not appear quite so radical or unreasonable as it may have done from the old viewpoint.

Computers as seen by users and as seen from an overall systems viewpoint present different appearances. In the following two sections we will consider first the user's view and then the modern system view. After this discussion of principle the last section of the chapter will consider the practical matter of the computer that we are going to discuss in detail.

I.1.   THE USER'S VIEWPOINT

Although the total image of what a computer should be is compounded from the views seen by a whole range of users, there are cases where the view of one group of users is the dominant concept behind the computer's architecture. In these cases the computer is designed as if it were to be used permanently for the one particular purpose. Other applications may be recognized but these are accommodated by slight modifications or extensions rather than by a radical alteration of the architecture. We will consider below a number of these views that can be clearly isolated. They are, for emphasis, expressed in an extreme form, although few people would hold such singleminded opinions.

I.1.1.   THE CALCULATOR

The oldest view of a computer is that it is a device for performing any numerical calculation; indeed, the term *computer* or *computor* was applied originally to any human calculator. Babbage's proposed analytic engine was designed specifically to perform arithmetic and it appears that Babbage knew that his machine could be programmed to perform *any* numerical task [2]. Most of the early model computer designs were also made from this viewpoint as is shown in the following extracts from the seminal 1946 report of Burks, Goldstine and von Neumann, which described a device which was to be the paradigm of the computer for many years and has come to be called the "von Neumann machine"[3]:

"In as much as the completed device will be a general purpose computing machine it should contain main organs relating to arithmetic, memory storage, control and connection with the human operator.

"In as much as the device is to be a computing machine there must be an arithmetic organ in it which can perform certain of the elementary arithmetic operations".

The above quotations introduce and effectively define the term "general purpose" as applied to computers, clearly assigning it the meaning of numerical calculator. This interpretation is confirmed by other early writings.

The first American computers had their origins in projects requiring vast amounts of calculation where the idea of a computer as a calculator was most natural. Nowadays most computers are used for commercial applications and computing professionals no longer consider their general purpose computers to be primarily calculating machines. There are computers designed for that purpose, such as great array processors like Illiac IV and small pocket computers more usually called programmable calculators, but these are considered to be very special purpose machines. Outside of the computing field, however, the public still has the simple view of a computer as a calculator.

Although we no longer think of a computer as primarily a calculator, this view still has the most profound influence on computer architecture. The majority of modern computers have been designed as if they were to be used as calculators, though it is recognized, implicit in the term "non-numeric computation", that some calculations will involve other than numbers. That this is true can be seen by inspecting manuals describing a computer to low level programmers. The important part of the machine is the central processor, other devices such as those for input and output are complications of detail and are left to the later chapters of the manual. The machine is defined by what the central processor can do.

Within the central processor of a computer-as-calculator each instruction is regarded as performing one complete step in a calculation. Each instruction is independent of others in the machine's repertoire and its effect is a meaningful, complete operation. There are many styles of instruction set possible (e.g. 1,2,3 or 4 addresses) but the format of the instruction always includes a unique operation code which defines the operation to be performed. Thus, apart from some preliminary details of the processor's organization, the description of the processor takes on the form of a list of instructions, giving for each its operation code and a description of what it does. Although, over the years, computers based on this line of reasoning have been augmented with special devices in order to make them more effective, the closed instruction form has remained in most machines and even the few that have not been designed from the calculator viewpoint are for the most part still described as if they were.

I.1.2. THE UNIVERSAL MACHINE

Although the development and production of modern computers has been in the main an American activity, many of the fundamental ideas of computer science have arisen outside the United States. Britain has been a major source of innovative ideas in computer architecture—after all, the whole subject was started by Babbage and the first modern computers to actually work were at Manchester and Cambridge. In modern times, perhaps the most important and definitely the most creative thinker in the computing field was the British mathematician A. M. Turing. In a paper published in 1946 Turing explored the limits of computation by defining and investigating the properties of a class of abstract machines which have now come to be called "Turing machines". Turing showed that it was possible to define a *universal* machine which could simulate the behavior of any other machine, i.e. a single universal machine could be constructed which could perform any mechanical algorithm.

Soon after the first modern computers were placed in operation it became accepted in the computing community that these machines were, in fact, universal. This is demonstrated by such names as UNIVAC (universal automatic computer) and DEUCE (digital electronic universal calculating engine). The term "general purpose", which always implied "universal" because a machine which can perform any numerical algorithm is certainly universal, became synonymous with the more general term. Throughout the fifties and sixties "general purpose" as applied to computers meant "universal" and it still has that connotation to some people today.

As well as being a theoretical genius, Turing was extremely interested in practical computing, particularly in non-numeric applications, for he was involved in using electronic computing equipment for cryptanalysis during the Second World War. In late 1945 Turing embarked on a project to produce a computer at the British National Physical Laboratory. Turing thought of his machine, although mainly to be used for numeric calculations, as being universal right from the start. In his first proposal of 1945 he lists chess and a variety of other possible applications [4]. In the following quote from his proposal he explains in simple terms how this can be:

> "... There will positively be no internal alterations to be made even if we wish suddenly to switch from calculating to energy levels of the neon atom to the enumeration of groups of order 720. It may appear somewhat puzzling that this can be done. How can one expect a machine to do all this multitudinous variety of things? The answer is that we should consider the machine as doing something quite simple, namely carrying out orders given to it in a standard form which it is able to understand".

Turing, because of his background in theory and non-numeric data processing (i.e. his involvement with wartime cryptanalysis), took a very different approach to the design of ACE (automatic computing engine) as his machine was called. He tried to design a universal machine by implementing a very basic architecture and providing application-oriented instruction sets as collections of subroutines. Now, although there is no direct connection, because Turing's work was largely ignored, this is just the approach taken with many modern computers where there is, "underneath" the outer computer seen by the programmers, a micro-machine or inner computer, which emulates the actions of the outer machine.

The essential features of a modern inner computer and Turing's 1945 design are much the same. An inner computer is extremely special purpose, being designed specifically for the limited application of emulation. As with the von Neumann machine the emphasis is on the central processor but an inner computer is designed at a lower level. The micro-programmer of such a machine sees a group of functional units each capable of performing some operation on data. The main purpose of instructions is to move data from unit to unit so that the correct sequence of operations is carried out. Instructions are not usually complete in themselves and many may have to be executed to perform a useful step in a calculation. Often the instructions contain fields of parameter bits each of which selects one option for controlling a particular unit. At one extreme, taken by Turing in his fifth design for ACE [5], it is possible to do away with instruction operation codes altogether, an instruction being solely for moving data from a source to a destination with the units and registers connected by data buses (a scheme used in earlier calculators such as the Harvard Mk I [6]).

One unfortunate misinterpretation of "general purpose" as universal is that a general purpose computer can do any calculation *practically*. No one would state such a blunder openly but it does seem to be a prevalent attitude and is partially responsible for the continuance of the von Neumann plus index registers model of a computer. It is hard to justify altering a computer's architecture when the feature desired can always be provided by software, particularly so at the design stage where the cost of the hardware to implement the feature is known, but its worth and the cost of software implementation are not so clear.

I.1.3. THE DATA PROCESSOR

The notion that a computer is fundamentally a data processing device came with the realization that commerce was to be the largest market for computers. Computers, starting with the UNIVAC and IBM 702 in the United States, and LEO in Britain, began to be designed specifically for the automation of business accounting.

The use of computers in business followed the techniques already evolved for unit record accounting equipment. The initial emphasis in data processor design was to increase the speed of the peripheral devices at handling unit records so that the fast electronic central processors could be used efficiently. As was stated in a paper introducing the IBM 702 [7]:

> "The characteristic of the 702 that soon becomes evident is its speed, particularly the speed of its input and output".

From the data processing viewpoint the peripherals are the really important devices and the flow of data through the machine the important concept: any computation is subsidiary and somewhat incidental to the machine's main purpose. The acceptance, though not necessarily the initial impetus, for many features of input/output was a result of data processing. Immediate examples are the use of buffers, I/O completion interrupts, and, eventually independent I/O processors. The central processor was not greatly influenced at all, the instruction set being slightly extended to deal with characters and to perform decimal arithmetic. These extra features were enough, however, for manufacturers to begin to market two lines of computers, commercial and scientific, the latter featuring binary arithmetic, maybe even floating-point hardware, but omitting decimal operations.

Later, computers designed for business started to develop in their own directions. The accumulator, which was included in the first data processors (the IBM 702 had a varying length accumulator up to 510 decimal digits long!), was eventually omitted with some machines, starting with the IBM 1401, which had character-addressed memories and instructions which referred to two or more variable-length fields of characters. There are many computers currently in use which are clearly of this special data processing type but most manufacturers have replaced them with series of machines (typified by the IBM System 360) which include both the commercial and scientific features. Most of these latter series include within their instruction sets a few extra instructions to help data processing, e.g. for translation and for editing in COBOL.

An interesting sidetrack in computer architecture was provided by the extreme data processing viewpoint of a computer as a "stream machine". The processor was viewed as a device which accepts input streams of characters and manipulates these to produce a continuous stream of output. This was implemented in the "Harvest" version of the IBM Stretch computer and as one of the two modes of operation of the Burroughs B5000 [8]. The idea was summed up in the paper describing the Harvest system:

> "The streaming mode is primarily a design attitude whose aim is to select bytes from memory according to some preassigned pattern and to keep a steady stream of such selected bytes flowing through a designated process or transformation and thence back to memory".

The concept seems to have died out, perhaps because it is stretching a point too far.

I.1.4. THE ALGORITHM EXECUTOR

It is implicit in the universality of a computer that it can be used to execute a wide variety of algorithms. However, the early concepts of a computer, as we have just seen, concentrated on the implementation of the basic steps of algorithms rather than on the overall form of programs or programming languages. The influence of programs on computer architecture did start very early with the introduction of instructions to facilitate subroutine linkage (first suggested in Turing's 1945 proposal) but, as far as the main manufacturers of computers were concerned, progress came to an equally early halt. In fact, most computer architectures nowadays incorporate few concessions to programmability, presumably because computers are not designed by programmers and at the time when most of the current lines of computers were conceived (in the early sixties) the importance of software was not fully realized.

The first computer in which high level programming languages were recognized as a significant component of the hardware/software system was the Burroughs B5000 [9]. One of the B5000's modes of operation was unashamedly designed to assist in the running of Algol programs, the other, the "streaming mode" mentioned above, was intended for string and data processing, in particular to assist with COBOL and compilation in general. The B5000 could fairly be termed an "Algol" machine, although many other factors were taken into consideration in its design. The design process was outlined in a 1961 paper [10]:

"As an example, for a computer to process applications expressible in the Algol 60 language, the system model group would interpret the language, specify a hardware representation and necessary language supplements, define speed or cost objects and the 'use image' the machine is to present".

A certain clue that the designers of a computer have had programming in mind is the appearance of instructions which are not complete in themselves but must work in concert with other instructions. For example, subroutine return must be preceded by subroutine entry, and the "add" instruction of a zero address machine must be preceded by instructions setting up the operands. One may also find instructions implementing quite complicated but often used subalgorithms. However, the form of a machine language program has otherwise been little changed even in computers designed expressly for high level languages. Programs are still represented as sets of subroutines each of which is a linear list of instructions, though explicit recognition of the structure within a routine has appeared recently [11].

Programming has also had little effect on the input/output side of machines, perhaps because high level languages have not themselves converged on an accepted approach to the process. However, there have been instructions included in some computers to help with the basic operations of scanning, formating and editing involved with I/O.

The majority of changes in computer architecture which can be attributed to the influence of programming languages have thus been made to central processors. The most significant influence is that many computers have been designed to make use of stacks for arithmetic, for subroutine linkage and for data storage. In these architectures the stack is regarded usually as an addendum to a more conventional architecture, but some have gone so far as to make the stack the fundamental feature of the machine. In the latter machines the von Neumann general registers and accumulators are replaced by registers for very specific purposes associated with the stack; in fact, there is no longer much resemblance to earlier architectures at all [12].

Since the software explosion of the late sixties, it has become apparent that the cost of software is the major expense in the development of a computer system. The importance of programs and programming implies that computers in future must be modified to help make the programmer's job easy; consequently, we can expect the view of the computer as an algorithm executor to become all-pervasive. It is significant that nearly all the non-imitative, larger computer lines announced since the mid-sixties have used stacks in one form or another.

I.1.5. THE COMPUTING UTILITY

This view of a computer's function is at a higher level than the previous, and is much more the attitude of an outside user. In its most blatant form, this view holds a computer system to be a source of a mysterious computational or control power.

Computers were put to work controlling real time devices very early [13] and it was not long before such use affected computer architecture. The artifice of a program *interrupt* was introduced in the UNIVAC 1103A expressly to assist with control. As was stated in a paper describing the feature [14]:

"The way Mr. Turner intended to run his machine, and in fact does run it, the wind tunnel has first claim on the services of the UNIVAC Scientific".

Of course, simple peripheral devices need to be controlled in real time and the interrupt concept spread to computers in general. In fact, the DYSEAC computer introduced interrupts for I/O completion somewhat earlier (though not called interrupts) [15].

Timesharing, where a computer's time is divided among several different users each of whom has the impression of using a dedicated machine, naturally invokes the image of computation power being shared. Coupled with remote communications, timesharing begat the concept of a *computing utility* [16], computing power for all who can afford it on the same basis as electric power and refuse collection. The concept is now a reality, for anyone possessing a terminal can connect by telephone to a variety of remote computer centers anxious to sell their service.

As well as interrupts for real time control, the idea of a computing resource has led to many other features which assist with the implementation of advanced operating systems. Mechanisms for virtual memory and protection of one user from another are examples, though most features derive indirectly through the ideas of sharing and multiprogramming. Some unusual architectures have arisen from a singleminded emphasis on sharing; these may have a permanent place in special purpose computers but are restrictive in general. Examples are the provision of separate sets of high speed registers for the users, as a group, and the operating system in order to speed interrupt response or even separate registers for each user to facilitate switching from user to user.

I.1.6. THE DATA BANK

Here the central purpose of a computer system is seen to be to act as a repository for large amounts of data. The system can have aspects of an archive in which new information is deposited or it can be oriented towards transactions where the data base models the real world and is being constantly updated. With both types of system, the data base itself is the fundamental component; the purpose of processors is to act in attendance on the data base, to maintain its currency and to assist in its interrogation.

The implementation of data base systems is still largely in its software, developmental stage, and the data bank viewpoint has not yet had much impact on computer architecture. All data base systems, to be useful, require that quick access be obtained to any item chosen arbitrarily from the massive quantities of stored information. Most hardware innovation in the data base area has been in the development of faster, larger capacity storage peripherals. For archival storage there are tape cataloging "robots" and other devices intended to replace magnetic tape libraries. Perhaps the most interesting development has been the introduction of micro-programmed controllers for rotating storage devices, especially discs, which can be used to minimize mean access times and also to perform local searches of files.

Data base systems are gradually replacing the older style data processing systems and are, in fact, becoming the dominant application of large scale computers. Problems involved with the development of such systems have prompted extensive investigation into the nature of data and its processing. There have been many suggestions for extensions to computers to assist the data bank; for example, large associative stores. Although nothing astounding has yet materialized, data base systems, realizing as they do the full potential of the computer in a commercial environment, are so important that we can expect them to exert a significant influence in future.

I.1.7.   THE COMMUNICATIONS DEVICE

We have already discussed two views of computers which concentrate on the flow of data, the first between registers of a simple inner processor and the second through the peripherals of a data processor. The view of the computer as a communications device is the same but from a greater distance. Data is routed through the computer from remote terminals; the fact that it gets processed is again regarded as somewhat incidental. This view has caused some excitement, as expressed in the following quotation [17]:

> "During this decade, a significant process is occurring—the marriage of two important technologies: computers and communications. The history of modern technology records few events of the importance and scope of this process—two giant industries, proceeding in the past on two independent courses, are now on a path of confluence...
>
> "From one point of view, the association between computer and communication technology is a most natural and expected one. The computer is in itself a communications system, although early computers had very elementary communications among the major components".

In communication systems, computers are used for switching. They may control special purpose switching devices; for example, an electronic telephone exchange where the computer's speed and flexibility can provide a better service, or, in digital communications networks the computer itself may receive messages and retransmit them to the addressed destination. The use of computers in communications is growing rapidly, particularly in the latter of the two roles above. However, such use has not had much impact on computer architecture, perhaps because it is an application of control for which computers are already designed [18].

The effect which use of communications has had on computer architecture is much more interesting. Given that there is a need for distributed computation with some sharing of data at different sites, the form of computer system which is most economical depends on a trade off between communication costs and computer costs. If communication is expensive and small computers are cost effective compared to large computers, then the system used tends to be distributed, i.e. lots of small computers, most computation performed locally and as little communication as possible. On the other hand, if communication is cheap or large computers significantly more cost effective than small computers, then the system tends to be centralized with one large computer center communicating to relatively unintelligent terminals. For many years, the centralized systems have been predominant, but recently distributed systems have become more common. Perhaps, because hardware is becoming a smaller proportion of the cost of a complete system, we are seeing a trend towards distribution of computation which is the most natural and convenient for any particular application.

The central computer has a critical role in a centralized system. Many remote terminals are in real time communication with the central computer which must be reliable and provide an adequate level of performance, else the remote users will all be very aware of its failings. Because it is so important, the central computer site can easily gather funds to provide better service and hence computer architecture has been adapted to provide solutions to its problems. The most universal change in central computers has been the inclusion of special purpose communication processors, or "front-ends", which take the burden of real time response away from the central processor itself. Architectural features to aid reliability can also be partly ascribed to the existence of centralized systems, redundant multiprocessing being a case in point.

I.2.   THE SYSTEM VIEWPOINT

Nowadays the term "general purpose" is still applied to computers but its meaning seems to have reverted back to ordinary usage, i.e. the opposite of "special purpose". It turns out that universality is a property enjoyed by even the most simple of computers [19]. Nobody would refer to a modern 8-bit microprocessor as being general purpose, although it certainly is universal. A computer system dubbed "general purpose" is now one which is intended to meet the requirements of most significant applications, satisfying all the user viewpoints discussed in the last section.

The fact that general purpose computers are produced at all demands some explanation. A computer designed for one specific application, such as numeric computation, must be more cost effective for that application than a general purpose machine. In fact, where the market is large enough, special purpose computers are produced; for example, there are computers designed for high speed numeric computation and others for low expense fixed control applications. The computer can no longer be thought of as a single concept but rather it is now a class of related, but different, types of machine. Despite this diversity, the majority of computers are general purpose because such generality does have advantages.

The advantages to the vendor lie in substantial savings. There are economies of scale in the manufacture of more of fewer models. More importantly, there is only one line of systems software to be produced. This advantage is compounded if the same architecture can be implemented over a range of hardware of varying speeds.

For the user the main advantage of a general purpose computer is that it is unusual for an installation not to require one. Most computers are used for some numeric calculation, and some data processing, with interactive use, if available, being a welcome feature. If one computer can be used for all applications it will be preferred over the use of multiple, special purpose machines because of the lower capital and operating costs.

It is then the aim of a general purpose computer design to be reasonably suitable for all major applications, or at least for those which were known at the time of design. It was once considered that this was impractical because scientific and commercial requirements were fundamentally different, but this turned out not to be the case. Are there, in fact, any contradictions implied by different uses of a computer which make it difficult to construct a general purpose machine?

When the question is restricted to a single processor then the answer must be that there are conflicts. The most significant is that real time response to interrupts is incompatible with a processor having sophisticated and therefore time-consuming instructions. For a complicated instruction the processor may have to construct a large temporary context which is awkward to save when an interrupt occurs.

As far as the whole computer system is concerned this conflict may be overcome by the simple expedient of including more than one type of processor. This was done very early in the case of special I/O processors or channels, although these were hardwired, not programmable, machines. It is quite common now to include a mixture of three or four different kinds of processor in the same system, some very special and hardwired, others programmable.

A general purpose computer system must then deal with the problems of *multiprocessing*, i.e. multiple processors executing simultaneously. Furthermore, in order to make efficient use of the processors and to allow interactive access, the system must deal with *multiprogramming* as well, i.e. more programs being actively executed than there are processors. The modern system-wide view of a general purpose computer is that it contains many programs executing (logically at least) in parallel, some of which may involve the use of special purpose processors, possibly being hardwired.

The system-wide view of the computer requires that something must control and coordinate the execution of the various programs. This controller has come to be called the "operating system" of the computer and the accepted view of its place in the system involves a startling change of position.

Rather than regarding a computer system as processors executing programs, it is considered as an operating system which coordinates other activities and allocates system resources, peripherals, memory and *processors*. Thus the processors take on a subsidiary role, even though the operating system (partly software, partly hardware) must make use of a processor to execute its own programs!

That is, in essence, the modern view of a general purpose computer. In the rest of this book we will consider in more detail how a computer architecture may be designed to fulfil the general purpose. We will not base the discussion on the user viewpoints of the last section, but we have picked out some common, fairly self-contained aspects of the hardware, and we will devote a chapter to each topic. The topics are:

(i) Algorithms: This is perhaps the most fundamental feature of a computer—that it can execute algorithms. A general purpose computer must be able to obey a variety of programs but even a fixed purpose or hardwired device can be thought of as following an algorithm.

(ii) Data Structures: For a program to perform any useful work, it must manipulate data. We will consider here the structure of the data use in some common applications and how it is accommodated architecturally.

(iii) Operating Systems: This chapter will review the many extra features of computers required to implement operating systems, particularly to deal with multiprogramming and other parallel activities.

(iv) Input/Output: Here we will handle features required by the system for it to communicate with its environment in real time. Topics will include the I/O aspects of computers and special interactive processors.

(v) Performance: This chapter will treat, briefly, perturbations made to computer architecture in order to produce a faster design. For the most part such details need not be known by systems programmers and therefore lie outside the field of architecture proper. Sometimes, however, the presence of speed-up devices has to be known if the programmer is to extract the best possible performance from the machine.

I.3. THE BURROUGHS B6700/B7700

For the example computer which we are to discuss in detail, it was essential to choose a machine which was designed with general purpose applications clearly in mind. There have been few computers about which we can say that their uses were clearly analyzed before they were developed, though there have been more such in recent years. Of the examples we could have used, we have chosen that which is perhaps the first and in the widest use [20].

The Burroughs B6700/B7700, which we will usually abbreviate to just B6700, has had an eventful career. Its predecessor, the B5000 (announced in 1962) was the first computer to be designed specifically for higher level programming, one of the first to include significant features to assist with implementation of an operating system, and definitely the first commercial computer to introduce "unlimited" virtual memory. An upgraded machine, the B5500, was announced in 1964 and continued to be produced until 1970 when it was upgraded to the B5700. As far as raw speed was concerned the B5000 was really obsolete by the mid-sixties, but what kept it selling was its software which provided a reliable operating system with very good timesharing.

Another source, within Burroughs, of ideas for the B6700 was the B8500. This was designed in response to customer request and was based upon a military computer, the D825 [21]. In the mid-sixties the B8500 was rumored to hold the title of the largest computer in the world! If it was, then it was so in terms of its capacity rather than its speed, for it could have up to 14 processors in one system. Although it was a commercial failure, it was an important influence on Burrough's later machines, particularly with regard to inter-module connections.

The successor to the B5000 was announced as the B6500 in 1966. As well as being much faster, the architecture had been redesigned to fix some of the obvious deficiencies of the B5000. The B6500 was something completely different from other computers and some papers delivered on it aroused considerable interest. It also seems to have been somewhat visionary, making a lot of sensible decisions in areas of controversy. The B6500 was upgraded to the B6700 in 1970 and a special feature called "vector mode" was made available. There are versions of various speeds available and one restricted model, the B6748. Most of our description will refer to the full B6700 with vector mode.

The B7700 (there was also a B7500) is a high speed version of the same architecture. In essence it emulates a B6700 but uses extra features such as associative memories to speed things along (it can also have more processors). The B7700 was made operational later than the B6700 and includes a few extra features to fix some oversights in the B6700 design. We will consider the B7700 specifically in the last chapter on architecture for high performance.

The B6700/B7700 is a middle to large scale computer system, but in its breadth rather than in the speed of its circuitry. Some systems being used for data base management and transaction processing have an astounding number of devices. One large B6700 system includes the following:

     3 central processors
     3 I/O processors
     8 data communications processors
    60 disk pack drives
    35 fixed-head disk memories
     2 card readers
    10 line printers
    48 magnetic tape drives
  2000 enquiry terminals
     6 million bytes of main memory

At the other end of the scale there are perfectly viable systems with one fixed-head disk and 250K bytes of memory.

One philosophical point inherent in the B6700 is that, apart from special real time processors, one central processor is adequate for all purposes. This, while true, can make a product unattractive for marketing purposes because many users may be forced to purchase far more generality than they need. One solution to this problem is to divide the processor into subsets, a method popularized in the IBM 360 where separate commercial and scientific extensions to the instruction set could be purchased. Burroughs does the same by making "vector mode" an optional extra for the B6700 and imposing restrictions in the B6748 for the same marketing purpose.

In the succeeding chapters the approach we will take is to introduce a general model of what computers are doing and then to see how the B6700 implements that model. Other computers which illustrate features missing from the B6700 will also be used as examples. The ratio of general discussion to detail will vary from section to section depending on how well developed the general ideas are. Although there is a lot of detail, we have tried to keep discussion of the B6700 separate so that the general points may be applied to any computer.

I.4. NOTES

1. Quoted by Knuth, D. E. (1968) p. 1, apparently from an early Burroughs computer manual.
2. Babbage's contributions are discussed by Randell in Randell, B. (1973).
3. Burks, A. W., Goldstine, H. H. and von Neumann, J. (1946).
4. Turing, A. M. (1945). For a discussion of Turing's report, see Carpenter, B. E. and Doran, R. W. (1977).
5. See Wilkinson, J. H. (1975) for an account of the ACE project and Wilkinson, J. H. (1954) for a description of the Pilot ACE.
6. Aiken, H. H. and Hopper, G. M. (1946).
7. Bashe, C. J., Buchholz, W. and Rochester, N. (1954).

8   The Burroughs B5000 stream mode is described in the manual of the B5500—Burroughs (1968)
The Harvest is described in Herwitz, P. S. and Pomerere, J. H. (1960). Note that in spite of the similarity between the streaming modes of the B5500 and Harvest, the latter was intended primarily for cryptanalysis.

9. The B5500 project, and other developments at the time, are discussed in Bulman, D. M. (1977).

10. Barton, R. S. (1961).

11. Particularly in so-called "High Level Language Machines"; see the survey by Carlson, C. R. (1975).

12. For surveys of stack machines, see McKeeman, W. M. (1975) or Doran, R. W. (1975).

13. The Whirlwind project, started in 1946, developed a computer specifically for real time flight simulation. See Redmond, K. C. and Smith, I. M. (1977).

14. Mersel, J. (1956). Univac Scientific Computer was another name for the 1103A.

15. Leiner, A. C. (1954).

16. Gruenberger, F. J. (1968).

17. Bauer, W. F. (1968).

18. The Plessey System 250 is a significant and interesting exception. Cosserat, D. C. (1972).

19. In fact the ability to add 1, subtract 1 and branch conditionally on zero is enough to make a computer as universal as any other. See Minsky, M. L. (1967).

20. The ICL 2900 is the other significant example. It is discussed briefly in Doran, R. W. (1976) and Huxtable, D. H. R. and Pinkerton, J. M. M. (1977) and, in more depth, by Keedy, J. L. (1977).

21. Anderson, J. P., Hoffman, S. A., Shifman, J. and Wilkes, R. J. (1962).

II.   Algorithms

Before a general purpose computer can perform any useful task it must be given a program which specifies the algorithm to be followed. It seems appropriate, therefore, to begin our examination of computer architecture by seeing how algorithms are presented to, and executed by, computers.

Throughout this book, and particularly in this chapter, we will·use tree structures a good deal; hence, we will discuss in the first section of this chapter the general properties of such hierarchies. The succeeding sections will introduce by stages the algorithmic aspects of computer architecture. Starting with the evaluation of simple arithmetic expressions, we will develop a model of the computing process to the point where it encompasses the Algol concept of block structure. The chapter ends with a brief account of aspects of the fuzzy boundary between algorithms and, the topic of the next chapter, data structures.

II.1.   TREES AND STACKS

In the sequel, whenever we discuss the general ideas behind what a computer is doing we will try to present a hierarchical model if it is at all appropriate. We do not believe that the processes we are dealing with are, in fact, tree structured; although some are, others are clearly a great deal more complicated. Rather, the main reason we use tree structures is that we seem to find them easy to understand. As H. A. Simon puts it [1]:

"The fact, then, that many complex systems have a nearly decomposable, hierarchic structure is a major facilitating factor enabling us to understand, to describe, and even to 'see' such systems and their parts. Or perhaps the proposition should be put the other way around. If there are important systems in the world that are complex without being hierarchic, they may, to a considerable extent, escape our observation and our understanding. Analysis of their behavior would involve such detailed knowledge and calculation of the interactions of their elementary parts that it would be beyond our capacities of memory or computation".

As well as being easy to understand, tree structured models are usually a good first approximation in that they accurately represent the systems being modelled in the majority of simple situations. Take, for example, family trees. Here the basis is that the descendant lineage of one person forms a simple tree if there is no intermarriage. In large populations, if only a few generations are considered, the model will be adequate for most families. However, there will be situations where it fails badly; for example, the model does not work very

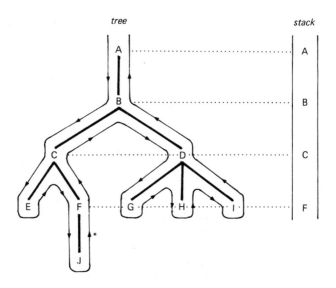

a)   Path of traversal with stack as at the point marked *

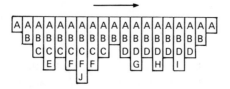

b)   Trace of stack contents during traversal

FIG. II.1. A tree and its associated stack.

well for the Egyptian dynasties where the Pharaohs married their own children and even the resulting grandchildren!

Of course, even if it is easy to understand, a model which doesn't work isn't much use. However, tree structures are so important to us that rather than embrace a more complicated model we prefer to "fiddle" the hierarchic model to make it represent reality. With family trees, for example, we show intermarriage and other unstructured events as links imposed on the tree diagram. The alternative is to represent a family as a list which indicates the relationships of each person. We find that such an alternative does not aid our understanding of the family structure and it is therefore unacceptable except as an additional reference. With computers, we can take the same course of "fiddled" tree structured model or we can, in certain cases because computer systems are "man-made", implement a pure tree structure and cause the user to modify his demands to fit in with the model.

We do not have space here to deal with the properties and representation of trees but there is one matter to get straight right from the start; that is the relationship between tree structures and *stack* structures. A stack is a data structure which is accessed in a first in/last out manner. For detailed discussion of the properties of trees and stacks we must refer the reader to established texts [2]; however, the reason for the close relationship between trees and stacks bears repeating here.

Consider as an example the tree structure of Fig. II.1(a). A computer often has to go through a tree in a systematic manner, usually from top to bottom and from left to right as indicated. While doing such a *traversal,* or in order to, it will be necessary to gather information concerning the nodes above the one currently being visited. If we trace this information in Fig. II.1(b), we will see that the item which varies at each stage is that on the bottom of the list. Hence the information could be held in a stack where the bottom entry shown in Fig. II.1(b) is the top item in the stack.

Whenever our model of what a computer is doing involves a tree structure we will find it convenient to make use of a stack and, conversely, whenever we use a stack there is a tree in the background somewhere. Sometimes, however, a stack is not adequate. Consider Fig. II.2(a) where we want to keep track of multiple activities in the same tree. In this case we need to use a multiple stack as in Fig. II.2(b). This can be regarded as a tree of stacks though sometimes it is considered to be a *cactus* stack, the origin of which name could perhaps be guessed if Fig. II.2(c) were to be covered in prickles and viewed upside down [3].

Although we will always draw trees with the trunk at the top, we will consider stacks to be the other way up. This is really a concession to convention, though we feel that upright stacks are more secure because information cannot so easily fall out of them!

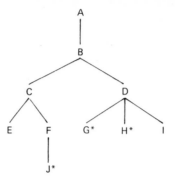

a)   Tree with three concurrent points of traversal (marked *)

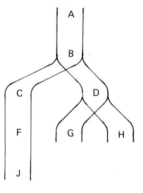

b)   The corresponding tree of stacks

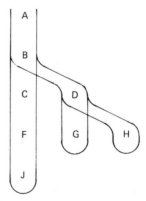

c)   The tree as a cactus

Fig. II.2. Multiple traversals of trees.

II.2.   THE ARITHMETIC STACK

An expression of mathematics or of logic has been designed to possess a tree structure with regard to the order in which operations are performed. The structure is exhibited in the expression by the use of matching pairs of parentheses or brackets and by implicit rules of associativity and priority among operators. For example, the expression $X + (Z + 6/T)^*Y$ has structure as in Fig. II.3(a).

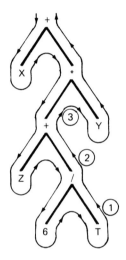

a)   Structure of the expression and its path of traversal

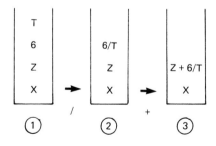

b)   Stack contents at marked points

FIG. II.3. Evaluation of expression $X + (Z + 6/T)^*Y$.

In this section we will see how stacks can be used to help evaluate expressions. After an introduction to the general model in the first subsection we will then discuss some of the practical problems involved in implementing hardware stacks for arithmetic, and, in passing, also discuss the evaluation of expressions in computers without stacks.

II.2.1.   EVALUATION OF EXPRESSIONS

In order to evaluate an expression a computer must traverse through its structure in the usual order. At each non-terminal node the computer must remember the operands so far evaluated for the operator associated with that node. Naturally, a stack may be used to hold these partial results; the stack contents at three positions in the execution of the example expression are shown in Fig. II.3(b). Note that an operator uses the top elements of the stack, as many as it has operands, and leaves its result there as well. If such operators are built into the hardware of a computer together with other instructions to place (*push*) values onto the stack, then the computer can readily evaluate any expression involving those operators.

There are many different ways of representing an expression in a machine language program, most of which have been tried at least in experimental machines. One extreme representation is to leave the expression exactly as it is, parentheses and all. In this case the computer has to "know" the priority and associativity of the operators and must determine the structure of the expression while it is being executed. The disadvantage of this approach is that the processor is somewhat more complicated than it need be for most applications.

Most systems then go to the other extreme of requiring that the structure of an expression has been determined before it is executed. An expression in a high level language has its structure evaluated when it is compiled and the computer executes a translated form in which the structure is fully evident, usually represented in the form of machine instructions which cause the computer to follow the exact order of traversal.

If we traverse through the structure of Fig. II.3(a) and represent the act of obtaining a value by writing down its name and the act of executing an operator by writing down the operator, we arrive at the following representation of the expression:

$$X \; Z \; 6 \; T \; / + Y \; * \; +$$

This form is called reverse Polish after Lukasiewicz who was its inventor (for formal logic) [4].

The simplest and most direct way of handling such representations is to use one computer instruction for each action, leaving the rest to the hardware.

TABLE II.1

Simple stack operators of the B6700.

(a) Instructions for pushing values into the stack

VALC address	— *value call*	}	*push contents of addressed location*
LT8 number	— *literal call 8 bits*		
LT16 number	— *literal call 16 bits*		
LT48 number	— *literal call 48 bits*	}	*push constants from program*
ZERO	— *literal call zero*		
ONE	— *literal call one*		

(b) Arithmetic operators

ADD	— *add*		
SUBT	— *subtract*	}	*dyadic*
MULT	— *multiply*		
DIVD	— *divide*		
CHSN	— *change sign bit*	}	*monadic*

(c) Relational operators

GRTR	— *greater than*		
GREQ	— *greater than or equal*		
EQUL	— *equal*		
LSEQ	— *less than or equal*	}	*dyadic*
LESS	— *less than*		
NEQL	— *not equal*		

(d) Logical operators

LAND	— *logical and*		
LOR	— *logical or*	}	*dyadic*
LEQV	— *logical equivalence*		
LNOT	— *logical negate*	}	*monadic*

Our example computer, the Burroughs B6700, follows this course and uses an arithmetic instruction set as in Table II.1.

In the case of the B6700 there are four groups of instruction used for expression evaluation. The first group is for fetching values to be pushed into the stack. The instruction "VALC address" (value call) pushes the contents of the addressed location into the stack. The others in this group are "literal calls" and are used for obtaining constants from the program. The operator LT48 pushes into the stack the following 48-bit word in the program, but, to save space in the program, for small constants the operators LT8 and LT16 may be used. Further savings are obtained from two special instructions ZERO and ONE which create and push into the stack two very popular constants.

The other three groups of instruction implement operators which take as operands the top elements of the stack, delete these and leave the result on top. Mostly, these have two operands, but CHSN (change sign) and LNOT (logical not) have only one operand. The three groups are: arithmetic, which operate on numbers to give numbers; relational, which operate on numbers to give logical values; and logical, which operate on logical values (true/false) to give logical values.

In the B6700 the example expression would be executed by the following piece of program:

```
VALC    X
VALC    Z
LT8     6
VALC    T
DIVD
ADD
VALC    Y
MULT
ADD
```

II.2.2.   IMPLEMENTATION OF STACKS

Most computers do not use such blissfully simple instruction sets as that of the B6700. Although this is partly due to historical circumstance, much of the blame may be laid on efficiency considerations, i.e. concern that a stack may cause a computer to be too slow or that the cost of the stack is not justified by increased performance.

The efficiency of a stack mechanism depends, of course, on how it is implemented. The most straightforward approach is to regard the stack as a fast push-down cellar-like device included in the processor. This was the approach taken in the English Electric KDF9, the first computer to implement a stack for arithmetic [5]. With a stack of this form there may not be an inefficiency as such, but the cost of the stack device may give rise to concern.

Unfortunately, for reasons based on other uses of stacks, it is not at all convenient to include a stack totally within a processor. The stack is far more useful in general if it is held in the main memory of the computer. In this case a stack may be implemented with little extra hardware, merely a register for addressing the top of the stack and the ability to move information to and from the stack as required.

Once the stack is relegated to the same memory as ordinary operands, its use may become very inefficient. The problem is that all stack operations will involve memory accesses; an addition operator, for example, requires two accesses to bring the operands to the central processor and one access to store the result back—three in all. A more conventional computer only requires one memory access to perform an addition, for it always takes one operand for an operator from a "high speed" accumulator and places the result in such a register as well.

Very few computer designers would be willing to live with such inefficiency because it is quite considerable. The example expression we have been using would require four memory references in a single accumulator machine, but 21 in a machine with a simple-minded stack (not counting instruction fetches). One computer which has a stack of this type is the PDP-11 [6] (but with the PDP-11 stack operations are just one part of a large instruction set and such operations are not the most efficient available).

There are two approaches to overcoming this inefficiency. One is to leave the instructions the same and alter the processor to make the stack operations more efficient. The other is to regard the stack as an additional aid to an ordinary computer, the stack being used only when necessary. The extreme version of the latter approach is seen in classical von Neumann machines which have no hardware stack at all.

II.2.3. STACKS IN VON NEUMANN MACHINES

Strange as it may seem, a stack is used for the evaluation of expressions even in a computer which does not implement stacks. For a stackless machine the programmer or compiler works out how large the stack will be and how it will vary, and uses a set of temporary storage locations in place of the hardware stack. In the transition from stage (1) of Table II.2 we see the stack for our example expression represented as temporary storage locations T1, T2, T3, T4, and evaluated using instructions typical of a von Neumann machine. The program to evaluate the expression is not left in such a verbose form but is optimized by a variety of tricks. The translation from (2) to (3) eliminates unnecessary temporary storage locations; (3) to (4) reverses addition which is commutative; and (4) to (5) eliminates stores followed by loads. The final result is in fact the direct translation of the equivalent expression

$$(6/T+Z)*Y+X$$

Not all expressions can be so simplified as to not require temporary storage and for an expression which does need temporary storage a hardware stack would be convenient. The MU5 and new ICL 2900 [7] both provide a type of stack which is thought of as a back-up to a conventional accumulator. In both machines the accumulator contents may be saved by being pushed into the stack at the same time as the accumulator is loaded, and the top value may be taken off the stack and used as the right operand in an operation involving the accumulator. Table II.3 compares the instructions to execute $(X - Y)/(Z - T)$

TABLE II.2

General of optimum code for an accumulator machine
(for the expression $X+(Z+6/T)*Y$).

(1)	(2)	(3)	(4)	(5)
VALC X	LD X / STO T1			
VALC Z	LD Z / STO T2			
LIT8 6	LD SIX / STO T3			
VALC T	LD T / STO T4			
DIVD	LD T3 / DIV T4 / STO T3	LD SIX / DIV T / STO T3	LD SIX / DIV T / STO T3	LD SIX / DIV T
ADD	LD T2 / ADD T3 / STO T2	LD Z / ADD T3 / STO T2	LD T3 / ADD Z / STO T2	ADD Z
VALC Y	LD Y / STO T3			
MULT	LD T2 / MPY T3 / STO T2	LD T2 / MPY Y / STO T2	LD T2 / MPY Y / STO T2	MPY Y
ADD	LD T1 / ADD T2 / STO T1	LD X / ADD T2 / STO T1	LD T2 / ADD X	ADD X

LD, *Load accumulator;* STO, *store accumulator;* ADD, *add to accumulator;* MPY, *multiplication of accumulator;* DIV, *divide into accumulator.*

for a pure stack machine, an accumulator machine and a machine of the MU5 type. Note that the MU5 approach needs special inverse instructions for non-commutative operators. The MU5 code, although requiring fewer instructions than a pure stack machine, is not as compact as it appears when the possibility of operation codes being of varying lengths is taken into account.

II.2.4.   AUTOMATIC SPEED-UP OF STACK ARITHMETIC

Many modern computers include devices called variously *cache* or *slave*

TABLE II.3

Evaluation of the expression $(X - Y)/(Z - T)$.

(1)	(2)	(3)
VALC X	LD X	LD X
VALC Y	SUB Y	SUB Y
SUBT	STO TEMP	LD Z *and stack accumulator*
VALC Z	LD Z	SUB T
VALC T	SUB T	*reverse divide the top of stack into accumulator and remove top element from stack*
SUBT	DIV TEMP	
DIVD		

(1) Pure stack machine (B6700). (2) Single accumulator von Neumann machine. (3) Machine of the MU5 type.

memories which reduce memory access time on average. These devices could also be used to improve the efficiency of transfers between stack and processor. However, the special nature of the stack allows it to be made faster by a less expensive but less general mechanism.

The Burroughs B6700 has a clever speed-up device which was first used in its predecessor, the B5000 [8]. As illustrated in Fig. II.4, the processor contains two high speed registers A and B which may be part of the stack. The main body of the stack is held in the memory, with the topmost entry pointed to by register S. Associated with registers A and B are flip/flops AROF, BROF (A,B, Register Occupied Flag) which indicate whether each register contains valid information and is considered as part of the stack.

All operations involving two operands take place between A and B registers, with the result being left in the B register and the A register marked as not valid. If A and/or B are not valid before an operation, transfers are made from the stack to fill them; however, no transfers are made after an operation is completed.

Table II.4 shows the stack transitions which take place during the execution of the code for our example, assuming that the A and B registers are initially empty. (M[S] is the contents of the memory location pointed to by the S register.) The stack mechanism requires four extra memory references for this expression. This is not optimal, for, as we have seen, no extra memory references are really necessary, but it is good compared with the 17 extra

TABLE II.4

Transitions in the B6700 stack registers while executing $X+(Z+6/T)*Y$.

	AROF	A	BROF	B	S	M[S]
(*initially*)	0	—	0	—	?	!
VALC X	1	X	0	—	?	!
VALC Z	1	Z	1	X	?	!
LT8 6	1	6	1	Z	?+1	X
VALC T	1	T	1	6	?+2	Z
DIVD	0	—	1	6/T	?+2	Z
ADD	0	—	1	Z+6/T	?+1	X
VALC Y	1	Y	1	Z+6/T	?+1	X
MULT	0	—	1	(Z+6/T)*Y	?+1	X
ADD	0	—	1	X+(Z+6/T)*Y	?	!

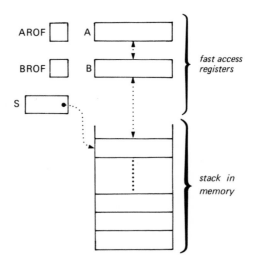

FIG. II.4. B6700 stack mechanism (simplified).

required with no special mechanism. As the average expression is even simpler than our example, the average performance of the B6700 mechanism is very good. It could be made even better by using more special registers like A and B; for example. the B7700 has 32 top of stack registers (though they are used in a different way).

Even with a speed-up mechanism, there are still opportunities to use patterns internal to expressions in order to make their execution even more efficient. Such tricks as are in common use with accumulator machines may also be adapted to stacks if there are a few extra instructions for fiddling the top items. The B6700 has some which are listed in Table II.5. With these for example $(A + B + C)/(A + B)$ could be evaluated with

$$
\begin{array}{ll}
\text{VALC} & \text{A} \\
\text{VALC} & \text{B} \\
\text{ADD} & \\
\text{DUPL} & \\
\text{VALC} & \text{C} \\
\text{ADD} & \\
\text{EXCH} & \\
\text{DIVD} &
\end{array}
$$

(Note that the last three operators of Table II.5 have very special purposes which will be explained later.)

TABLE II.5

B6700 instructions for manipulating the stack.

EXCH — *exchange (swap top two items in the stack)*

DLET — *delete (remove top of stack)*

DUPL — *duplicate (duplicate top of stack)*

RSUP — *rotate stack up* ⎫ (*interchange top three items in the stack by*
RSDN — *rotate stack down* ⎬ "*rotation*")

PUSH — *push down stack registers (push A and B through to memory)*

II.3. MACHINE LANGUAGE PROGRAMS

An expression in a programming language is, from one point of view, merely an algorithm which is used to calculate a value. The structured nature of such expression algorithms is not unique to them but carries over to algorithms in general. The formal syntactic definitions of high level languages force a tree structure on the form of each program but the flow of execution of such a program is not necessarily bound to follow the syntactic structure. One can condense much of the brouhaha about structured programming to the statement that the abstract form of a program should be tree structured as far as execution is concerned, and that the static form of a program should represent this structure. We will follow the trend by regarding programs as fundamentally tree structured and the places where a program is not so well formed will be treated as aberrations to be mapped into the tree structure. For an example of a program outline and its structure see Fig. II.5.

Once this point of view is accepted there is little point in making much

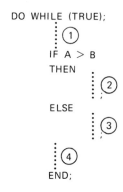

a)   Program in PL/I (outline only)

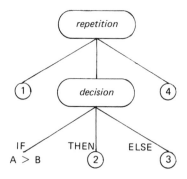

b)   Structure of algorithm

FIG. II.5. A program and its structure.

distinction between programs which represent expressions and those which represent algorithms. It is reasonable to allow any program to calculate a value, and the arithmetic stack may be used to hold partial results for any programs, not just for expressions. The main difference between expressions and algorithms, in general, is that for one of the latter a simple pass through a program is not enough to execute it. Repetitive parts of programs may need to be traversed more than once and some alternatives may not always be used. Reverse Polish notation is not enough by itself and so the structure has to be represented to the computer in a more general manner.

There are two extreme ways of representing program structure to the computer. One uses branch instructions to "flatten" the program so the execution is as linear as possible. The other represents the tree structure as much as possible. Most computers use a mixture of the two methods.

II.3.1. BRANCHING INSTRUCTIONS

In Fig. II.6(a) the program of Fig. II.5 is shown "flattened" by use of some of the B6700 branch instructions listed in Table II.6. This process is used in almost all computers and requires little comment except to note that the B6700 has only a limited set of conditional branch instructions. These are adequate because the B6700 is able to evaluate logical expressions in its stack and the branches need only test the logical value on top of the stack. The B6700 branch instructions come in two versions—ordinary where the destination address is part of the instruction, and *dynamic* where the address is the top item in the stack (the logical value in this case being next to top). Before completion, the branch instructions remove from the stack the logical value (for the dynamic instructions the address as well) because it is not required again.

TABLE II.6

B6700 branch instructions.

	Address in instruction	Address in stack (dynamic)
Branch if true	BRTR	DBTR
Branch if false	BRFL	DBFL
Branch unconditionally	BRUN	DBUN

Expressions with algorithmic components may be executed by keeping intermediate values in the expression stack. For example, b*(if m > n then e else f) may be translated as

```
          VALC    b
          VALC    m
          VALC    n
          GRTR
          BRFL    over
          VALC    e
          BRUN    out
over:     VALC    f
out:      MULT
```

The B6700 design treats assignments statements as expressions. Using the

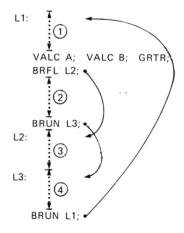

a)   Program 'flattened' using branch instructions

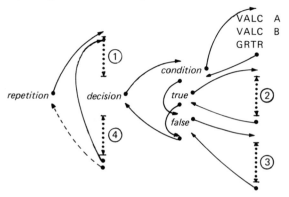

b)   Program with structure retained

Fig. II.6. Alternative representations of a program.

NAMC (name call) instruction the address of the variable which is to be "stored-into" is pushed into the stack. An expression is then evaluated to give a value on top of the stack immediately above the destination address. Then the instruction STON (store non-destructive) is executed to perform the store. At the same time, STON removes the address, leaving the expression value on the stack. The instruction STON thus takes the form of operator which uses the top two items in the stack as operands and leaves behind a value. If the value is not required then the instruction STOD (store destructive) may be used instead. To summarize with an example, a := b := c + d could be translated as:

$$
\begin{array}{ll}
\text{NAMC} & \text{a} \\
\text{NAMC} & \text{b} \\
\text{VALC} & \text{c} \\
\text{VALC} & \text{d} \\
\text{ADD} & \\
\text{STON} & \\
\text{STOD} & \\
\end{array}
$$

(See Table II.7 for a reference list of B6700 instructions used for assignment.)

TABLE II.7

B6700 storing instructions.

NAMC	— *name call (places address in stack)*
STOD	— *store destructive (also OVRD)*
STON	— *store non-destructive (also OVRN)*

An alternative method to the B6700 way of handling assignments is to use an instruction which removes the top of the stack and places it at the address specified in the instruction. This is conventionally termed a "pop" instruction in contrast to the VALC which is termed "push". The pop instruction has the advantage that the destination address does not have to be pushed into the stack (with the overheads that could cause) and it has the disadvantage that addresses in a machine language translation of a high level language assignment statement are used in a different order to the corresponding symbolic addresses in the assignment statement. It is interesting that in its special "vector mode" of operation where stack adjustments must be kept to a minimum the B6700 makes use of a pop operator (see Section III.3.2).

II.3.2.   SUBROUTINE STRUCTURE

The alternative approach to program structure is illustrated for comparison in Fig. II.6(b). Here each level of the program tree is kept to itself in ascending locations with branch instructions leading to and from subsequences (the branches shown as arrows). As such, this representation has little to commend it. However, note that, because branches returning up the tree are always to locations where the computer has been before, the upwards branch addresses could be placed in a stack and such branches could obtain their addresses from the stack. Thus, each program segment does not need, internally, any knowledge of from where it is entered [9].

It is not yet the time to make any definite statements about the best representation of machine language programs. It may be considered desirable that machine language programs have a structure similar to their high level forms but both the extremes we have introduced are removed from high level forms—the first because it is indeed "flattened" and the second because the sequence in which statements occur in the program is discarded in favor of their structure. Of course, the sequential presentation of our programs is dictated by the limitations of computer input media and it could be that some time in the future, when on-line development of structured programs at video terminals is commonplace, the second structured representation will come into favor. At present, however, the flattened form is the usual and while efficiency of execution remains important it still will be because the structured form is difficult to manage with optimizing compilers which usually grossly rearrange program structure. However, the structured representation is essential when the program is extended to include subroutines. A subroutine cannot return to a fixed address for it may be called from differing points. In fact, the most common use of a stack is to handle subroutine return addresses.

The simplest stack for this purpose would require two instructions with the effects "branch and save return address" and "branch to address on stack and remove address from stack". Most conventional computers without stacks have similar instructions which refer to a special register but this must be stacked programmatically if subroutines are to call further subroutines.

At this stage of our development a computer needs two stacks, one for return addresses and one for temporary storage. Two distinct stacks are necessary if the use of subroutines and the use of temporary storage for arithmetic are not related; indeed, some computers, e.g. the KDF9 [5], have been built with two stacks. However, when programming in a high level language it is not normally permissible to initialize a temporary storage location inside a subroutine and then use it after returning from the subroutine. This and similar restrictions are summed up by saying that the uses of subroutines and temporary storage (or expressions) are not independent but are *mutually well-nested*.

This relationship between the two stacks can impose complications. It is usual in error situations to allow a subroutine to jump to an error exit while in the middle of a calculation. As the expressions and subroutines are well-nested, unwanted temporary values must be removed from the arithmetic stack in order to return it to its form before the subroutine was called. For this to be possible, the subroutine stack entries must also contain pointers into the arithmetic stack (as illustrated in Fig. II.7(a)) as well as return addresses.

An advantage of the use of two stacks is security—there is no risk of a bad program inadvertently confusing temporary values with return addresses. If one is willing to forego this protection, or to guarantee it in other ways, it is possible to combine the two stacks together. The return addresses can be mixed in with the temporary values just as if in Fig. II.7(a) they were inserted at the locations to which they are pointing. The processor must maintain pointers to the tops of both the whole stack and the embedded subroutine stack. The latter pointer may be restored when a subroutine exits if the items of the subroutine stack are linked together, as illustrated in Fig. II.7(b).

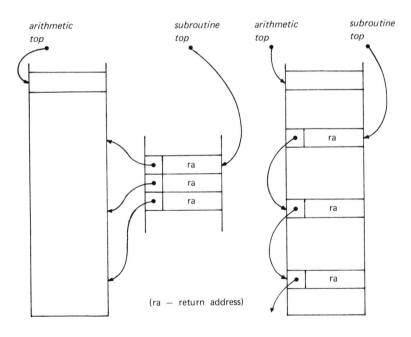

a)   Two separate stacks   b)   Two stacks in one

FIG. II.7. Stacks for both arithmetic and subroutine linkage.

Whether one or two stacks are used, function subroutines may return values by arranging that they are left on top of the arithmetic stack. There are various ways of doing this but we will not go into them here [10]. With this extension, a subroutine call may be used in any place where a push (VALC) instruction may occur.

The B6700 uses one stack for the two purposes but its mechanism is rather complicated and is closely entwined with the mechanisms for storage allocation and parameter passing. We will discuss the B6700 mechanism in the next section, but basically the process of subroutine linkage is to first place the address (in fact, usually the address of the address of the address) of the subroutine into the stack, then to execute the instruction ENTR to branch to the subroutine, with the instructions RETN (leaving a function value) or EXIT (leaving no value) being used to branch back.

II.3.3. INSTRUCTION FORMATS

There have been many different forms and lengths of instruction chosen for computers. From a general point of view there can only be one guideline— that an instruction should be as long as is necessary to encode the information it contains. This may have to be modified because of practical considerations, but there seems little doubt that instruction length and form should not be too strictly limited [11].

The B6700 instructions, for example, come in 8-bit chunks, which Burroughs terms *syllables*. The two instructions NAMC and VALC are two syllables long consisting of a 2-bit opcode and a 14-bit address. Other frequently used operators are one syllable long but forms used less often are of diverse lengths (the average instruction appears to be about 1·8 syllables long). The average instruction length is also kept low by using the same codes for different operations when the computer changes mode.

A B6700 subroutine or mainline program is an array of syllables. The machine's memory has a word structure (48 bits per word) but this is almost completely ignored within programs. The most glaring exception is the operator LT48 where the 48-bit constant has to be within the bounds of the next word.

II.4. ADDRESSING ENVIRONMENTS

In all of the example machine language programs given so far, both the operators and addresses were written symbolically. The impression may have been gained that the symbolic operators and addresses represented simple numeric fields in actual machine language instructions. For the operators that impression is correct, but for addresses the relationship between symbols and the numeric addresses of a computer's memory is not so simple. In fact, the relationship is so complicated that we must leave its full discussion to Chapter IV where we treat the topic of virtual memory.

However, at this stage we can make a start by looking at the form of addressing used to refer to objects "close" to an executing program—an addressing mechanism which is quite adequate for most single programs executing in isolation. The first three subsections below gradually introduce a model of addressing, starting with the form of addresses within a program, then showing how such addresses can be structured, first for simple programs, then for complete, very general programs. The last two sections modify the model in order to capitalize on the restrictions of block structure, the final section explaining the B6700 mechanism.

II.4.1. ENVIRONMENTS AND RELATIVE ADDRESSES

For an algorithm expressed as a high level language program it is usual to term the set of names which may be used at any point in the program the *addressing environment*. The environment, for short, normally only includes names which do not involve computation, e.g. identifiers of arrays belong to the environment whereas array elements such as $A[3 \times i + j]$ do not. The identifiers in an environment are a long way removed in form from the addresses used to refer to computer memory locations: the identifiers in the environment change as the program executes; they are symbolic, of varying lengths and not restricted in quantity, whereas the computer memory's addresses are unchanging, numeric, of fixed lengths and limited in quantity by the size of the memory. One of the most important functions performed by the combined software and hardware of a computer system is the conversion of identifiers to memory addresses and the resolution of the conflict in the ways that they are used.

In general, a program requires new variables and finishes with others in such an erratic manner that the only way of dealing with its environment is to leave identifiers symbolic in the machine language (not necessarily in the same character form but as a unique name or number not related to memory addresses). When a name is first used, the hardware or system software can set up an entry in a table in order to associate the name with a memory address. Subsequent uses of the name require that the address be found from the table. When the name is no longer used, it is removed from the table.

Eventually this may become an accepted method (it has been used in some experimental computers [12], but, at present, a fast associative table is too expensive for such a purpose). The associative table is especially hard to justify when it is considered that most programs use names in patterns which make its use unnecessary.

At the other extreme the simplest and most direct form of address to use in machine language is the absolute or real address. This form requires that all identifiers be converted to absolute addresses before a program executes. This is clearly very efficient and is quite justified in many applications, especially for a special purpose, fixed program computer. However, with multiprogramming it cannot be guaranteed that programs and data will occupy the same locations from run to run, or for that matter during a single execution. When subroutines are allowed to recurse or to be shared, the same names will need to refer to different locations.

If an object cannot be located at a fixed address before execution of a program the solution which immediately springs to mind is to alter the address as the program executes. There are many disadvantages associated with such a modification; hence, it is normal to instead make use of an *indirect* address. A fixed address is used in the instruction but the contents of the addressed location are altered to reflect the variable address. It would be a bit cumbersome if every name was treated indirectly, and, happily, this is also unnecessary. Names may often be clustered into invariant areas and the whole area accessed through one direct or *base* address. Such base addresses are selected from a special array or submemory thought of as being fast (we will use the name "D" for the array). An address generated at compile time will then be a *relative* address, consisting of a base address register number d and an offset i; the address calculated at run time being $D[d]+i$. Use of relative addressing is less efficient than use of a known absolute address, but it is not too bad if the memory D is much faster than the main memory of the computer.

For the remainder of this chapter, when we use the term *environment* we will mean the current set of in-use base registers (or their contents) because the relative address equivalents of all identifiers in the high level environment are obtained from these registers.

II.4.2. STRUCTURED ENVIRONMENTS

Some of the very first computer designs relied solely on absolute memory addresses but since then almost all larger computers have provided some registers which may be used for holding base addresses. In fact, most designs have followed the Ferranti Mk I [13] and have included index registers expressly for this purpose. Some computers have provided general registers to be used for holding both addresses and data, while others have specialized by using base registers for program addresses, index registers for data addresses and even further types. All these registers, if they indeed do contain addresses, are part of what we are now calling the environment.

The number of environment addresses which may readily be used on a particular computer is restricted by the number of index/base registers the computer provides. As this number is not infrequently small, the programmer or compiler must go to considerable trouble to ensure that environment addresses are in the correct registers when they are needed, moving addresses from main memory to the registers (and *vice versa*) as required. Some computers attempt to circumvent this problem by providing a very large number of index-type registers—hundreds in extreme cases [14]. Unfortunately, the presence of a very large set of index registers creates problems of its own. The index registers are local to a processor and whenever the processor switches from executing one program to another, or even changes its locale within one program, the index register contents must be changed (the local registers of a processor are often called its *context,* a switch like that just described being referred to as a "change of context"). Either all index registers must be swapped and the implied large overhead tolerated or some account must be taken of the way the index registers are used in order to minimize the overhead. We mentioned earlier that, in general, the environment changes very erratically, but is there some pattern which can be taken advantage of without imposition of excessive restriction?

We can again make use of our first approximation to reality and specify that environment addresses be used in a tree structured manner so that we can then organize the environment as a stack—Fig. II.8(a) illustrates a sequence of demands for storage which is so structured. Such tree structured use of storage is often implied by the structure of programs but this is not necessarily so. For example, if a program uses storage areas A and B in the sequence "want A; want B; finished with B; finished with A" then such use is definitely tree structured, but the sequence "want A; want B; finished with A; finished with B" is not so structured, although both programs could be tree structured with respect to execution. Tree structured environment sequences certainly subsume constant environments and are clearly adequate for the block structured allocation required by many high level languages (see Section II.4.4 for a discussion of block structure). Sequences which are not so structured will have to be modified, most likely by anticipating storage use, assigning environment registers before they are actually needed and keeping them active longer than is necessary.

We will from now on assume that the computers we discuss have a stack of registers to be used for relative addressing. Such computers must have instructions for placing another address on to the environment stack and for removing the top unwanted address. In a program, for the time being, we will restrict data addresses to the relative form (register number, displacement). For example, in Fig. II.8(b), the 16th item (counting from zero) from the base area C would be referred to as (1,16). (Sometimes, if a special register is assumed for a special purpose, such as the instruction counter when

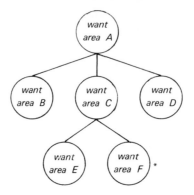

a)   Structure of changes in environment

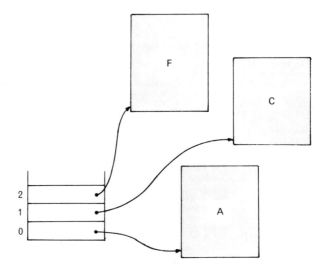

b)   Stack of base addresses at point marked *

FIG. II.8. Structured environments.

addressing within a program, then the displacement may be all that is necessary.)

II.4.3.   EXECUTION RECORDS

Although an environment stack is adequate for handling small changes in the environment, it is not, by itself, capable of dealing with the situation described earlier where a processor makes a complete change of context. Here we will see how the environment stack must be extended so that subroutines may be accommodated. In the following description we will be thinking in terms of high level languages with well developed subroutine structure; because such languages tend to call subroutines *procedures* we will switch to using the latter term.

There are some programming languages which specify that a procedure may use names from the environment from which it is called [15]. However, a procedure may be called from many different environments. Most languages therefore, especially those which are to be compiled, specify that any names which are not considered to be local to a procedure must be from the environment of where the procedure was declared or defined. This is the reason why the environmental context of a processor changes suddenly when a procedure is called or when one finishes. Figure II.9 illustrates a typical situation. The written form of the program includes the definition of two procedures P and Q at the points shown. The procedure P is called at point (1) and passes another procedure Q as a parameter. Inside P, Q is used at point (2). The environment at point (1) is shown as the central stack of Fig. II.9(b). When the transition is made to procedure P, most of what may be addressed at point (1) becomes unavailable. However, the environment stack builds up again until point (2) is reached. The transition to Q makes some items available in P not available and *vice versa*—the stack builds up until it is at point (3).

The first extension needed to deal with these context changes is to replace the simple environment stack with a cactus stack, as illustrated in Fig. II.9(b). The cactus stack in this case defines three points of traversal although only one is active (later, in Chapter IV, we will see cactus stacks that represent many traversals active simultaneously). The processor must be able to identify the environment "substack" which is being used at any time and must therefore have some mechanism for "remembering" the old stack in use before a procedure was called in order that the environment may be restored when the procedure is finished. Only the current stack is required to be held in high speed registers; this is called the "current environment display" or just *display* for short.

With the inclusion of recursion or sharing it becomes impossible to associate a constant environment with a procedure when it is declared. Figure II.10 illustrates a procedure P which is called recursively from within a procedure Q declared inside P. Note that the initial environment of Q is quite different each time it is called. We come to the conclusion that a procedure must be specified by a program which is fixed, coupled with an initial environment which may vary, before the procedure can be executed. Because the initial environment cannot be determined until the program is executed, this coupling must be created during the course of execution. We will call a

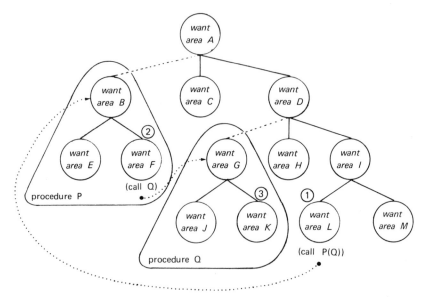

a)   Structure of storage requirements for a program with embedded procedures.

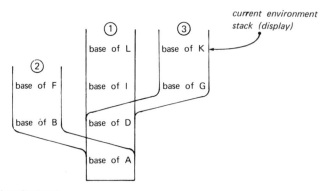

b)   Cactus stack of environments

FIG. II.9. Environments with procedures.

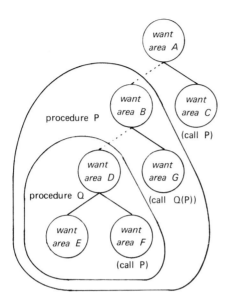

a)   Structure of storage requirements

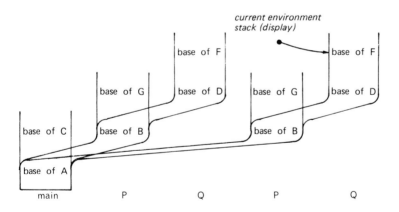

b)   Cactus stack when main program calls P — which calls Q — calls P — calls Q

FIG. II.10. Environments with a recursive procedure.

word of data which defines the procedure address and its environment a *procedure constant*.

We have now built up quite a complicated situation for executing programs. There are three stacks—two simple stacks for temporary storage and return addresses, and the cactus stack of environments. The stacks are closely related and we can extend the idea introduced in Section II.3 of including pointers into the temporary storage stack with return addresses so that the return addresses are also associated with pointers defining the environment to which each procedure returns. For the program of Fig. II.9, the total setup is as in Fig. II.11. At any point of execution the information required to enable the program to run to completion is defined to be its *execution record*—clearly the execution record is defined completely by the troika of stacks together with the context held in a processor.

A scheme for implementing procedures must also be able to deal with procedure parameters. It is necessary for a procedure to be presented with some data from the point from where it is called. This may readily be accomplished using a stack mechanism. The parameters constitute the first area to be required inside a procedure and, because the calling routine can determine the initial environment from the procedure constant, the obvious

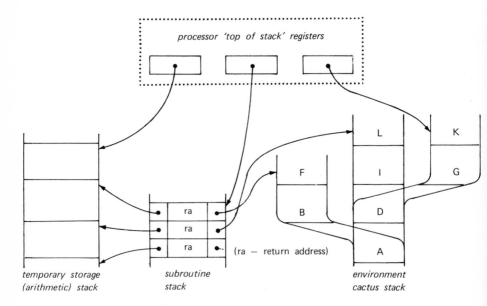

FIG. II.11. An execution record (based on Fig. II.9).

convention is to arrange for the called procedure to "find" that its next environment display register points to the location of the parameter area. We will not elaborate on such schemes at this point, as we will soon describe the B6700 mechanism [16].

One last situation to consider briefly is where an "unexpected" change is required from one point in an execution record back to some previous situation. This could be caused by, heaven forbid, a branch to a global label, or by a more sophisticated event mechanism; but, either way, it is an important facility to cater for. A stack mechanism can handle such sudden changes if the program addresses representing the destination of such a leap include similar information to a procedure constant so that the stacks can be reset when the abrupt exit is taken.

II.4.4. BLOCK STRUCTURE

Execution records of the form that we have just described are necessary for programs where the usage of temporary storage, procedures and base registers is independent. In fact, the behavior of most programs is constrained to exhibit much more regularity than we have made use of. One kind of regularity which is often imposed on programs, especially on those written in high level languages, is that of *block structure*.

Block structure, as introduced in Algol, had simplified storage allocation as its main rationale. This is not so important nowadays with computers sporting virtual memories, but block structure is nonetheless still a feature of most advanced programming languages. Without going into details as to what it actually is, block structure is equivalent, from our hardware point of view, to requiring that the three parts of the execution record are mutually *well-nested*. By this we mean that when an item is deleted from one stack the other stacks are in the same condition as when the item was first placed on the stack. A high level restriction corresponding to *well-nestedness* is that block structure would not allow entry to a procedure P, allocation of storage A, exit from P, and still have A available; rather A must be de-allocated before return from P. [17]

The advantage of block structure from the architectural standpoint is that the three stack structures may be embedded in one stack in a similar manner to the way the two stacks were combined in Section II.2.3. For example, the base addresses and return addresses of Fig. II.11 could be embedded in the temporary storage stack as shown in Fig. II.12. Only the current display is contained in high speed registers in the processor, the rest of the environment cactus stack being embedded in the execution record. (An alternative approach to that of Fig. II.12, which is used in some computers [18], is to replace the whole display stack at the location where we have placed a single register in the record, a scheme particularly designed for computers with

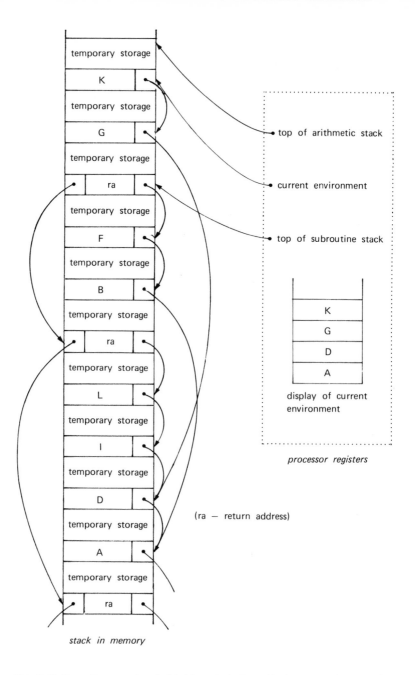

Fig. II.12. Execution record embedded in a stack (for a block structured program).

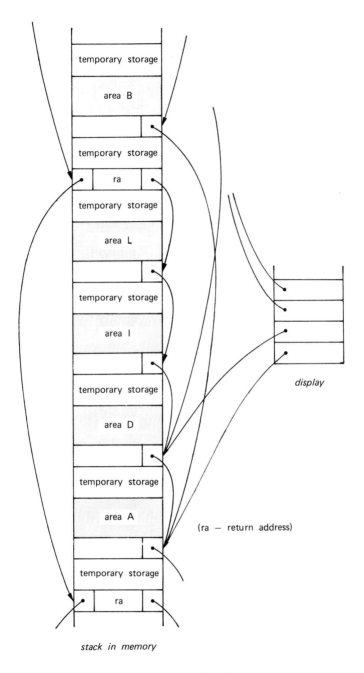

FIG. II.13. Execution record including data storage areas.

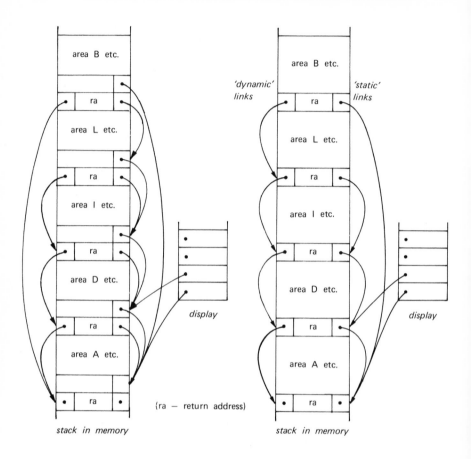

a) Stack when all blocks are procedures
    and all procedures are blocks

b) Stack with redundant links removed

FIG. II.14. Execution record with blocks and procedures combined.

instructions for moving a group of fast registers to and from main memory.)

It is possible to make further use of details of Algol block structure and impose a couple of more stringent restrictions on the stack. The first restriction is to require that storage for each block be held in the stack. The net effect of this change is shown in the transition from Fig. II.12 to Fig. II.13—note that the display now points into the execution record stack.

The second restriction goes beyond the requirements of Algol. In Algol, procedures and blocks are not strictly related; however, it makes no difference semantically if every procedure is regarded as being a block. If, further, a block is treated as a degenerate procedure called from where it is defined, the two constructs may be combined—all blocks are procedures and all procedures are blocks. The changes caused by this last restriction are shown in Fig. II.14(a) where each block is a procedure and every procedure has block storage (some temporary storage areas in Fig. II.13 are removed in the transition because no storage is required between procedure call and block entry). In Fig. II.14(b) is shown the same setup, but now simplified by the removal of redundant links. In this final stack scheme the words containing the links are called *blockmakers* or *stackmakers* and the links themselves are often referred to as *static* and *dynamic* links, static defining the storage structure and dynamic the procedure calling history [19].

This final scheme is the one essentially followed by the B6700. It is, of course, fine for Algol programs but for other languages the lack of freedom in allocating base registers is irksome. The B6700 does not require that all storage be in a stack but merely that each declared name in a program be given one stack location and other addresses calculated using in-line code. However, there are times when it would be very convenient to have address registers which point into arrays remote from the stack but such are not permitted with the restricted scheme.

II.4.5.   THE B6700 STACK

In the preceding sections we have seen how programs use base addresses and relative addresses in order to make access to their environments. The discussion went as far as the general model needed to deal with block structure and the particular restrictions used by the B6700. Now we can proceed with a discussion of the more idiosyncratic detail of the B6700 stack (the B6700 instructions for stack management are listed in Table II.8).

In the B6700 each block of a program is assigned a level number corresponding to its depth of nesting, starting from 2. Named items in each block are assigned relative addresses within the block again starting from 2. At run-time each item named is assigned a stack location and may be accessed by a relative address based on the display register of the appropriate level. Figure II.15 shows a program with its corresponding stack setup. Note that the block marker links are again spread over two words—the MSCW and RCW. The register F is used to point to the topmost of these pairs and so defines both the procedure stack and the addressing environment.

In Fig. II.15 we see that corresponding to P, which is a procedure but nonetheless a declared name, there is a stack location. This corresponds to, as we promised earlier, the procedure constant which should contain both the

TABLE II.8
B6700 subroutine and block structure instructions.

MPCW— *make program control word (LT48 but with tag set to 111)*

MKST — *mark stack (creates MSCW on top of stack)*

ENTR — *enter into procedure*

RETN — *return (leaves value on stack)*

EXIT — *exit (return from procedure with no value)*

IMKS — *insert mark stack*

STFF — *stuff environment (converts IRW to SIRW)*

PUSH — *push (top of stack registers into memory)*

---

address and the pointer to the initial environment in which the procedure should run. With the B6700 this location contains instead a *program control word* (PCW), which is the address (of the address) of the start of the procedure. A pointer to the environment is available, however, from the block marker below the PCW and this may be obtained while the address of the PCW (2,3 in this case) is evaluated. (The unfortunate side effect of this is that a PCW, once created, must always stay where it is if it is to be meaningful; hence procedure variables are not directly catered for.) To create a PCW on the stack the instruction MPCW (make PCW) is used.

The protocol for entering a procedure (or a block) is as follows:

1. Execute the operator MKST (mark stack) which places into the stack the first word of the block marker, an MSCW (mark stack control word). The MSCW is the link word; when created by MKST it contains a self-relative link to the old F register setting and the F register is set to point to it, i.e. the dynamic link is set.

2. Push into the stack a reference to the PCW of the procedure to be entered (a reference because the PCW itself cannot be moved). There are two main forms of address—the one created by the NAMC operator is a simple address couple called an indirect reference word (IRW).

3. Push any parameters into the stack.

4. Execute the operator ENTR to transfer control to the procedure, e.g. for a procedure with two parameters the sequence used would be

MKST; NAMC; VALC; VALC; ENTR

begin
      integer i;   (2,2)
      procedure P (j,k)   (2,3)
          integer j,k; (3,2), (3,3)
              ⋮
              ⋮ ;
        ⋮
      begin
          integer m,n; (3,2), (3,3)
            ⋮
          P (m,i);
            ⋮
      end
        ⋮
end

a)   Skeleton of an Algol program

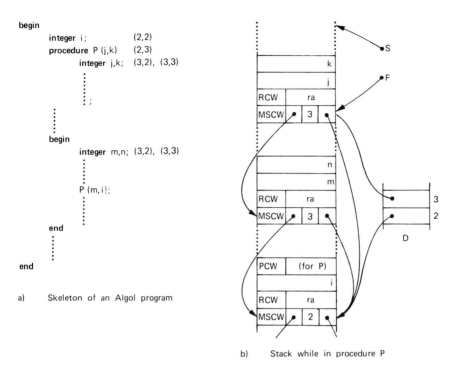

b)   Stack while in procedure P

FIG. II.15. The B6700 stack.

5. Reserve and initialize any local variables in the stack.

The action of the ENTR operator is to transfer control to the new procedure and new environment, and to update the display registers. The old environment was, in effect, saved by the MKST operator. ENTR locates the PCW and the MSCW beneath it which defines the environment of the new procedure. The unused field of the new MSCW (previously created by MKST) is set to point to the procedure's MSCW and the return address is saved in the location above the new MSCW in the form of a "return control word" (RCW). The display registers are then reset by chaining down through the MSCW's and ensuring that each display register is set correctly. This process continues until a display register is encountered which already points to the correct MSCW and which is of a lower level than the level before the procedure was called.

There are two typical stack setups encountered by ENTR. The first, illustrated in Fig. II.16, is when the procedure called has its PCW in the current environment. This could be caused by

```
A : begin
        ⋮
           procedure P(a,b,c,d);
           ⋮
    B :  begin
             ⋮
                P(x,y,x,t)
                ⋮
         end
         ⋮
    end
```

The other situation, illustrated in Fig. II.17, is where the procedure has been passed as a parameter and is therefore not in the current environment. This could be caused by

```
A : begin
          procedure Q(P); procedure P;

          Comment P is a parameter of type procedure;

                  B : begin
                         ⋮
                          P(a,b,c)
                         ⋮
                      end;
C : begin
      D : begin
                procedure R(x,y,z)
                ⋮
                 Q(R);
                ⋮
          end
      end
end
```

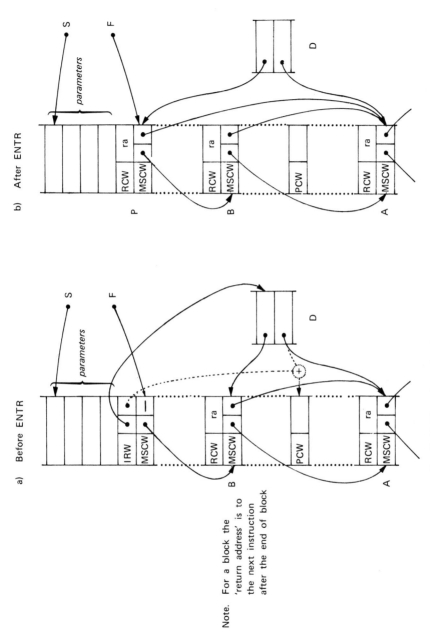

Note. For a block the 'return address' is to the next instruction after the end of block

Fig. II.16. Entry into a local procedure on the B6700.

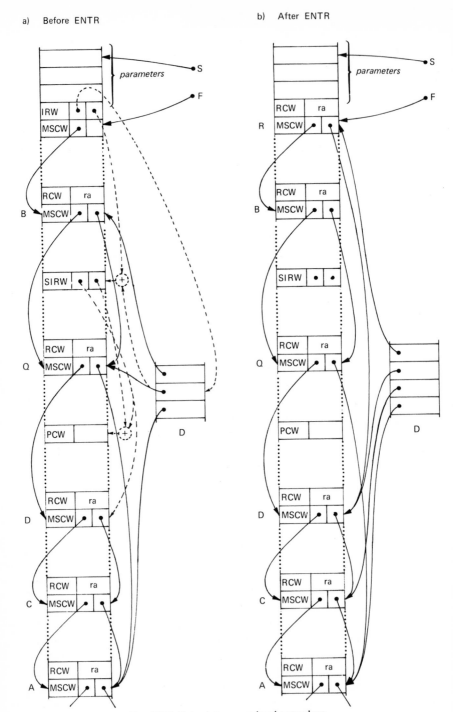

a) Before ENTR

b) After ENTR

Fig. II.17. Entry into a non-local procedure.

Here the simple address couple of an IRW is not adequate to refer to the PCW, so instead a stuffed IRW (SIRW) is used (see Fig. IV.4(a) for the format of an SIRW). This contains an "absolute" address of an MSCW plus a displacement. (An IRW on top of the stack may be turned into an SIRW by use of the operator stuff environment (STFF).)

An interesting variant of this sequence is possible by using an instruction which allows the insertion of the control words when the parameters are already in the stack (used by the hardware for interrupts). This is "insert stack marker" (IMKS) which inserts the MSCW below the top two elements in the stack; thus the following sequence equivalent to the above could be used:

$$\text{VALC;VALC;IMKS;NAMC;RSDN;ENTR}$$

There are two operators for returning from procedures, return (RETN) and exit (EXIT). Both of these use the links in the MSCW pointed to by the display register of the current level (usually also by F) to reset the stack and display registers to the situation before procedure entry. Both remove all parameters, the MSCW, and RCW, and restart execution from the address in the RCW. RETN, as opposed to EXIT, leaves the top value on the stack thereby returning a result from a function procedure.

The last operator in Table II.8 is the only one in the B6700 repertoire which refers to the physical rather than the logical stack. PUSH ensures that the contents of the high speed A and B registers are pushed through into the stack in memory. It is required in some circumstances where the hardware does not adjust the stack automatically. For example, on entry to a block the "top" two local variables could be in the A and B registers and may not be addressed until placed into the stack in memory. This is because stack addresses are not checked to ensure that they are not greater than S—the stack top pointer.

II.5. Operand-Dependent Instructions

In our discussion of computer instructions so far we have always assumed that the operands to the instructions are correct and sensible. We have not discussed what happens when the operands are not what is expected. The fact is that most computers following the von Neumann model have no way of determining that operands are what they are supposed to be; hence an instruction which receives garbage as input "unknowingly" continues to propagate rubbish as its result. However, the reader may have noticed that some instructions we have run into do take different courses of action depending on the type of their operands. Such instructions are called *operand dependent.* Most instructions exhibit operand dependence to a certain extent (e.g. ADD subtracting a negative operand) but once a computer has the capability of distinguishing between different types of data the character of its instructions alters dramatically to take advantage of the new information. One example just touched on is that instructions may take sensible action on "garbage in" situations, thus assisting in isolating software errors.

In this section we will look into the ways that operand-dependent instructions can be used, but first we must discuss how the operand types may be distinguished.

II.5.1. TAGGED MEMORY

An instruction may determine the type of its operands by examining the operands themselves or by noting how they were addressed. When we discuss data structures in Chapter III we will see that the latter method, use of the so-called *access path,* is adequate to determine the properties of most operands. However, when different types of item are directly accessed using the same base addresses, it becomes necessary to use the first method of finding the properties of an operand.

As mentioned in the introduction to this section, in the classic von Neumann machine different types of item are held in memory in the same binary representation and there is an ever present chance of an instruction unwittingly operating on the wrong type of object, e.g. another instruction rather than a number. Placing too much trust in the correctness of an operand is therefore risky and it is not surprising to find that instructions in a von Neumann machine are kept very simple. The dangers of operand incorrectness are particularly serious in a stack machine where the stack contains items of many different types, such as program constants, block markers, data, etc. If a faulty program confused these different items it would execute chaotically and be very hard to debug. It is therefore essential in a stack machine that the instructions can immediately distinguish between different types of item in the stack.

For a stack machine, items in a stack need to include information specifying their type, though the same items elsewhere may not need to include such information. This implies that either items in the stack are of a larger, different form to the same items outside the stack or that the same information is included in all items even where it is redundant. As the stack is included in the same memory as other data, the latter course is usually taken—some space is "wasted" in each word in memory. The few bits of each word which allow resolution of the type of data at the highest level are called a *tag* [20]. Every word in the computer's memory then contains the same sized tag but further parts of some words may be used to refine the classification even further (see

TABLE II.9

B6700 tag types.

Tag bits			Word type
50	49	48	
0	0	0	single precision operand
0	0	1	indirect reference word (IRW) stuffed indirect reference word (SIRW)
0	1	0	double precision operand
0	1	1	word of program code return control word (RCW) mark stack control word (MSCW) program segment descriptor
1	0	0	step index word (SIW)
1	0	1	data or array descriptor (DD)
1	1	0	used by software (uninitialized operand)
1	1	1	program control word (PCW)

(Note: 1. that bit 48 is considered the memory protect bit; 2. the hardware can also distinguish between integer and non-integer single precision operands and between IRW and SIRW stack addresses but cannot immediately distinguish among tag 3 words.)

Table II.9 for the initial part of the B6700 classification which uses a 3-bit tag).

The first proposal for tags was made by von Neumann in his 1945 design for EDVAC [21], where he used one bit in each word in order to distinguish instructions from data. Since that early beginning tagged memories have not been used very much, probably because the "waste" of space for tags is hard to justify at the engineering level. There is increasing need for their use, both for the security they provide and because, with one form of virtual memory, it is necessary for an operating system to be able to distinguish addresses from data.

When operands have tags, instructions can be made much more intelligent and begin to resemble little subroutines in the extent of what they can do. This capability has not yet been fully explored so it is not sensible to discuss it in general. Let us instead look at some of the uses the B6700 has made of tags for arithmetic. (Note that all of the B6700 instructions already discussed check the type of their operands and cause error interrupts if anything is amiss.)

II.5.2. "INTELLIGENT" ARITHMETIC

The B6700 uses tags to distinguish between data words which may be of two different sizes, single and double precision. As illustrated in Fig. II.18 a single precision operand is a floating point, octal based, binary number of length 48 bits and a double precision operand consists of two words, 96 bits in all. (The octal representation is apparently a hangover from the old B5500, as is the unused bit 47 which was the single tag bit in the B5500 where it was called a "flag" bit.)

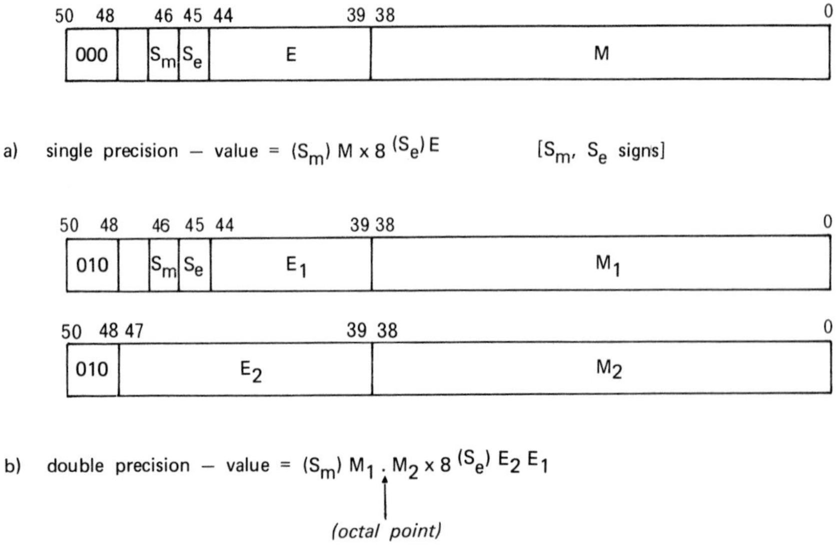

```
50   48     46 45 44         39 38                            0
 ┌──┬──┬──┬──┬──────────┬──────────────────────────────────┐
 │000│  │Sm│Se│    E     │                M                 │
 └──┴──┴──┴──┴──────────┴──────────────────────────────────┘
```

a)   single precision — value = (S_m) M x 8 $^{(S_e)}$ E   [S_m, S_e signs]

```
50   48     46 45 44         39 38                            0
 ┌──┬──┬──┬──┬──────────┬──────────────────────────────────┐
 │010│  │Sm│Se│   E1     │                M1                │
 └──┴──┴──┴──┴──────────┴──────────────────────────────────┘

50   48 47                   39 38                            0
 ┌──┬──────────────────────┬──────────────────────────────┐
 │010│         E2           │               M2             │
 └──┴──────────────────────┴──────────────────────────────┘
```

b)   double precision — value = (S_m) M$_1$. M$_2$ x 8 $^{(S_e)}$ E$_2$ E$_1$

(octal point)

FIG. II.18. B6700 number representation.

The stack mechanism of Fig. II.4 is extended to that illustrated in Fig. II.19. Each of the two top of stack registers A and B has a full word extension, X and Y respectively. The operands in A and B include tags as do words in the stack, hence the hardware automatically deals with just A or both A and X (just B or both B and Y) depending on whether the operands are single or double precision. The only difference with double precision is that two adjacent locations are used in the stack for each operand and two transfers are required to load or fetch each item.

All of the arithmetic operators discussed so far (listed in Table II.1) take

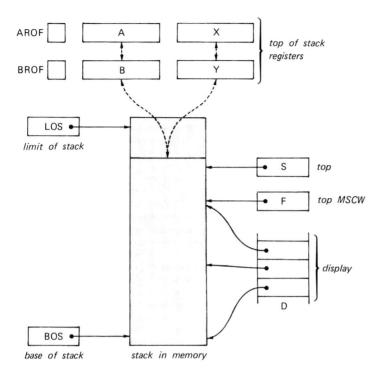

FIG. II.19. Complete B6700 stack setup (for one process).

account of the precision of their operands. The rule they use is that if one of the operands is double precision then the result will also be double precision. The store operators (STON and STOD) take note of the current contents of the location being stored into and adjust the precision of the value being stored if necessary. Thus, the B6700 has no need for different sets of instructions for different precisions as is necessary in a more simple machine which can make less use of operand dependence.

Some extra instructions are required for converting between single and double precision operands. For the B6700, these are listed in Table II.10. The instruction "extended multiply" (MULX) leaves the product of two numbers in double precision form. "Set to single precision, truncated" or "rounded" (SNGT, SNGL) convert double precision numbers to single precision (the numbers are normalized first to save significance). "Set to double precision" (XTND) upgrades a single precision operand to double precision by appending a word of zeros. The two instructions "set two singles to double" (JOIN) and "set double to two singles" (SPLT) are used for converting

TABLE II.10

B6700 double precision instructions.

MULX— *extended multiply (gives double precision result)*

SNGT — *set to single precision—truncated*

SNGL — *set to single precision—rounded*

XTND — *set to double precision*

JOIN — *set two singles to double*

SPLT — *set double to two singles*

between single and double precision when no normalizing is desired in the cases when the B6700 software may wish to regard an operand as other than a number (the top operand in the stack is exchanged with the least significant word of the double precision pair). Note that there is no instruction equivalent to LT96.

One aspect of the strange representation of numbers (Fig. II.18) is that any number which is an integer can be represented as a floating point number with a zero exponent. The B6700 uses a zero exponent to distinguish integers from other numbers so that, as in real life, the integers are a subset of the reals. As a consequence the B6700 does not need to provide a separate set of instructions for integer arithmetic. Rather, integers are treated as real numbers, and instructions (see Table II.11) are provided to convert the result to the

TABLE II.11

B6700 instructions for integer arithmetic.

IDIV — *integer divide*

RDIV — *remainder divide*

NTIA — *integerize truncated*

NTGR — *integerize rounded*

NTGD — *integerize rounded double precision*

recognizable integer form. The two instructions "integerize truncated" (NTIA) and "integerize rounded" (NTGR) convert reals to integers (and also convert any double precision operands to single precision). Because the B6700 does not normalize its operands before or after most operations, any integer calculation (apart from division) will give a recognizably integral result unless overflow occurs. Thus if i, j and k are integers, $i := j + k$ is translated as

```
VALC    j
VALC    k
ADD
NTGR
NAMC    i
STOD
```

and the NTGR instruction would normally be a null operation (its real purpose is to detect integer overflow).

The result of dividing two integers is not, in general, an integer, and even if it were the DIVD operator would not leave it with a zero exponent. If an integer result is required, the instruction "integer divide" (IDIV) must be used; this is equivalent to "DIVD;NTIA". The remainder on integer division may be obtained instead of the quotient by using the modulo operator "remainder divide" (RDIV).

The form of B6700 double precision numbers is rather unusual in that the octal point comes in the middle. This has the advantage that the first word of a normalized double precision number is also a normalized single precision number. It has the disadvantage that the largest double precision integers have an exponent of 13 rather than zero. For this reason there is a special instruction "integerize rounded double precision" (NTGD) to integerize double precision numbers (IDIV is "DIVD; NTGD" if one of the operands is double precision).

It should be pointed out here that because the B6700 hardware is able to distinguish integers from other numbers, most instructions will accept any single or double precision operand where an integer is required, the operand being integerized automatically before use. An example is the case of DBUN and other dynamic branch operators which make use of an operand in the stack representing a branch destination. The operand is converted to a single precision integer which is used as a half word address in the current program (a PCW, or a reference to one, may be used to branch to another separate program).

The reader may have noticed that, in the example of arithmetic just given, the address and the value to be stored were placed in the stack in the opposite order to that which we used previously. Because the tags for operands and addresses are different, either order is acceptable to the STOD and STON instructions. If there are no side effects the second order is preferable, for fewer items are held in the stack and fewer stack memory transfers are required. The alternative translation of $i := j + k$ is

```
NAMC    i
VALC    j
VALC    k
ADD
NTGR
STOD
```

and would require two extra transfers between the top of stack and the stack in memory than the other translation (which does not need any stack adjustments).

Although it is out of place in this section, for the sake of completeness we will discuss here the B6700 instructions which treat operands as other than numbers—the "bit manipulation" instructions. These are mainly intended for systems programming although other uses may be found for packing data into words. Other instructions which deal with bits are conditional branch operators, which only test the lower bit of the top stack word (1 true, 0 false) even if it is not a number, and the logical operators, which operate on a whole single or double precision word as a string of bits.

The bit manipulation instructions are mainly operators which map the top of stack to itself and are listed in Table II.12. The first group are of two forms, ordinary where the bit positions being dealt with are included in the instruction, and dynamic where that information is expected to be in the stack on top of the operands. The first two pairs are for setting or resetting a specific bit in the top of stack word. The "field transfer" instructions take a field from one word and place it in another. The "field inserts" are similar but always insert the right most field. The "field isolates" extract a field from the top of

TABLE II.12

B6700 bit manipulation instructions.

Ordinary	Dynamic	
BSET	DBST	*bit set*
BRST	DBRS	*bit reset*
FLTR	DFTR	*field transfer (B,A, length)*
ISOL	DISO	*field isolate (start, length)*
INSR	DINS	*field insert (start, length)*

LOG2 — *leading one test*
CBON — *count binary ones*
SAME — *logical equivalence*

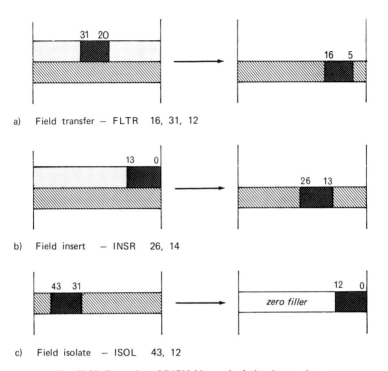

a) Field transfer — FLTR   16, 31, 12

b) Field insert   — INSR   26, 14

c) Field isolate   — ISOL   43, 12

FIG. II.20. Examples of B6700 bit manipulation instructions.

stack word. Examples of these instructions are given in Fig. II.20. (Note that bit positions are identified by number, 50 the most significant, 0 the least, and fields are given as a most significant bit position and a length.) Only bits 47–0 are affected by the bit operators except for the "isolates" which set the result tag to zeros, thus representing an operand.

There are three miscellaneous bit manipulation operators; these are "leading one test" (LOG2) which determines the position of the first set bit in an operand; "count binary ones" (CBON) which counts the number of set bits in an operand; and "logical equal" (SAME) which (as opposed to EQUL) compares the top of stack elements as bit strings.

II.6.   DATA STRUCTURES AND ALGORITHMS

In the next chapter we will be looking at the features of computers intended to facilitate the processing of data. At first glance, the subject of the structure of data would seem to be quite distinct from that of algorithms, the subject of this chapter. However, the two topics are very closely related. One aspect of this relationship we have already run into, the fact that algorithms are represented as structured programs. In fact, the relationship also goes the other way—data structures exhibit many of the properties of algorithms. In this section, serving as a cadenza linking the two subject areas, we will discuss some topics from the fuzzy boundary between data structures and algorithms.

From one extreme point of view, data structures are nothing more than sets of algorithms. As an example of why this view is at all tenable, consider a procedure P (k) which adds 1 to its parameter k. We know then that P (A[i]) should add 1 to the ith element of the data structure (array) A. However, internal to P the argument is still just k and from this inner viewpoint we are not dealing with an array but with some method or algorithm for calculating an address. This view, natural from within the procedure, can be extended to cover arrays everywhere—we could always regard A[i] as being a call on the algorithm with parameter i.

Of course, an array has many other properties besides providing access to a value; for example, it has a length, its elements are related by the order of the subscripts, and operations such as addition have extended meaning when applied to arrays. It becomes difficult to regard such properties as being inherent in the definition of the data structure type array and so, instead, the properties are embodied in the definition of the operations from which they result. Operations like addition take on the character of being "generic", i.e. they apply to different types of data and take different courses of action depending on the type. Whenever a new type of data structure is defined (explicitly or implicitly) it is necessary to extend the definitions of all applicable generic operations so that they do in fact apply correctly to the new type.

However, the operations resulting in "value" and "address of value" apply to most data structures. For such properties the opposite stance becomes reasonable, to indeed include the properties in the definition of each new data structure type. In terms of implementation the definition of each type includes procedures which are called automatically wherever a structure of that type is accessed, such invocation delivering as result a value appropriate to the operation causing the access. Such a facility is sometimes referred to as an *escape mechanism,* a term perhaps more appropriate than the corresponding B6700 *"accidental entry* to a procedure" considering that the procedure call is always quite deliberate.

II.6.1.   ESCAPE MECHANISMS

This ability to escape to a procedure when referencing data is implied by the Algol "name" procedure parameters. For example, the procedure we

just used as an example could be written in Algol as
"procedure P(k); real k; k : = k + 1;".

The interpretation of the name parameter k is given by the "copy rule"—
essentially to replace a call of the procedure by the definition of the procedure
with the actual parameter substituted for the dummy parameter. For the
above P(i) is interpreted as i : = i+1 and P(A[i]) as A[i] : = A[i]+1.
Reasonable implementations of Algol do not invoke the copy rule but insert
calls on escape procedures wherever a name parameter is used; such escape
procedures are termed *thunks* in the accepted jargon of Algol [22].

The name parameter mechanism has fallen into some disfavor because, if
used unintelligently, it is inefficient. For example, consider:

procedure place_total_in (sum);
       real sum;
       for i : = 0 step 1 until 99 do
         sum : = sum + A[i];

Here, "place_total_in (B[l,m,n])" will go through the process of calling a
procedure to calculate the address of B[l,m,n] 200 times when in fact it is constant for the whole process and need be evaluated once only. "Call by name" is
often replaced by "call by reference" to overcome this inefficiency. However,
the Algol call by name has the advantage that it does not involve the
programmer with the concept of *reference* which, as far as he is concerned, is fairly irrelevant [23]. It can be implemented more efficiently; in
the preceding example a smart compiler would know that B[l,m,n] is a constant address and treat the "name call' as "call by reference" behind the
programmer's back.

With the procedure setup introduced in Section II.4, it is very easy to
implement an efficient escape mechanism which is only invoked when
absolutely necessary. As procedure constants include references to their
environment, escape can be caused whenever a procedure constant is
encountered by the computer where some other operand was expected.
However, as procedure constants could themselves be values, an "escape
procedure constant" would be flagged as such because when encountered it
could be entered and not treated like other procedure constants.

It will be noticed that a thunk procedure is expected to provide different
results in different circumstances; in the example procedure P above which
could be translated (using B6700 mnemonics although the B6700 instructions,
as we will see, work somewhat differently to what we are now describing) as

```
NAMC    k
VALC    k
ONE
ADD
STOD
```

the thunk would have to provide an address if entered when executing NAMC and a value if entered when executing VALC. It would be desirable for the thunk in such cases to be passed a parameter (perhaps the code of the instruction invoking the thunk) telling it just what is required of it, because address and value are just two results of many which might be envisaged.

For referencing, however, the results required are all related and the expedient may be taken of returning the most general item as the result of the thunk, which is therefore parameterless. The task of obtaining the property required (address of address of value, address of value, value, etc.) must be left to the calling program. A neat expedient may be used here to eliminate unnecessary thunks and to avoid duplication of instructions. Each instruction which may cause thunks is extended to deal with chains of addresses as well as simple values. The thunk is caused to return, not to the instruction following that which caused it, but to the instruction itself which is thus re-executed and obtains the appropriate item. Re-execution must not be right from the start of the instruction, however.

As an example, the VALC operator could be extended as follows:

```
VALC address:
    top ← top+1 ; stack [top] ← M [address];
*repeat
        if stack [top] is a value then exit else
        if stack [top] is an address then
            stack [top] ← M [stack [top]] else
        if stack [top] is an escape program constant then
            enter thunk procedure else
        error
    end
```

In this case P(1) would involve VALC in just one memory reference, P(i) would take only 2. However, P(A[i]) would cause VALC to enter a procedure which would deliver the address of A[i] and return to the repeat in the above algorithm causing VALC to continue and fetch the value of A[i].

Note how important operand dependence and tags are for the efficient implementation of operators like VALC. Without tags it would be necessary to invoke an escape procedure for every reference to a name parameter regardless of whether it was really required.

II.6.2. B6700 "ACCIDENTAL ENTRY"

The B6700 VALC instruction behaves as we have just described. We gave the impression that NAMC was similar but this is, in fact, not the case, mainly because of efficiency considerations. If NAMC were to check that the location it points to does indeed contain a value and is not part of a chain of addresses, then a memory reference would be used which in the majority of cases would be unnecessary. However, the operation of storing into such an addressed location requires that the location be accessed and the contents may then be checked before they are altered (for memories of magnetic core technology a location *must* be read before being written). The B6700 thus performs thunks and "address chasing" when a location is accessed for STON or STOD. NAMC then does nothing but place the address on the stack.

Thus I : = J would be translated as:

VALC J ; NAMC I ; STOD

with any thunks being entered from the VALC or STOD. However, Algol requires that side effects caused by thunks occur in the written order. Thus provision is made for checking an address by using the operator "evaluate descriptor" (EVAL—see Table II.13), e.g. NAMC I ; EVAL ; VALC J ; STOD. In fact, the escape action using STOD and STON is seldom used by B6700 software.

TABLE II.13

B6700 address manipulation instructions.

LOAD — load (*loads top of stack with the value it addresses*)

LODT — load transparent (*load but regardless of tag*)

EVAL — evaluate descriptor (*reduces an address chain to a single reference to an operand*)

Of the four operators which may cause thunks to be executed only one, VALC, has an address. Thus, on return from a thunk, the other three, EVAL, STOD and STON, are re-executed as if for the first time—the items on top of the stack being in the correct order (STON and STOD re-arrange the order of the top elements if necessary to place the address on top). Return is not made to a VALC operator but a bit is set in the MSCW so that the RETN and EXIT operators will cause the VALC operator "micro-program" to be re-entered at the correct point.

Another peculiarity of the B6700 is caused by its PCW's not including an environment pointer. This is adequate for Algol because procedure constants usually cannot be passed around but must occur in very special places. Thus the B6700 does not need to distinguish between ordinary PCW's and those for accidental entry because they are never required to be used ambiguously. PCW's stay fixed in the location where they are created and, instead, references are created to them. Such references must be SIRW's, formed using STFF, if they are to be passed as parameters.

The B6700 is heavily Algol-oriented in its escape mechanism and it has to be admitted that other languages cause it some problems. For example, it is awkward to handle addresses as values (and therefore procedures as values) because addresses are always evaluated by VALC. Software gets around this where it is necessary by converting addresses to values by changing the tag, passing them and then converting them back again. Alternatively, address chains can be stepped through using the operator load (LOAD) which only performs one level of de-referencing.

II.7. NOTES

1. Simon, H. A. (1969).
2. Knuth, D. E. (1968).
3. "Cactus stack" is a term originating with the Burroughs B6700. See Cleary, J. C. (1969) and Hauck, E. A. and Dent, B. A. (1968).
4. Lukasiewicz, J. (1929).
5. Davis, G. M. (1960), Allmark, R. H. and Lucking, J. R. (1962).
6. Bell, G., Cady, R., McFarland, H., Delagi, B., O'Laughlin, J. and Noonan, R. (1970).
7. For the MU5 see Kilburn, T., Morris, D., Rohl, J. S. and Sumner, F. H. (1968), and Ibbett, R. N. and Capon, P. C. (1978). The ICL 2900 is based directly on the MU5 and has a similar stack organization.
8. Carlson, C. B. (1963).
9. A representation of this form is used in one of the interpreted machine languages of the Burroughs B1700—Wilner, W. T. (1974) and in some paper designs: Berkling, K. J. (1971), and Doran R. W. (1972).
10. Alternative examples are compared in Doran, R. W. (1975).
11. See Wilner, W. T. (1972) for a discussion of instruction length design.
12. Chu, Y. (1975).
13. For a discussion of the early Manchester University computers, see Lavington, S. H. (1975).
14. The Ferranti Atlas for example; see Lavington, S. H. (1978).
15. The LISP language for example; see Allen, J. (1978).
16. Such a parameter-passing scheme is developed as an example in the tutorial by Doran, R. W. (1975).
17. For a discussion of programming language block structure, see Barron, D. W. (1977).
18. As used in the MU5; see Linsey, C. H. (1971).

19. This semantic model is that introduced in Dijkstra, E. W. (1960) and developed at length in Randell, B. and Russell, L. J. (1964).
20. For a discussion of the importance of tags see Feustal, E. A. (1973).
21. von Neumann, J. (1945).
22. Ingerman, P. (1961).
23. Hoare, C. A. R. (1975).

III. Data Structures

In the preceding chapter, we noted that a data structure type is effectively defined by the algorithms which access and manipulate data specified to be of that type. Such algorithms may be implemented as machine instructions or performed by subroutines with or without the programmer's knowledge. Although the boundary between algorithms and data structures is fuzzy, a computer architecture, in a sense, draws the line between data structures which are algorithmic figments and those which actually exist, the latter being those built into the hardware of the computer. This chapter is devoted to discussion of such real, hardware-implemented data structures.

While there is no doubt that programmers need to be able to use quite sophisticated data structures directly, these may be provided by software as well as by hardware, and as this is the case, it is reasonable to question whether any data structure instructions other than the most primitive should be built into hardware at all. Such an approach is taken by most computers anyway but the question does not have such a simple answer. Rather, a decision on what to include in hardware must involve a compromise between the cost of including features to handle data structures and the performance advantage thereby obtained. An algorithm implemented as a single instruction is usually much faster than an equivalent program as it requires no memory references for instructions and is able to make use of low level parallelism, especially in checking for error conditions (such as exceeded array bounds). It may well be justified to deal with much-used structures directly if the computer's work load is such that the new instructions are used frequently enough to have a significant impact on performance.

There is a danger when incorporating an algorithm into hardware that the resulting instruction may not be adequate. It is very annoying not being able to use a sophisticated and expensive feature of your computer because it does not do quite what you want—for example, if it implements COBOL pictures yet you are using PL/I pictures which are slightly different. On the other hand, it is extremely pleasing when your computer provides just the feature that you do want. Although there are features which are fundamental and which should be incorporated in all general purpose computers, the detailed requirements of users are varied, even conflicting. What is required in order to satisfy everyone is some way of providing the effect of sophisticated instructions without fixing them inflexibly into hardware.

This is exactly the effect given by subroutines, but these, as we have noted, tend to be inefficient. What is really required is the ability for the computer to temporarily change from emulating a machine language program to executing a "micro-routine" designed to give the effect of a new instruction. This ability could be provided to the users of a machine such as the Burroughs B1700 which executes its micro-routines directly from main memory. However, it is not usual to make micro-code widely available, both because of the complexity involved in micro-programming and because the integrity of a complete system is in danger if micro-programming is not carefully controlled. However, some machines, the B6700 we shall see is an example, take a step in this direction by providing sets of special "mini-instructions", useless by themselves, but which may be combined to build up little subroutines having much the same scope as a single instruction.

Unfortunately, if such micro- or mini-routines are held in the main memory of a computer then instruction fetches are still required for their execution. As we shall see in Chapter VI, some larger computers have devices called program buffers which automatically arrange that small programs are kept local to the processor and are executed without excessive overheads in fetching instructions. For such machines then, the significant increase in performance obtained by elimination of instruction fetches for an algorithm placed into hardware no longer applies. Hence, for such machines the important goal when introducing instructions for handling data structures is to try and reduce memory references to data, an approach which, of course, also improves performance on a computer without a program buffer.

In this chapter we will investigate first what common structures are required for all general purpose computers and then go on to consider two particular types, strings and vectors, that are in such common use that special hardware for their processing is justified. We will make heavy use of the B6700 as an example, although we will attempt to keep explanation of B6700 details separated from more general discussion.

III.1. BASIC STRUCTURES

Taking the basic data items such as numbers as being atomic, what are the most important basic structures which we can build from them? The most fundamental abstract type is that of the *set*—an amorphous collection of items. Although the set is the most fundamental structure we can think of, it is not really the simplest for us because we (and computers) perceive objects as having spatial inter-relationships. In the first dimension then, the *list* is the most basic structure which computers should handle, where a list is a sequence of basic items arranged in a particular order.

Lists with no further restrictions are important data structures, and we will treat them in more depth in Section III.2. For many purposes, though, a list is too simple because it is necessary to extract any item from the list more or less at random. Most programming languages therefore implement as the basic data structure the *record,* which is a list with certain items in the list having names by which they may be identified and accessed. It is usual to immediately let the definition of a record recurse and to allow a record to be a basic component of a record, thereby making the fundamental data structure the *record structure* or tree structure. Figure III.I(a) is an example of such a basic structure which the architecture of a general purpose computer should assist in accommodating. Note that each item in the structure may be fully identified by a *compound name* e.g. "week.start-date.month" or "week. rainfall.daily.mon".

III.1.1.   ARRAY STRUCTURES AND DESCRIPTORS

Although it is possible to envisage record structures as being implemented directly in hardware, such a course is not followed in most computers because a much more special type of structure is quite adequate in the majority of circumstances.

The main restriction imposed on record structures is to change symbolic names to indices in order to fit in with the random access property of computer memories. The items in a record are considered to be placed at adjacent ascending locations so that the address of any item may be calculated by adding an *index* number onto the address of the first item in the record. Such a record is called an *array.*

Record structures can by definition contain records. To obtain the same effect for arrays, each array is fully specified by a block of information called its *descriptor*. A descriptor may be thought of as containing the base address of its array, the length of the array and other pertinent data about the array. Each descriptor occupies a fixed amount of storage space and thus can be included in an array. Record structures are then represented by *array structures,* e.g. the structure of Fig. III.1(a) is represented by Fig. III.1(b).

If an array contains different types of item then any index into the array has to be given in terms of a unit which is a factor of lengths of all types in the array. The size of the indexing unit is a property of an array rightly included in its descriptor so that the size can be taken into account when turning an index into a real address. In Fig. III.1(b) we have used items of four different lengths,

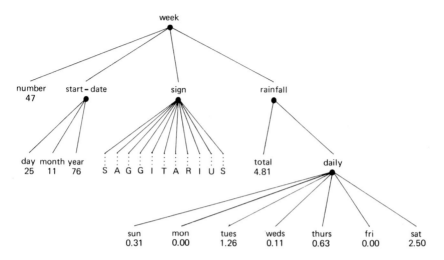

a) A record structure

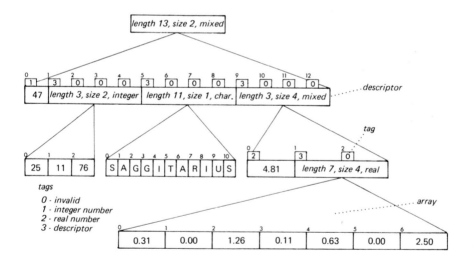

b) The corresponding array structure

FIG. III.1. Basic data structures.

characters of length one byte, integers of two bytes, real numbers of four bytes, and descriptors themselves of eight bytes. Two of the arrays contain items of two different sizes, of lengths 2 and 8 in one and 4 and 8 in the other. The indices are therefore given as multiples of 2 bytes and 4 bytes respectively.

For array structures, compound names are converted to a sequence of indices, each index standing in place of a name in the corresponding record structure. For example, "week.rainfall.daily.thurs" is "@week.9.2.4" where "@week" represents the actual address of the descriptor for the structure. If descriptors contain lengths then any such name may be checked when used in order to ensure that no array bound is exceeded.

We have been assuming since Section II.6 that each basic item of data has a tag which is used to indicate its type. Now with descriptors it is not always necessary to associate a tag with each item because common tags may be included as a property in a descriptor. When there are different types of item in an array, tags will still be necessary; however, tags are not logically "system-wide" constants but really should be defined anew in each descriptor. For example, even if there were 16 different types of basic information, a particular array might only use two of these and thus merely require 1-bit tags.

If items in an array vary in size as well as in type, then it is inadequate to attach tags to the items themselves. Rather, every item obtainable by indexing must be tagged, e.g. if items are of lengths sixes and sevens then it would be necessary to be able to tag every bit. In Fig. III.1(b), three arrays require no tag bits because one contains character only, one integers only and the other contains real numbers. Two arrays require 2-bit tags, one with tags attached to every 2-byte group, the other with tags on each 4-byte group. Note that index boundaries within an item must receive a special tag to indicate that they are invalid.

Although such a scheme as we have just illustrated is quite practical, most computers restrict the forms of array structures quite seriously, usually in order to fit in with the real memory word size. The restrictions usually take the form of requiring that:

i. the length of each basic item be a divisor or multiple of the word length;

ii. in mixed arrays, subsequences of items of different types start on word boundaries and extend over a whole number of words;

iii. tags, if they exist, are of fixed size and are associated with real words.

These restrictions are imposed in the name of efficiency; there is concern that an architectural word may stradddle a physical word boundary and thus take twice as long to access. However, the restrictions do not always have the desired effect because most computers in fact have a different physical word size to that of the architecture they implement, a submultiple in a small computer and a multiple in a large computer. If architectural words were to be of natural lengths then they would be smaller on average and multiple accesses would be necessary less often than would otherwise be expected.

Most computers do not implement descriptors but merely provide index registers to point into arrays. However, our example computer does; in fact, the concept originated with the B6700's parent, the B5000 (and independently in the work of Iliffe [1]). In the B6700, tags are of three bits attached to each real memory word and are as listed in Table II.8. In fact, apart from bit 48, the memory protect bit, they have little meaning outside the stack because descriptors are used to define the contents of arrays. As illustrated in Fig. III.2 there are two basic types of descriptor, one for programs and the other for data (note that programs and data must be kept separate in the B6700). Both types of descriptor include a base address for the array they describe and the number of items in the array. Data descriptors also include the size of the items in the array (which may be of lengths 4,6,8,48 or 96 bits) and a flag stating

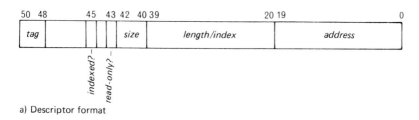

a) Descriptor format

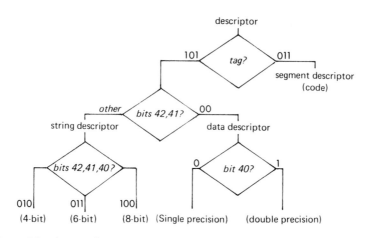

b) Types of descriptors and arrays

Fig. III.2. B6700 descriptors.

whether or not the array is protected (*read-only*). Only arrays of word (48-bits) size may include descriptors; however, descriptors may be mixed in the same array with items of other types.

III.1.2.   BASIC OPERATIONS ON ARRAY STRUCTURES

It would be nice to be able to translate a compound name such as "rainfall.daily.fri" into a similar internal name, e.g. "9.2.5", and deal with it directly. Although this is indeed possible we will have to leave discussion of such names to the next chapter because their use impinges on the topic of "virtual memory". For the moment let us gloss over the actual representation of names and assume that a name is an address. This will allow us to make some progress in describing operations on array structures.

In Chapter II we introduced the use of relative addresses which specify a base register (or display register) together with an offset to be added to the contents of the register. If access is to be made into an array, then its descriptor must be specified, usually by an address in relative form. Once the descriptor is obtained, it can be manipulated in various ways; most importantly, it may be *indexed* with an integer value to give the address of an item in the array. In the notation of the B6700, the address of A[i] could be calculated on top of the stack with:

VALC	A	*places the descriptor for A on top of the stack (warning, the B6700 VALC does not work like this, as we will see)*
VALC	i	*places the value i on top of the stack*
INDX		*operates on the top elements to give the address of A[i]*

The index operation, INDX, may be thought of as the simple addition of a value on to a base address (and so it remains in most machines), but the descriptor contains other information enabling the indexing process to be smarter than mere summation. The descriptor contains the length of the array and any indices may be checked to ensure that they do not exceed this limit. Hidden to the programmer, the INDX operator can use the size of items in the array when calculating the address. The final address is not necessarily simple as it may still contain descriptor information defining the item to which it points. Although an *indexed descriptor* is a more complex object than a simple (display, offset) address couple, the two forms of address may be used interchangeably in most situations.

If the value of an item in an array is required, it is necessary, once the address has been evaluated, to replace it with the value to which it points using a LOAD operator. Thus the value A[i] could be placed onto the stack with

VALC   A

VALC   i

```
        INDX
        LOAD
```

Now, if the addressed item is itself a descriptor, the process may be repeated, e.g. if the array A[1:4,0:2] is regarded as a structure (cf. Fig. III.6), then the value of A[j,2] may be obtained with

```
        VALC    A
        VALC    j
        ONE
        SUBT
        INDX
        LOAD
        LT8     2
        INDX
        LOAD
```

If, rather than dealing with a single element of an array, it is necessary to traverse the whole structure, then the stack may be used to contain indexed addresses giving the place where the calculation left off in much the same way as return addresses indicate where program execution had reached before a procedure call. For these indexed descriptors to be useful it must be possible to further adjust their indices. For example, using an operator "ADJ", it should be possible to form B[i + 1] by executing "B[i] ADJ 1". To ensure that such an operator cannot produce addresses lying outside the bounds of an array, each indexed address must still include all the properties of its original descriptor, especially its length and size. If this condition is met, then to set the whole array A[1:4,0:2] to zero, one could use

"VALC" A ; ZERO ; INDX ;	*create address into array of descriptors*
repeat 4 times;	
DUPL ; LOAD ; ZERO ; INDX ;	*create address into row of array A*
repeat 3 times:	
DUPL : ZERO : STOD :	*zero the array element*
LT8 1 ; ADJ ;	*form address of next element*
end;	
DLET:	
LT8 1 ; ADJ	*form address of descriptor of next row*
end;	
DLET	

(Note the ADJ at the loop's end could be included in a special instruction to terminate the loop when the array bound is exceeded.)

Another useful facility would be to allow any descriptor to be restricted so as to point to a subarray of the original. If such a restricted array could be produced then it would be a reasonable requirement that it is extendible again within the limits of the array from which it was derived. For this to be safe, a restricted descriptor would have to include all the information in the descriptor from which it was derived. As this is a recursive process some alternative mechanism is needed or we would have to allow for descriptors of infinite length. We will consider in Chapter IV a relative descriptor mechanism which has the correct effect.

The B6700 calls a halt before it gets going on this process of modifying descriptors. An indexed descriptor retains all the properties of the original with the important exception of its limit. There is, therefore, no "ADJ" type of instruction because the limit cannot be checked. The indexed descriptors are still held in the form of "base, index" (for reasons to do with virtual memory), so presumably it would be safe to "ADJ" backwards but this is not catered for. (See Section III.3.1 for the B6700's alternative mechanism.)

The functions of the B6700 INDX and LOAD instructions are essentially as described above, but their details are complicated because the B6700 VALC instruction cannot be used to bring a descriptor to the top of the stack. If this is necessary, it can be done by using the sequence NAMC; LOAD. (The LOAD operator de-references an address and is capable of dealing with both indexed descriptors and address couples (IRW's).) However, the B6700 INDX instruction expects to find the address of a descriptor on top of the stack rather than the descriptor itself. Hence, if a descriptor is to be indexed the sequence NAMC;VALC;INDX (or VALC;NAMC;INDX) is used, where NAMC specifies the address of the descriptor. INDX requires that one of the two operands on top of the stack be a numeric value, while the other operand cannot be a descriptor but may be a chain of indirect references which eventually leads to a descriptor. For the commonly used sequence INDX;LOAD the B6700 provides the extra instructions NXLN and NXLV (index and load name, value respectively) which also check that the item loaded is of the correct type (a descriptor or an operand respectively). In all the indexing instructions, wherever an integer index is required any number may be used and will be automatically rounded. (See Table III.1 for a summary of the B6700 index operators (STBR and OCRX will be discussed later).)

The reason the VALC operator cannot be used to load a descriptor is that whenever it finds one it tries to index it with the next item in the stack, e.g. if A[3,2] is required, then, rather than the seven instructions, all that is required is

LT8 2
LT8 3
VALC A

This may be viewed as a verbose way of packing the symbolic address "A.3.2." into an instruction stream without having to handle instructions of arbitrary lengths.

TABLE III.1

B6700 instructions for basic array operations.

LOAD — *load*
INDX — *index*
NXLN — *index and load name*
NXLV — *index and load value*
STBR — *step and branch*
OCRX — *occurs index*

III.2. STRINGS

The term *string* is really a synonym for list but in computers it tends to be applied to arrays in which the identification of items by indices is unimportant compared to identification by properties of and between items. Furthermore, the name string is usually restricted to refer to arrays of digits or characters. Whereas an item in an array is located by its index, a character or component of a string is specified by its matching pattern (e.g. "the first blank"). Although string processing based on patterns has been thoroughly investigated in SNOBOL, it has not yet passed through to hardware (except in paper designs [2]).

Any sophisticated string operations based on pattern matching must be very complicated if they are to avoid inefficiency. For example, an operation such as "set 'word' to the first substring in S which is surrounded by blanks" is fine by itself but is not adequate when considered in the context of other operations. For example, succeeding operations may wish to use the rest of S with or without "word" and even, possibly, the string up to the position of "word". All these substrings could be located in one operation whereas a sequence of instructions of the type above would unnecessarily repeat the same work many times. Such considerations lead to the conclusion that string operations should be capable of producing more than one result and require some mechanism for identifying a substring within a given string.

Rather than implementing sophisticated string operations, computer designers have been satisfied with providing very basic instructions from which more complex operations can be created as subroutines. Instead of implementing a method of dealing with substrings and subdescriptors provision is made for scanning through a string to find the location of the substring with the required property—usually, in fact, merely the index of a character. Such an address into a string is often termed a *pointer*.

All computers do some string processing and all therefore require some method of scanning strings. The simplest approach is to treat a string as just another array and use programmed loops to perform scanning. However, general purpose computers do a very large amount of string processing, for example, in the scanning phase of compilation and for I/O editing. It is quite reasonable, therefore, to build in some instructions to assist with these tasks. As well as for the above two uses, strings are also used to represent decimal numbers and operations are required for their manipulation. Discussion of these three topics (string scanning, editing and decimal operations) follows but it is oriented towards the B6700 as an example of the state of the art.

III.2.1.   STRING SCANNING

The B6700 descriptors contain a field which specifies the size of the data items in the array. When the unit size is 8, 6 or 4 bits, the descriptor is called a string descriptor. Most string operators of the B6700 will apply to strings composed of characters of any size though usually strings of characters of different sizes may not be mixed in one operation.

A string is defined by a pointer, which, for the B6700, is an indexed string descriptor. Because it is indexed, a pointer specifies the character size and the base address of the string but not its length. Now, pointers can be adjusted and, as there is no bound to check, an adjusted pointer could be an invalid address pointing outside the string. The system is protected from these invalid addresses by a restriction on adjustment and a system convention. Adjustment is restricted to being by a character at a time. The convention is that a special word with the tag memory protect bit set is placed at the end of each string. All operators which adjust pointers fetch each new word pointed to and check its tag, causing a "segmented array" interrupt if a boundary word is encountered. This mechanism certainly works but is very restrictive; for example, if a pointer is to be increased by 100 then each intermediate word must be fetched and checked (though this is all done by one instruction).

Pointers identify strings which need to be used as operands, hence it must be possible to store them in variables. The B6700 does not normally recognize addresses as valid values and tries to de-reference them whenever they are stored. However, the necessary exception is made for indexed string descriptors and they may, for the most part, be treated as values.

The string (and edit) operators expect that the top of the stack be set up to contain the operands. The order of operands in the top of the stack is:

i. the character scanned for (or pointer to a table);

ii. character count;

iii. source pointer (or a single or double precision operand which may be used repetitively as character data);

iv. destination pointer.

Each operator requires only as many of these operands as are applicable. The "count", which specifies how many characters are to be scanned, is usually optional if the operation can be terminated by some other condition.

The instructions, listed in Table III.2, are of two varieties. "Destructive" instructions do their thing and then completely remove the initial operands from the stack. "Update" instructions leave on the stack as results the count, destination and source, all of which have been updated to reflect the position of the scan when the operator terminated.

The first group of instructions (Table III.2(a)) performs three operations:

i. source characters may be transferred to a destination;

ii. two strings may be compared character by character;

iii. a source string may be scanned for a specific character.

All these operators may be conditioned on the truth of a character relationship, e.g. "while no character = 'X'". An example is given for a "transfer while not equal update" in Fig. III.3.

These operators may be terminated in three ways:

i. by count becoming zero;

ii. by the condition failing;

iii. by running off the end of the array.

The first two types of termination are distinguished by a flag (sometimes called a "toggle") TFFF being set for the first and reset for the second. This flag may be pushed into the stack by use of the RTFF operator of Table III.2(b). The last method of termination causes the "segmented array" interrupt; however, if the operator was "update" then the pointers are left in

TABLE III.2

B6700 string processing instructions.

(a) Instructions for scanning character strings

		while <	while ≤	while =	while ≥	while >	while ≠	uncon-ditional
destructive	transfer	TLSD	TLED	TEQD	TGED	TGTD	TNED	TUND
	compare	CLSD	CLED	CEQD	CGED	CGTD	CNED	—
	scan	SLSD	SLED	SEQD	SGED	SGTD	SNED	—
update	transfer	TLSU	TLEU	TEQU	TGEU	TGTU	TNEU	TUNU
	compare	CLSU	CLEU	CEQU	CGEU	CGTU	CNEU	—
	scan	SLSU	SLEU	SEQU	SGEU	SGTU	SNEU	—

(b) Instruction to determine type of termination of scan

RTFF — *read toggle (or true/false) flip/flop*

(c) Transfer words (between character strings)

	with protection	overwrite
destructive	TWSD	TWOD
update	TWSU	TWOU

(d) Transfer while in (or while not in) a specified set

		while true	while false
destructive	transfer	TWTD	TWFD
	scan	SWTD	SWFD
update	transfer	TWTU	TWFU
	scan	SWTU	SWFU

(e) Translate instruction
TRNS — *translate*

(f) Instruction for fetching a substring
SISO — *string isolate*

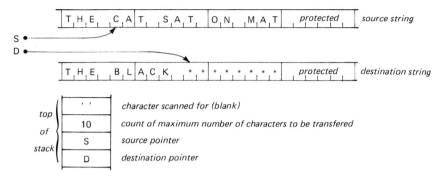

a) Before execution of TNEU

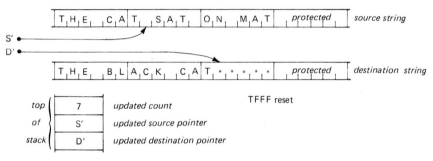

b) After execution of TNEU

FIG. III.3. Execution of an example B6700 string transfer.

the stack and the instruction may, in certain cases, be restarted (this was included for the B6700 version of paging).

Naturally it is more efficient to transfer words rather than characters and for this purpose the instructions of Table III.2(c) are provided. These may be used for any single or double precision array whether or not it is a string. The "overwrite" operators store into the destination regardless of whether its descriptor or tags indicate that it is read-only.

With the scanning operators a particular character may be found in a string, but more complicated instructions are required if the character sought is one of a class. These instructions, listed in Table III.2(d), use in place of the character operand a descriptor of a *table* which defines the class of characters being sought. The numeric value of each character being scanned is used to "index" into the table to locate a bit which indicates whether or not that character is in the class (for 4-, 6- and 8-bit characters the tables use 2^4, 2^6 or 2^8 bits respectively packed up to 32 bits per word).

Another similar instruction, TRNS (translate), is used to translate characters from one form to another. In this case the table contains characters rather than bits (the tables are of length 4, 16 or 32 words with 4 characters packed per word).

The final instruction, SISO (string isolate), is used to place a small substring (up to 24, 16 or 12 characters) on top of the stack as a single or double precision operand. A length and base pointer are the initial parameters required by SISO, which is used, for example, to fetch a computational binary number held as characters in the middle of a COBOL record.

III.2.2. STRING EDITING

String instructions like those described in the last section are complete basic operations from which more complicated routines may be constructed. However, in setting up each operation there is considerable overhead and performance would be seriously impaired if each string manipulation instruction had to be preceded by a long prolog to set up the various operands. In the B6700, with update operations, this overhead is not visible to the programmer but it is still of concern because operands have to be moved from the stack to the processor's local memory (such overheads could be eliminated by smarter hardware). In order to minimize overhead there should be some way of making a sequence of instructions work on the same source and destination strings. The descriptors of the source and destination strings could be held in the execution record in memory or could be part of the local context held by the processor. The latter approach is that taken by conventional machines which use index registers to point to strings and is also used by computers that provide micro-operators from which to build compound instructions.

Micro-operators are often used to implement the "picture" editing feature of COBOL or PL/I. For example, the IBM 1401, and later the IBM 360, used an edit instruction which processes a raw numeric string using an edit picture represented as another string [3]. The B6700 takes a different stance and regards the editing picture as itself being a program which is executed in a special *edit mode*. Although editing instructions and modes are both useful and efficient, it is perhaps questionable whether a special mechanism is required for editing rather than making editing part of a good string processing design. Leaving that question aside, let us see what the B6700 provides.

The B6700 must be in the special edit mode of operation before it can execute edit instructions. The entering of a special mode is merely a trick used to compress the size of instruction operating codes and while in edit mode conventional instruction codes are used to mean something different; hence fewer, and therefore smaller, codes are required by the whole machine. Before executing any edit instructions, their operands must be set up in the stack in the same order as for other string operations. Because the stack setup is the same, provision is made for executing any single edit instruction during ordinary string processing. In this case the edit instruction is preceded by one of the temporary mode changing operators EXSD or EXSU (execute single edit instruction, destructive or update). There is another instruction EXPU which is unusual in that it uses the one pointer as both source and destination. (See Table III.3 for edit related instructions.) For a single edit instruction the character count, if applicable, must be dynamic, i.e. in the stack not in the instruction.

It is perhaps more usual to execute a sequence of edit operations using one

TABLE III.3

B6700 edit mode instructions.

(a) Initializing edit mode

	enter table	execute single	execute single on one string
destructive	TEED	EXSD	—
update	TEEU	EXSU	EXPU

(b) Control of flags

RSTF   — reset float
ENDF(neg,pos)   — end float and insert sign if its off
SXSN   — set external sign

(c) Character transfers

MVNU count   — move numeric characters (insert zones)
MCHR count   — move characters
MINS count,ins   — move with insertion of fill character for zero
MFLT count,ins,neg,pos — move with floating sign

(d) Literal insertion

INOP   — insert overpunch
INSG neg,pos   — insert sign
INSU count,ins   — insert character unconditionally
INSC count,ins, 1,ins 2 — insert character depending on float

(e) Skip

	forward	reverse
source	SFSC	SRSC
dest.	SFDC	SRDC

(all followed by a single parameter giving the number of characters to be skipped)

(f) Ending edit mode

ENDE — end edit

of the two operators TEED and TEEU (table enter edit). In this case the operands set up in the stack include a pointer to the table (i.e. string) of edit operators. The instructions in an edit table are designed to deal with COBOL-like pictures and are executed in linear sequence, with no branches, until the instruction ENDE (end edit) is encountered. Although the execution sequence is linear, individual instructions take different courses of action depending on two flip/flops. The external sign flip/flop (EXTF) should be set before entering edit mode to reflect the sign of the number being edited—a binary operand on top of the stack can have its sign transferred to EXTF by use of the operator SXSN (set external sign—see Table III.3(b)). The other flip/flop, FLTF, controls what is called *float,* which is basically the actions involved in eliminating leading zeros from a number in character form. Float takes place when FLTF is off, and it may be placed in this condition by using the edit operator RSTF (reset float). Edit mode makes the B6700 behave rather like a finite state machine where source characters may alter the state of FLTF and thereby cause different actions.

The simple edit operators MVNU (move numeric characters) and MCHR (move characters) just move characters from the source to the destination with MVNU also adjusting zone punches in the process. Up to 256 copies of the same constant character may be inserted into the destination string by use of INSU (insert unconditional). Two further insert operators depend on the sign flip/flop EXTF. INOP (insert overpunch) modifies the destination code to make sure that an overpunch is included if EXTF is on, i.e. if the number is negative. INSG (insert sign) inserts one of two sign characters depending on EXTF. The skip operators allow characters in the source or destination string to be skipped over or rescanned.

The other edit operators make use of the float flip/flop FLTF. MINS (move with insert) will replace zeros by the insert character while float is active (i.e. while RSTF is off); however, a non-zero character will cause float to be inactivated (i.e. RSTF set on). MFLT (move with float) is similar except that a sign, depending on EXTF, will be inserted when float is ended. INSC (insert character) will insert multiple copies of one or the other character depending on whether or not float is active. That float has ended may be ensured by use of ENDF (end float) which again inserts one of two sign characters in the destination string.

Some examples of COBOL pictures, corresponding edit tables and the transformations they cause are given in Fig. III.4.

III.2.3.   DECIMAL ARITHMETIC

It may seem out of place to deal with decimal arithmetic in this section considering that binary arithmetic was discussed under the heading of

picture	edit table	examples
$***9.99CR	RSTF INSU 1,'$' MINS 3,'*' MVNU 1 INSU 1,'.' MVNU 2 INSG 'C',' ' INSG 'R',' ' ENDE	012345 → $*123.45 000001 → $***0.01 000001 → $***0.01CR (negative)
+++9.99	RSTF MFLT 3,' ','-','+' ENDF '-','+' MVNU 1 INSU 1,'.' MVNU 2 ENDE	012345 → +123.45 000001 → +0.01 002346 → -23.46 (negative)

FIG. III.4. Example B6700 edit tables.

algorithms. However, computers have traditionally allowed decimal numbers to be of varying lengths, which implies that they have to be treated as strings whether they are represented as ordinary characters or are held packed as 4-bit binary encoded decimal digits.

The reason for treating decimal numbers as variable length strings is not that such numbers are expected to be arbitrarily large. Most computers treat their binary numbers as being of fixed size and therefore impose a strict maximum which is seldom exceeded. These limits are not much more restrictive when applied to decimal numbers. Rather, the reasoning is that, for commercial applications, the values of the numbers are seldom manipulated but the numbers are most often used for display purposes when they are just strings like any other. The reason why decimal arithmetic is usually implemented directly rather than requiring conversion to a binary form is simply that the time taken to convert from decimal to binary and back is greater than the speed advantages of binary arithmetic.

Because temporary storage stacks usually deal with constant-sized data items, the variable size of decimal data has been used as an argument against stack machines [4]. Of course, this is not really a strong argument as a stack *must* be used, or simulated, to evaluate a decimal expression even if all instructions are of the two address memory/memory variety. Furthermore, although stacks do have a fixed width, which is usually the physical word size of the memory, basic data items may be of variable sizes in multiples of the width of a memory word. The B6700 double precision operands, for example, use two words. If decimal data is to be held in such a stack, it must be mapped into the word size somehow. One approach to this is to have a special packed decimal data type but in a limited range of precisions—a method used, for example, in the ICL 2900 computer where decimal data may be of three precisions, 8, 16 or 32 digits (1, 2 or 4 words). As well as extending the arithmetic unit to handle decimal numbers, this approach requires some instructions for packing 8-bit characters into 4 bits and conversely for unpacking.

The alternative to decimal arithmetic is to insist on binary arithmetic only but provide extra instructions to assist with binary/decimal conversion (if not already available) and for aligning the decimal points of binary numbers (i.e. for multiplication and division by powers of ten). The B6700 follows this second course. Conceptually, this is an unfortunate choice because the operations for converting between binary and decimal are intrinsically slower than simple operations, such as addition, executed with decimal operands. However, it is not at all clear that the choice is an unsound practical tradeoff in the case of a machine of the B6700's performance class, considering that decimal arithmetic is not necessarily the major performance inhibitor in COBOL environments. Let us now work through the B6700 decimal-related instructions listed in Table III.4.

The operators shown in Table III.4(a) for bringing decimal numbers into the stack expect to find on the stack a length and a pointer into a string. They take a decimal number of the specified length from the string (composed of 4-, 6- or 8-bit characters) and place it into the stack. The *pack* operators produce a packed decimal number (with its sign in the special toggle flip/flop TFFF) but the *input convert* operators go one step further and convert the decimal number completely to binary.

Once the number is in binary form the operators in Table III.4(b) may be used to adjust the decimal point. There is one kind of operator for scaling left, i.e. multiplying by some power of ten. The scale factor may be obtained from either the instruction or, dynamically, from the stack. If scale left operators cause overflow an interrupt does not result, rather a special overflow flip/flop is set.

Scaling right, i.e. dividing by a power of ten, is more complicated because of the question of what to do with any remainder caused by the division. In the B6700 there are four options. Both the quotient and remainder can be *saved* in the stack, or the remainder can be discarded and the quotient either *rounded* or *truncated*. The remainder is always converted back to packed decimal form; thus the last option discards the quotient and is called *final* because it is used to convert a binary number to decimal. The final scaling instructions also set the external sign flip/flop and if the quotient is not zero set the overflow flip/flop.

There are two operators for dealing with flip/flops involved in decimal arithmetic—these are listed in Table III.4(c). The overflow flip/flop may be read into the stack with the instruction ROFF (which also resets the flip/flop).

TABLE III.4

B6700 decimal instructions.

(a) Instructions for bringing decimal numbers into the stack

	pack	input convert
destructive	PACD	ICVD
update	PACU	ICVU

(b) Scaling instructions

	left	right			
		save	round	truncate	final
ordinary	SCLF	SCRS	SCRR	SCRT	SCRF
dynamic	DSLF	DSRS	DSRR	DSRT	DSRF

(c) Instructions for controlling flip/flops

ROFF — read overflow
SXSN — set external sign

(d) Instructions for transferring decimal numbers from stack to strings

	signed (from EXTF)	absolute
destructive	USND	UABD
update	USNU	UABU

The sign of the number on top of the stack may be placed in the external sign flip/flop (EXTF) by using the operator SXSN. The external sign, as we saw, is used for editing and is also required for the unpacking operators which are listed in Table III.4(d). A packed decimal number, the second operand in the stack, is placed as a string of characters at the location pointed to by the third operand. The top operand is the length of the number to be transferred. The unpacking can be absolute, i.e. regardless of sign, or the sign can be taken from the external sign flip/flop and placed as appropriate zone bits in the character string.

In Fig. III.5 is illustrated a translation of a fairly complex COBOL statement. Note that the code could be optimized by replacing the index calculations by the use of pre-calculated pointers.

III.3. VECTOR PROCESSING

Much of large scale numeric computation involves the processing of physical phenomena represented as mathematical constructs called vectors and

```
1 S.
   2 A PIC S999.99.
   2 B PIC S9.9999.
   2 C S999.999.
```

a) Cobol structure

```
ADD A,B GIVING C ROUNDED
```

b) Cobol statement

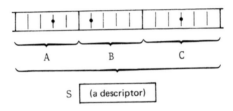

c) Storage layout for structure S

reset overflow flip/flop	ROFF; DLET;
get A and convert to binary	NAMC S; LT8 0; INDX; LT8 5; ICVD;
adjust decimal point of A	SCLF 2;
get B and convert to binary	NAMC S; LT8 5; INDX; LT8 5; ICVD;
add A to B	ADD;
round to three decimal places	SCRR 1;
convert to decimal	SCRF 6;
form address of C	NAMC S; VALC 10; INDX;
set up operands in	EXCH;
correct order	LT8 6;
and store 6 digits in C	USND;

at this point the result in C is valid unless overflow is set

d) Translation of Cobol statement to B6700 machine code

FIG. III.5. Example of B6700 decimal arithmetic.

matrices. Regarded as data structures, vectors are merely arrays of numbers and have the common properties shared by all arrays. What makes vectors special, and provides opportunities for adapting computer architectures to facilitate vector processing, is the way in which vectors are manipulated by algorithms. Very often, but not always, each element in the vector is processed by the same algorithm and its processing is independent of the processing of other elements.

When each element of a vector is processed independently the algorithm being applied to the vector can make great use of parallelism, even to the extent of processing all the elements simultaneously, if that is practicable. If a computer has special vector processing instructions then it will know, when it executes such instructions, that parallelism may be applied. However (as we will see in Chapter VI), there are mechanisms which are included in fast computers to introduce local parallelism automatically where it is appropriate in all programs for vector processing or otherwise. Furthermore, some vector algorithms process vectors in a serial manner and such serial algorithms must be allowed for in any special vector processing design. Thus, apart from a few significant exceptions [5], most computers that are oriented towards vector processing require that vector operations be expressed as serial programs, though some have a few basic parallel operations built in.

Although few machines have a rich set of vector operations, the most widely used vector processing languages, such as APL, have many basic operations built in. Though this is of no direct consequence, as operators may be implemented as subroutines, there are significant advantages to be gained by executing or interpreting a language like APL directly rather than requiring its compilation into machine language. For example, it is particularly important with vector operations to leave optimization of expressions until run-time, e.g. "from $X + Y$ take elements m up to n", if translated as it stands with X and Y being length 1000 vectors is rather inefficient if $m = n$. Of course, much optimization can be performed at compilation but there are situations where adequate optimization can only be performed once execution is under way. Some techniques for automatically optimizing expressions as they are executed have been investigated, at least in paper machine designs [6].

Facilities for processing vectors as a whole may filter through to general computers eventually but, for the time being, we will only consider how current computers handle vector processing programs. As with strings, there are two approaches: to explicitly introduce vector descriptors into the execution record and operate on individual elements with ordinary instructions; or to manufacture "micro-programs" to make whole programs into single new instructions. The former method is the most usual and we will consider it first, in Section III.3.1, along with the particular problems of multidimensional arrays.

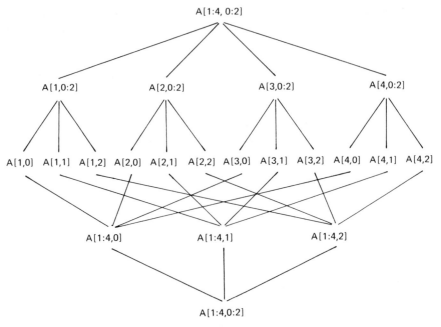

FIG. III.6. Mapping a matrix into a linear array.

III.3.1. MULTIDIMENSIONAL ARRAYS

It is not really practicable to implement matrices, i.e. multidimensional vectors, as simple array structures. A matrix can be represented as arrays of arrays as is illustrated for a two-dimensional array in the upper half of Fig. III.6. However, it is implicit in the definition of a matrix that rows and columns should receive similar treatment. If they are of the same lengths, it should take no more time to scan a column than to scan a row, but, when a matrix is represented as a "row of rows", columns take much longer to deal with. For example a program, in an Algol dialect, for initializing column j of A [0:9, 0:9] could be

> for i := 0 step 1 until 9 do
>   A [i,j] := 0;

but to initialize row j we would use

> B := A [j,0:9] ; *i.e. the descriptor of row j*
> for i := 0 step 1 until 9 do
>   B[i] := 0 ;

In this example columns require repetitive double indexing but rows need only single indexing and therefore require many fewer indexing operations and memory references.

This is not at all satisfactory and in order to make the treatment of rows and columns equal it is usual to represent a matrix of two or more dimensions as a simple linear array. For rectangular matrices the rows are packed into the array one after the other, in a canonical order. It is easy to show then that the location of any element $A[x_1, x_2,...,x_n]$ of a matrix A represented as an array starting at "base" may be calculated as a "vector product" of form

$$\text{"base} + x_1 s_1 + x_2 s_2 + ... x_{n-1} s_{n-1} + x_n s_n \text{"} \quad (\text{where } s_n = 1).$$

In the example of Fig. III.6 for the array A of dimensions [1:4, 0:2], the expression for the location of A[i,j] within the array A is $-3 + i \times 3 + j \times 1$ and thus A[2,1] is at location 4. Elements of the same row or column are spaced in the array at equal intervals given by the coefficient of each dimension which is termed the *stride*. A particular row or column may be stepped through by calculating the offset of its first element and using the appropriate stride. Thus the column A[1:4,1] in Fig III.6 starts at $-3 + \text{lower\_bound}*3 + 1$, i.e. $-3 + 1 \times 3 + 1$, i.e. 1, and elements are distance 3 apart. The row A[2,0:2] starts at $-3 + 2*3 + 0$, i.e. 3, and elements are 1 apart.

Thus a vector can be defined completely within an array if the offset, stride, lower bound and upper bound of each dimension are known. This information, confusingly called a *dope vector,* could form part of a descriptor. This is not usual, however, as the dope vector contains a lot of information. Rather than providing indexing instructions which use dope vectors it is usual to explicitly program the calculations to access any element of a matrix. To make this efficient, bounds of individual dimensions are not checked and the only security provided (if any at all) is given by the bounds of the array in which the matrix is embedded.

Our example machine does not include index registers or allow its display registers to be treated as such, but it does make provision for vectors with its "step index words". A step index word (SIW) as illustrated in Fig. III.7(a) contains three values—a current index, a stride and a maximum index. An instruction STBR (step and branch) is provided for incrementing SIW's. STBR expects to find the address of an SIW on top of the stack, it fetches the SIW, increases its current index by its stride and stores it back in memory. If the new current index is not greater than the maximum then the branch is taken. To make use of the value in an SIW the VALC instruction is extended further so that if it comes across an SIW it converts the current index of the SIW into an ordinary numeric operand. Note that an SIW may be located via a chain of addresses.

This mechanism is quite similar to that of other computers, allowing for the

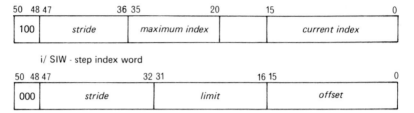

i/ SIW - step index word

ii/ ICW - index control word

a) Word formats

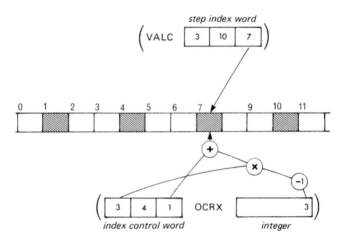

b) Use of step index words and index control words

FIG. III.7. B6700 multidimensional array mechanisms.

lack of index registers and the nature of the stack. As an example of its use the column A[1 :4,1] of Fig. III.6 could be set to zero with the following program:

$$\left\{ \begin{array}{l} \text{place into location S the SIW with stride 3,} \\ \text{maximum index 10, and current index 1} \end{array} \right\}$$

```
LOOP    :    NAMC    A ⎫
             VALC    S │
             INDX      ⎬ Set next array element to zero
             ZERO      │
             STOD    ⎭
             NAMC    S ⎫ increment address and branch
             STBR      ⎭
```

When matrices are packed into arrays it is possible to define any particular row, column, etc. by specifying its base and stride, i.e. as a restricted dope vector. The B6700 allows for simple one-dimensional dope vectors with its *index control words* (ICW's) which contain a stride, maximum index and base offset (see Fig. III.7(a,ii)). If an index value is placed in the stack on top of an ICW, then the instruction "occurs index" (OCRX) will multiply the (index − 1) by the stride and add it to the base offset to form an index into the array defined by the ICW. It is the index before the operation (rather than index after, as with STBR) which is checked against the maximum. ICW's are no doubt useful but do not fit in with the SIW setup—the "occurs index" mechanism was apparently designed to deal specifically with arrays of structures in COBOL.

The two methods of indexing into a multidimensional array are illustrated in Fig. III.7(b) using the same example as Fig. III.6.

III.3.2. SPECIAL VECTOR PROCESSING FACILITIES

The mechanisms just discussed do not go very far towards making vector processing more efficient and are really representative of the minimum which is needed in an architecture to allow vector processing. We now want to look at ways that general architectures can be extended to further facilitate the processing of vectors. As with strings, there must be some way of making pointers into arrays part of a processor's context so that the pointers do not have to be explicitly accessed each time they are used. However, the hardware of many high performance computers is such that frequently used items, including pointers, are stored in fast local memories and thus taken into the context automatically, without programmer intervention. It is therefore questionable, if speed is the aim, whether special facilities for vectors are justified at all in a *general purpose* computer, where execution time of arithmetic operations, especially floating point, is fairly slow. If there is much parallelism and power in the arithmetic section of the processor then special facilities are more warranted but the computer is then scarcely in the general purpose category [7].

With it understood that all of this may be unnecessary, let us now see how vector processing may be made to appear more efficient. A typical vector calculation will involve stepping through a number of arrays and, in order to eliminate memory references or to facilitate parallelism, facts about each array will have to be available locally to the processor. These facts will include for each vector its current address, stride and limits. Index registers serve the purpose of holding this array information in most computers which go no further than the basic mechanisms of the last section. To make such machines more suited to vector processing, it is necessary to introduce new instructions which specify a number of parallel operations on different registers at once. Although the B6700 is a stack machine without index registers, it is a good illustration of the changes required for any computer.

The B6700 solution to vector processing is to include a special mode of operation called *vector mode* which is very similar to edit mode in its attitude. Vector mode appears to be a late addition to the B6700 (although it has been stated [8] that the B5000 was intended to have some such feature). Vector mode uses registers required for other purposes during normal operation— the problem of context switch on interrupt is met by disallowing irrelevant interrupts while vector mode is in operation. This must reflect a change in B6700 design philosophy; the edit mode allowed interrupts, presumably because real time response to interrupts was considered important. By the time vector mode was produced such response was considered unnecessary and vector mode is only limited by the 2 sec maximum which is applied to any instruction. This could seriously downgrade interactive performance of the system but it can be controlled by adjusting the priority of vector processing jobs so as to make them background tasks.

As with edit mode, the B6700 vector mode is treated as a step down to "micro-code" to create a new instruction. With edit mode there are always two pointers needed, one for the unedited text and one for the result, but with vector processing things are not so simple as there could be many or few vectors. Here the B6700 imposes the severe limitation of three vectors (actually three addresses into vectors which is even worse).

Before entering vector mode, again like edit mode, parameters are placed in the stack. These are indexed descriptors pointing into arrays, strides for the three arrays, and an optional length in the following order:

   i.   pointer C
   ii. length (if bit 44 of pointer C is on)
  iii. pointer A
  iv. pointer B
   v. stride C
  vi. stride A
 vii. stride B

Vector mode is entered by the execution of one of the two instructions VMOS or VCOM (see Table III.5(a)). Rather than being included in a special table as for edit mode, vector mode instructions are part of the ordinary program (starting on the next full word boundary after VMOS, VMOM). A vector mode "micro-routine" is really just an ordinary program and most of the ordinary arithmetic instructions may still be used. What is different is that some of the string processing opcodes have been used to apply to the three vectors set up on the stack before vector mode started.

TABLE III.5

B6700 vector mode instructions.

(a) Vector mode entry

VMOS — *vector mode single*
VMOM— *vector mode multiple*

(b) Load/store of vector elements

	Load			Store			
ordinary	LDA	LDB	LDC	STA	STB	STC	*single precision*
	DLA	DLB	DLC	DSA	DSB	DSC	*double precision*
increment	LDAI	LDBI	LDCI	STAI	STBI	STCI	*single precision*
	DLAI	DLBI	DLCI	DSAI	DSBI	DSCI	*double precision*

A	B	C	A	B	C

(c) Load/store of scalars

FTCH (address couple) — *fetch*(= *VALC*)
STOR (address couple) — *store*(= *NAMC;STOD*)

(d) Control instructions

VEBR *vector mode branch*
VXIT *exit vector mode*

The special vector instructions, all 8 bits long, are listed in Table III.5(b). For each of the vectors A, B and C, the current element may be pushed into the stack or popped from the stack. At the same time the current address may be incremented by the stride (the instruction must also specify single or double precision operation). As well as elements from the three vectors, simple scalar variables in the current environment may be pushed or popped using the operators of Table III.5(c), FTCH (a restricted VALC) or STOR (an operator with the effect of NAMC; STOD).

The vector mode program is considered to have an overall loop structure where the same operation is repeated for each element of the vectors. If a "length" was included in the initial stack setup, the loop is repeated until this is counted down to zero. In vector mode multiple (VMOM) the instruction "VEBR" is used to decrement the length and conditionally branch out of the loop and so end vector mode. If the program ends with some instructions not in the loop then vector mode must be exited by the use of the VXIT instruction of Table III.5(d).

In vector mode single (VMOS) there can only be one word of vector mode instructions; this is held locally to the processor and is repeated with count down performed automatically until the count reaches zero when the vector mode is exited.

For example, the code for $A := B + C$ is:

```
          set up vectors in stack including length
          VMOS
          LDBI ⎫
          LDCI ⎪
          ADD  ⎬ single vector mode word
          STAI ⎪
          NOP  ⎪
          NOP  ⎭
```

for $SUM := \sum_i A_i$:

```
          ZERO
          set up vector in stack including length (all are required
                                                although two are unused)
          VMOS
          LDAI ⎫
          ADD  ⎪
          NOP  ⎬ single vector mode word
          NOP  ⎪
          NOP  ⎪
          NOP  ⎭
          NAMC    SUM
          STOD
```

for $A := X*B + Y*C$:

```
          set up (using length − 1)
          VMOM
loop:     LDBI
          FTCH    X
          MULT
          LDCI
          FTCH    Y
          MULT
          ADD
          STAI
          VEBR    out
          BRUN    loop
out:
```

Another unfortunate feature of vector mode is that protection from exceeding array bounds is lost, and consequently compilers are expected to check that "length" repetition of incrementing does not give an address outside an array. If the length option is not used then the number of repetitions is unknown and this check cannot be made. It is expected in this case that the increments should all be unity and the same trick as for string processing of running into protected words at the end of the array is used. When no length is specified the vector load and store instructions all include two bits which specify whether to leave one or two values on top of the stack when a "segmented array" interrupt occurs on loading a vector element (this use of the two bits conflicts with the FTCH and STOR operation codes which are therefore not available in "no length" vector mode).

Although B6700 vector mode is not very pretty it is extremely effective at speeding up vector operations. Earlier we had an example of a program to set an array column to zero using SIW's; this takes six memory references for each element—in vector mode, after the initial setup, only one reference is required to store zero (code VMOS; ZERO; STAI).

Apart from its rough aspects the main fault with vector mode is that it is not really necessary on machines that have relatively slow, non-pipelined floating-point operations. This is illustrated with the B7700 where, because of memory speed-up devices, many array processing programs would execute largely without unnecessary reference to main memory. Thus although the B7700 has vector mode the advantages from its use are minimal. Vector mode does provide extra indexing instructions which reduce the size of repeated loops, but the same effect could be obtained with instructions to refer to vectors in the execution record, e.g. if SIW's contained a current address then a set of instructions of form "$^{STORE}_{LOAD}$ top of stack $^{into}_{from}$ address given by SIW in location 'address couple' and optionally increment current address and branch if limit exceeded" would give some of the compactness of vector mode code without its complexity.

III.4. Notes

1. In the Rice University computer, Iliffe, J. K. and Jodeit, J. G. (1962) and the Basic Language Machine, Iliffe, J. K. (1968).
2. Shapiro, M. D. (1972).
3. The 1401 is discussed briefly in Bell, C. G. and Newell, A. (1971).
4. For example, see Amdahl, G. M., Blaauw, G. A. and Brooks, F. P. (1964).
5. Griswold, R. E., Poage, J. F. and Polansky, I. P. (1971).
6. See Abrams, P. S. (1970).
7. Examples of computers designed around fast arithmetic units are the IBM

360/91—Tomasulo, R. M. (1967)—the CDC 6600—Thornton, J. E. (1970)—and the Cray-1—Russell, R. M. (1978).
8.   Barton, R. S. (1967).

IV. Operating Systems

If a computer has the ability to both execute algorithms and manipulate data then it can certainly be used to perform useful work, providing it has some way of performing input and output. It would, therefore, be quite logical to deal with the I/O architecture of computers at this stage. However, because I/O usually involves special processors, we must leave its discussion until we have dealt with computers with more than one processor. The control of multi-processing is one of the functions performed by a computer's operating system which becomes, naturally, the topic of this chapter.

At the present state of development of operating systems it is difficult to place a firm boundary between what should be done in hardware and what should be left to software. The principles involved in the detailed design of operating systems have been dealt with extensively in recent texts [1] and much detail concerning the B6700 operating system has been included in Organick's monograph [2]. It is not the intention to repeat this material here, rather discussion will be restricted to the overall functions of operating systems and how the B6700 operating system is assisted by its hardware.

IV.1. THE OPERATING SYSTEM CONCEPT

The concept of what an operating system *is* greatly influences the architecture used for its implementation. The notion of "Operating System" has, like "Computer", gone through many stages since it was introduced, and it is therefore important that we have a clear idea of what it means to us before we start elaborating on the subject. To understand the modern view of operating systems it is helpful to trace the history of their development. This we will attempt in this section, though be warned that the history is again highly idealized.

Although we think nowadays of an operating system as being composed largely of software, such was not always the case.

In the early days of computers, programmers had to operate the machine themselves if they wanted to test or run their programs (a situation which still exists with small computers). Because operating a computer is a skill quite different from programming, and because there needs to be quite strict discipline in managing a computing shop (for example, in the maintenance of a tape library), these "hands on" computers were soon protected by an administrative procedure which forced the programmers to communicate the instructions for running their jobs to a professional computer operator. These "closed shops" were the first operating systems even if they did depend on an intelligent human operator.

The rapid increase in the speed of computers created difficulties for human operating systems. Because unit record peripheral devices were too slow for the central processors, faster peripherals were used, for example magnetic tapes, and jobs were batched onto tape off-line. Even so, it soon became impossible for human operators to keep up with the machines they were operating, the operators themselves becoming a major bottleneck. Happily, many of the operators' functions were mechanical and could be taken over by a device capable of obeying simple instructions—the computer itself.

Thus, the first automated operating systems consisted of a program, resident in the computer's memory, capable of interpreting commands written in a simple language and sequencing the jobs of a batch run and the steps within a job. The operating system was thought of as a program. This is shown by some alternative names, e.g. the *executive program* or the *master control program*. To the user programmer the system did not change very much (and hasn't since for batch systems) except that he had to learn the special language in which to give commands to the operating system. Some instructions, such as for mounting a tape, still had to be given to the human operators. These instructions could be given directly in handwriting or via the operating system program. As the operating system was a program it could start up a user program but, in the simpler systems, it was the user's duty, in turn, to start up the operating system when his program had finished (this is still with us as the "CALL EXIT" of Fortran).

The first operating systems processed batches of programs but dealt with only one at a time. Multiple activities were introduced later, apparently to accommodate two different features. The first, maybe the second chronologically, was *timesharing,* i.e. where a processor is switched between jobs so quickly that each user gets the impression that it is devoting itself solely to his job. The second feature was another result of the input/output problem. In order that the central processor could be put to work while waiting for I/O, the task of transferring blocks of data between memory and I/O devices was relegated to simple subsidiary activities implemented by "channels". This was primitive *multiprocessing* (i.e. the use of more than one processor). However, it became apparent when using channels that the design of programs which work in parallel with their I/O operations is difficult and unnatural. Thus the only easy way to make use of channels was to have a number of programs available for execution at the same time so that when one program was waiting for I/O others would still be able to proceed. This intermingling of the execution of different programs became known as *multiprogramming*.

The gradual acceptance of multiprogramming as the normal mode of computer operation led to some important changes in the way we view a computer system. It became clear that the operating system was allocating resources of the system to competing programs, and that those resources had to be shared dynamically. Because memory space could be saved by sharing programs the concept of a set of executing programs being resident in the computer became replaced by that of a set of tasks where a *task* is the coupling of a program possibly shared with an execution record and a processor (the term *process* is often used for task [3]). It was found easier when sharing memory (including files) to make the memory virtual, i.e. the tasks referred to a (sort of) symbolic memory which was mapped at run-time into the actual memory (and, similarly, files were spooled, i.e. were automatically transferred from slow to fast peripherals).

It was clear that subsidiary processors, such as channels, were also resources to be shared. However, there was at first some reluctance to completely share the processor which ran the operating system. Thus we find systems like the Burroughs B5000 and the Control Data CDC6600 [4] where there are multiple identical processors but only one processor runs the operating system. This imbalance is unattractive, esthetically, because two identical processors are treated differently, and, more importantly, because it impinges on reliability. If a two-processor system is to be able to recover automatically from the failure of one processor, it cannot afford to dedicate a processor to the operating system. For these reasons it became accepted that all processors are resources to be allocated by the operating system.

This was a major change of viewpoint because it implied that an operating system dominates the processors and is not a mere program being executed by a processor. In fact nowadays it is usual to regard an operating system as a cooperating set of parallel tasks rather than as a program. What makes the operating system tasks special is that they are designed to deal directly with the hardware which handles communication between processors, in particular with the interrupt system. The interrupt system is a small piece of hardware which coordinates processor activities at a very basic level. It communicates with the operating system only and may even be regarded as part of the operating system if we are willing to consider an operating system as being partially hardware and partially software.

We have been giving the impression that there is just one operating system in a computer, but really the situation is more complex. In the next section we will consider what is going on in a modern computer in the ideal situation when the operating system has no restrictions on available resources. It seems convenient to consider resources to be of two varieties, those which act, i.e. processors, and those which are passive, e.g. memory and files. We will consider them in that order. Section IV.3 deals with the allocation of processors when they must be shared, and Section IV.4 discusses the form of virtual memory and how hardware can assist in mapping the virtual to the real. The final Section, IV.5, will consider the problems involved in protecting the various tasks in the system from each other and from themselves.

IV.2. UNLIMITED SYSTEMS

In this section we will look at a computer system while assuming that it has no shortage of resources. As there are no shortages, there will be no question of allocating memory or processors and all tasks will be executing continuously for the duration of their life in the system. Furthermore, we can regard resources as being discarded after being used because there are unlimited quantities of replacements. This is an unusual viewpoint and is rather unrealistic; however, it is largely how a user programmer views a modern computer system, where as much virtual memory may be used as is required and where multiple parallel tasks may be created at will.

IV.2.1. THE DYNAMIC STRUCTURE OF TASKS

There are many activities taking place in a computer system at any time. First, let us consider some individual examples of typical activities.

A typical user of a batch processing system submits to a computer center a deck of cards or other records. The user thinks of the actions he wants performed as a *job* composed of individual steps called *tasks*. The user's deck (or job file) contains instructions written in a *job control language* which specify the sequence in which the tasks are to be performed, the files they are to use and generally how they are to be controlled. An example job deck is given in Fig. IV.1 (the job control language being B6700 WFL—"work flow language") for a job to compile an Algol procedure and a Fortran main program in parallel, bind the resulting object programs together and then execute the combined program.

One common attitude toward job control instructions is that they are orders to the operating system of the computer. However, it is quite possible for the user to be unaware of the operating system's existence and instead think of job control instructions as a program to be executed by the computer. In a sophisticated job control language, very complicated control programs can be

```
?JOB EXAMPLE; USER = CU0021FRED; CLASS = 2;
BEGIN
        PROCESS COMPILE MAIN/A WITH ALGOL[TA] TO LIBRARY;
        DATA
```

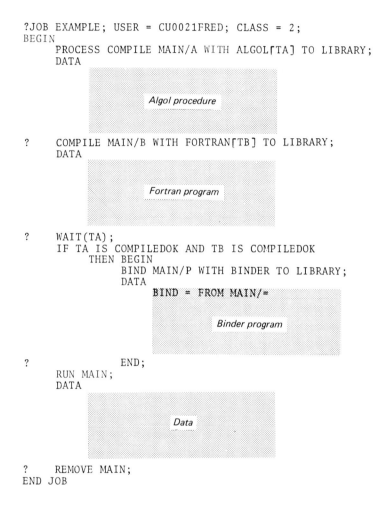

```
?       COMPILE MAIN/B WITH FORTRAN[TB] TO LIBRARY;
        DATA
```

```
?       WAIT(TA);
        IF TA IS COMPILEDOK AND TB IS COMPILEDOK
            THEN BEGIN
                    BIND MAIN/P WITH BINDER TO LIBRARY;
                    DATA
```

```
?                   END;
        RUN MAIN;
        DATA
```

```
?       REMOVE MAIN;
END JOB
```

FIG. IV.1. An example job control program (written in B6700 WFL—note that ? represents an invalid character that is used to flag the end of data files embedded in the WFL program).

written, for example, a batch processing system to process programs written in just one language. The line between an operating system and a job control program is hard to draw. Let's not draw it, and instead take the other view that job control statements form a program which is executed to control the tasks of the job.

A "picture" taken of a job at some stage in its course of execution will reveal a number of parallel activities. One activity will be the job's control program which is always executing and monitoring the execution of other activities which are the individual tasks of the job. In Fig. IV.2(a) is shown a typical stage where two compilations are being run by the one job. Note that the job not only controls the tasks but also provides or modifies their environments, e.g. the files on which they operate.

Let us now look at a task while it is executing. An atypical Algol task could initiate parallel activities or subtasks, as in Fig. IV.2(b), for example, to message input or to send output to remote stations. One task may act, therefore, as a controller of other tasks which it initiates. The subtasks obtain their initial environments in the form of subroutines, global variables, etc. from their parents.

Let us go down a step further and consider one of the subtasks of the previous example, for example, the subtask communicating to remote terminals. At some stage it could perhaps be required to send a message to three different terminals. It therefore sets three data communications tasks to work sending the same message. Here we have a task using one sort of processor controlling tasks possibly using a different type of machine (see Fig. IV.2(c)).

Rather than following this down the peripheral hierarchy, for it does go further, let us now go back up and look at the operating system of the whole machine. This is receiving job files from batch input peripherals and from remote terminals. It spools the jobs to back-up fast-access storage and then runs them. The operating system, at this level of discussion, controls the jobs because it is always monitoring them for error situations (via the interrupt hardware). It also provides special subroutines and tables for each job. From the point of view of the jobs being executed, the operating system resembles some form of deity which is ever ready to punish sinners who divide by zero or commit some other transgression. However, the operating system is willing to delegate control to other demi-deities, for example, a special batch controller. (Any operating system may well be further divided into different levels of control within itself.) This is illustrated in Fig. IV.2(d).

Now put all this together to get a structure showing all the various jobs, tasks, activities, run-time support packages, monitors, etc. which are all executing at one given time, for example as in Fig. IV.3. Each node in the structure may be thought of as an executing combination of program and processor. Each node controls its subnodes and modifies the initial environments in which they, in turn, execute. Let us call these nodes *regimes*. It is not good practice to introduce new terms but there does not seem to be an epithet in common use. "Regime" seems to be an apt term for an entity which provides part of the environment and also exercises some control over objects under it.

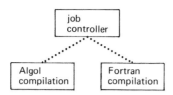

a) A job

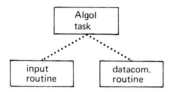

b) Control within a task

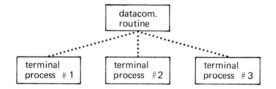

c) Control of I/O processes

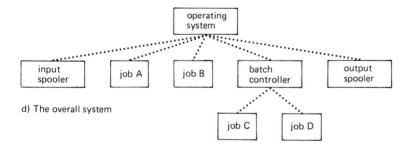

d) The overall system

FIG. IV.2. Example activities within a computer system.

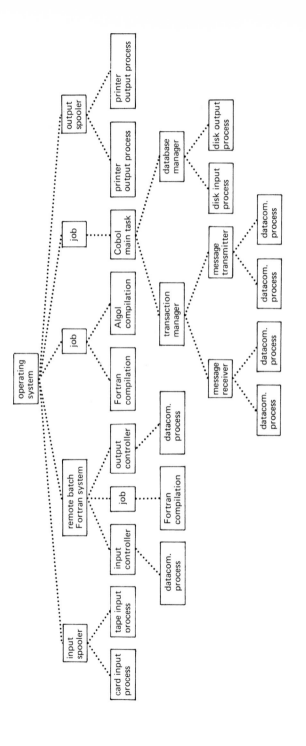

Fig. IV.3. Typical dynamic task structure.

The nodes under a regime may still be called *tasks*. From a regime a task is viewed as a complete entity although it may itself be a regime and view things under it as tasks. Looking upward from a task, the successive regimes of which it is a part may all contribute to both the control of, and the initial environment for, the task (we suffer under city, county, state and federal laws, not to mention the UN). Sometimes a regime may exercise no control over its immediate tasks but delegate this function to an outer regime—at the other extreme a regime may exercise complete control over its tasks and hide their activities so that higher regimes know nothing about them.

Our example system, controlled by the B6700 MCP, follows the general concepts just outlined. However, the structure of tasks is maintained by software rather than hardware. There are two classes of processors—central and others used for I/O. I/O tasks are an entirely software construct but the B6700 hardware caters directly for tasks which execute on central processors. (The B7700 hardware deals directly with I/O tasks but we will leave description of this to the next chapter.)

In Chapter II we noted that the execution record of a B6700 task was maintained in a single stack. Tasks and regimes are therefore identified with stacks. Each task has a unique number called a "stack number", which is used as an index into an array of descriptors of the stack areas (called the *stack vector*). Addresses which refer to an item within an execution record, and which are not accessible via a display register, must include a stack number. The SIRW's (stuffed indirect reference words) illustrated in Fig. IV.4(a) are of this form, consisting of: i. a stack number, ii. the displacement from the stack base of an MSCW and iii. the displacement of an item above the MSCW. Evaluation of an SIRW, illustrated in Fig. IV.4(b), takes two memory references. The first reference is to find the descriptor of the stack vector, the descriptor being stored in memory rather than local to each processor. The second reference is used to obtain the descriptor of the appropriate stack. The address of the base of the stack is incremented by the sum of the displacement d and the index i to give the real equivalent of the SIRW—note that the MSCW given by the displacement is not accessed or checked. If the stack number from the SIRW is that of the stack currently being used by the processor, then the hardware can bypass these two memory references because the base address of the stack is held local to the processor in register BOSR.

The dynamic structure of tasks is maintained by the MCP system as "stack number" links from stack to stack. This information, and other data concerning the state of each task, is kept in, or may be accessed via, a storage area in the base of each stack but is not part of the environment of the task.

Although the structural links are software-maintained the execution records and environments are handled by hardware. Each MSCW includes a stack number as part of its static link. This allows the cactus stack of display

46 45			36 35		20	12		0
tag 001		1	stack s	displacement d			index i	

0

a) Form of a 'stuffed indirect reference word' (SIRW)

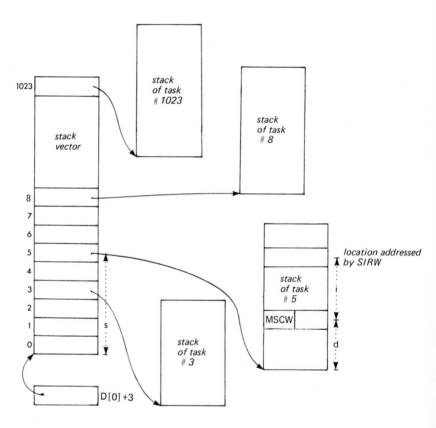

b) The stack vector and evaluation of an SIRW

FIG. IV.4. Addressing across B6700 tasks.

110

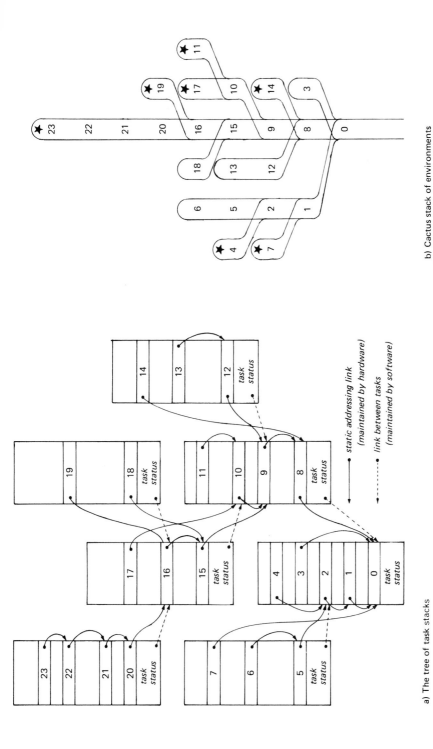

a) The tree of task stacks

static addressing link
(maintained by hardware)

link between tasks
(maintained by software)

b) Cactus stack of environments
★ = actively executing branch

Fig. IV.5. Mapping of addressing environments across the tree of tasks in the B6700 (idealized).

registers to extend over several execution record stacks, in particular, the current display may contain addresses into higher regimes. When a lower-level task is initiated it expects to use an initial environment of display registers set up by other regimes. Burroughs' literature talks of the structure of tasks as being *the cactus stack* but one may equally view the structure of static links as the cactus. Note that, now we have multiple tasks, more than one branch of the cactus stack may be in use—see the example of Fig. IV.5. Though we will soon see that the B6700 task structure is not quite as general as Fig. IV.5 would indicate, the idea definitely is very general, especially if, as discussed in Chapter II, the block markers may point to data areas rather than actually being the start of those areas.

<h2>IV.2.2.   CONCEPTUAL MACHINES</h2>

At this stage of the development of our understanding, we regard a computing system as a hierarchy of tasks and regimes. With no shortage of processors to consider, a task may be regarded as an actively executing program and is therefore an association between a computer processor or *machine,* a program the machine is executing and the execution record of that program. We have already discussed the form of programs and execution records in some depth so it is high time to look at the machines, which, after all, do all the work.

Consider the machine from the programmer's viewpoint. A machine language program is composed of instructions as basic steps and the collective definition of the instructions effectively define the machine. However, once the programmer gets to use more advanced tools, the basic steps in the program are no longer all instructions. The program is still, as far as the programmer is concerned, a sequence of basic steps, which implement the bottom limit of refinement of the algorithm which the program represents, but some of these basic steps may well be calls on subroutines. Some of these subroutines may be written by the programmer and have known internal structure but some could have been provided by other programmers or the operating system and the construction of these is probably completely unknown to the programmer.

Even given that the basic steps in a program are a mixture of hard, machine-executed instructions and subroutine calls, the programmer's view of the machine is still concrete because he knows which instructions are hard and which are soft. Or does he? It is clear which steps are in fact hard instructions in some cases but in other situations the programmer does not know at all. One example of this is the so-called "extracode" or "programmed operator" instruction which automatically converts a machine instruction into a subroutine call. Another example is given by the subroutines provided by high level languages: the programmer has no way of telling, unless he examines the compilers, which are subroutines and which are implemented as single instructions.

Rather than try to distinguish between subroutines and instructions it has become usual to unify the two concepts by postulating the existence of a *conceptual machine*. By a conceptual machine we mean that computer which a "program" can think that it is being executed by, i.e. the machine which executes all the basic steps of the program as indivisible atomic changes in the program's execution record [5]. There will be steps in the program which everyone knows are performed by software, others which we all agree are done by a hardware machine and many other steps which we are not sure whether are hard, soft, firm or otherwise. Rather than regarding a task as a program being executed by a real processor we will in future think of the task as being executed by a conceptual machine. A conceptual machine, subroutines and processor, is supplied to a task by its initiating regime as part of its initial environment.

As a task executes, so its environment changes. The task may select new parts of its program to be addressed as subroutines or it may even create new subroutines to execute. Hence, rather than being fixed like a processor, the conceptual machine associated with a task may vary as execution proceeds. The execution record of the task is also the execution record of the conceptual machine and changes in the machine will be embedded in the task's execution record. Some changes will be changes in the environment, other changes will reflect the state of the real machine (for example the edit and vector modes of the B6700), and there will be some changes, such as the switching of interrupt routines, which apply to the imaginary part of the conceptual machine, yet are not changes of environment as such.

While it is clear that some conceptual machines must at some time be real if anything is to get done at all, it must also be accepted that the other extreme is possible, i.e. that a conceptual machine can be entirely imaginary. Sometimes the user is aware of this, for example it may be known that a SNOBOL program is being executed by an interpreter, but in other situations, such as when a computer is micro-programmed, the user may not know that interpretation is taking place. Although it may seem strange to regard a completely imaginary machine as existing like any other, this last example shows that it is a practice which is quite common.

Activations of interpreters are also tasks and they have execution records and their own conceptual machines. It seems reasonable to regard the interpreter tasks, whether hardware or software, as being subsidiary tasks of the regimes they interpret. A typical situation is illustrated in Fig. IV.6. Here, a main task P controls three subsidiary tasks—Q, R, S. The task Q, like P, is executed by processor C; task R, perhaps an I/O operation, uses a different processor D; and task S, maybe a SNOBOL program, is interpreted by a

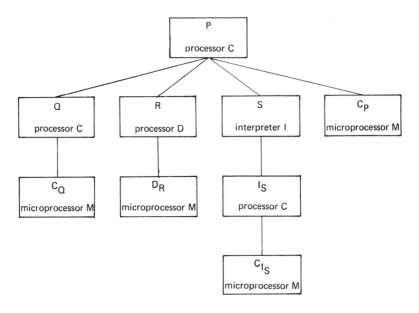

FIG. IV.6. Task hierarchy extended to include interpreters.

C-program I. To complicate matters further the machines C and D are both emulated by the same kind of micro-processor though of course each has a different micro-program. In the figure the hierarchy is shown terminating in tasks which are interpreted by real processors, or at least, ones which we think of as being real. Note that there can be two or more levels of interpretation as in S being interpreted by I_S, which is interpreted by ^CI_S.

Because the B6700 processor is not micro-programmed there is no provision made in its architecture for dealing with interpreters. The general method by which environments are handled was described in Section IV.2.1; however, there are some important details and restrictions to be considered.

To start with, the operating system stack at the root of the tree of tasks is always pointed to by display register D[0]. In this way the operating system provides procedures and constants which may be used by each and every task. However, only one other regime between the operating system and a task can contribute to the task's environment in the same way. This restriction is imposed, apparently, to facilitate memory management.

A procedure in the B6700 is addressed by a program control word (PCW) which gives the address of the procedure relative to the start of a segment of memory. The environment in which the procedure is to execute is determined from the MSCW below the PCW. Now, the PCW does not specify the address of the memory segment directly but via a so-called *segment descriptor* (rather like an array descriptor). Segment descriptors are limited to being located at addresses relative to the display registers D[0] and D[1], thus imposing the restriction mentioned above that only one regime apart from the operating system can contribute programs to the environment of a task. Any routines which an intervening regime would like to supply directly must be squeezed into the D[0] or D[1] stacks (usually called *segment tables*). Thus one finds routines supporting Algol or PL/I run-time environments provided as D[0] routines even though they are not required universally.

Figure IV.7 illustrates a typical B6700 situation where there are six tasks

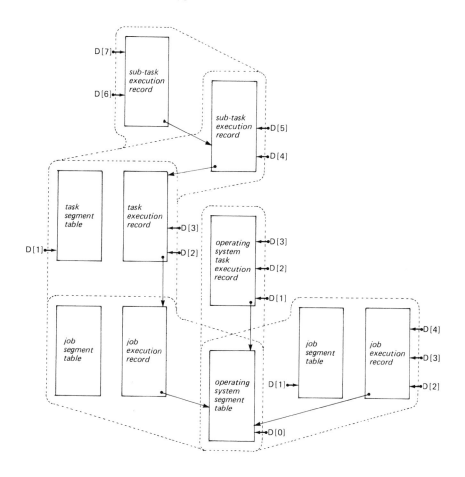

FIG. IV.7. Restricted treatment of B6700 D[0] and D[1] stacks (display registers for three processors shown only).

which can be considered as active. At the bottom is the stack of the overall operating system regime which controls three tasks, two of which have their own program segment tables and one of which executes an operating system program. One task has spawned another task which has its own segment table; that in turn has spawned a subtask which has in turn spawned yet another, the subtasks being distinguishable from tasks by their not using new program segments. Note the following points:

1. although there are many levels of task only two (or one) segment tables are directly addressible;

2. although they could be used as execution records the D[0] and D[1] stacks never serve that purpose;

3. any task or subtask may start up tasks having new segment tables or start up subtasks sharing the same segment table.

IV.2.3.   INTERACTION BETWEEN TASKS

Our model of a computer system has now progressed to the stage where we regard all computational activity as being distributed in a hierarchy of tasks. We have a good understanding of the nature of tasks, their execution records and conceptual processors, but, so far, we have considered tasks as only executing by themselves. Now we must look at how a task fits into the hierarchy, how it interacts with other tasks.

Interaction between tasks has two aspects which are treated in two separate sections below. The first, and conceptually the most simple, is mere passive communication—how tasks "talk" to each other. The second is the more active communication of how one task controls another. It is implicit in the model of tasks as a hierarchy that some tasks are more important than others. The controlling tasks must be able to keep track of what their subjects are doing and be able to order them to take specific courses of action. Methods of control in the task hierarchy are central in the design of operating systems.

1.   *Communication*

The information exchanged between tasks can be of large or small quantities. If the data exchanged is small, as with one task signalling another that a buffer is full, then there may possibly be special interprocessor data paths for its communication. However, if the data is of larger magnitude, for example an I/O buffer record itself, then communication is usually by means of intermediate memory to which both tasks have access. If the task's execution records both reside in the same memory then that is also used for intertask exchanges.

That is not very interesting at all but the situation is given some color by the problem of mutual exclusion. If one task is using a certain section of memory in which to place a message for another task, then it is necessary to deny the second task access to the message area until the message is complete—otherwise garbled information could be obtained. Because even the most simple message could take more than one memory access to complete, it is necessary to restrict access to any area, even a single location, which is used for communication between tasks; in other words, access to such an area must be mutually exclusive.

The problem of mutual exclusion has been extensively studied and many solutions developed [6]. At our current stage of discussion the problem is amenable to a less general solution than is required when processors are shared. Because all tasks are always active, all that is required is some way for a task to appeal to the memory hardware to grant it exclusive use of an area of memory until otherwise stated (conflicts for exclusive access to be resolved by some simple hardware algorithm which guarantees each task a turn).

Such a scheme is, because of its simplicity, open to abuse. A task having exclusive use of an area may fail and stop, or perhaps just be greedy and permanently inhibit access to the area by other tasks. If the tasks are arranged in a hierarchy then matters can be set right by appeal to a higher regime. If A and B are communicating as equals and, for example, A cannot obtain access to an area used by both A and B, than a common regime which controls A and B can resolve the conflict; the regime after all supplies the resources, including processors and memory, used by A and B. In fact, the use of memory hardware to aid mutual exclusion is an example of this very action, for the hardware itself is ultimately controlled by the operating system. Of course, at the highest level, between parallel tasks of the operating system, there is no higher authority available to arbitrate and special action is required when conflicts arise.

Rather than having a complex instruction for reserving a memory area for exclusive use, most computers use a very simple instruction in conjunction with a convention. Any task desiring to reserve an area is required to test a lock. Only one task can find the lock open and the action of testing, if the lock is open, locks it again—the action of testing is mutually exclusive. When a task has finished with the area it executes a complementary instruction to open the lock.

The B6700 has a "read with lock" instruction (RDLK) which exchanges the next to top of the stack with the contents of the word addressed by the top of the stack, all in one memory cycle—the memory access hardware guaranteeing that only one processor accesses the lock at once.

With RDLK a critical section of program or an access to a resource may be made exclusive by designating a location to be a lock. The lock contains true or false indicating that the section or resource is being used or not. The critical item may be made exclusive to one processor at a time by preceding its access with the macro "lock" and following it with "unlock":

```
lock(LOCK):                          unlock(LOCK):
        L:ONE                                ZERO
        NAMC LOCK                            NAMC LOCK
        RDLK                                 STOD
        BRTR L
```

2. Control

The nature of the hierarchy of tasks is such that a regime is much more powerful than the tasks within its domain. Regimes must be able to create tasks, to control their activities while they execute, and finally to terminate them if necessary. The creation and termination we will not discuss yet (or at all as it happens) because we are still regarding tasks as always executing—that leaves control as the topic of this section.

Because a regime provides the initial environments for its tasks it has close control over a task's capabilities. However, once a task has begun, it executes, to a greater or lesser extent, freely and is not directly tied to the state of execution of the regime itself. In such circumstances, imposition of control must be based on the regime's intelligence of its tasks' activities. The first subsection below deals with monitoring—how a regime keeps tabs on its subjects. This leads on naturally to the topic of interrupts—sudden changes in the normal path of execution of a task when something untoward occurs. The final subsection below mops up some details and discusses the B6700 interrupt mechanism.

(a) *Monitoring.* In order for a regime to be able to control its tasks the regime must have knowledge of what its tasks are doing at any time. The regime must monitor the activity of each task and ideally this monitoring should be complete and continuous; the regime should be looking at all of its tasks all of the time.

Such ubiquitous omniscience is usually reserved for spiritual regimes (the silent listener at every conversation) and is certainly not possessed by mere mortal programs. However, the ideal is approached closely in some special situations where a regime is much "faster" than the tasks that it controls. The regime can look at each task in turn and, although monitoring is not continuous, it certainly appears that way to the slower tasks. This method of imposing control is used for dedicated hardwired controllers, for example, where a data communications front-end processor is controlling a set of modems.

If a regime is not fast enough to fool all of its tasks all the time, then it cannot control its tasks completely without help. One obvious way for a regime to re-assert its authority is for it to make multiple subcontrollers in its own image—one for each task. Control is restored (as long as the regime can trust itself) but some coordination is required between the controllers. Although adequate at this stage, this multiple manifestation scheme does have the practical disadvantage that, because every task has a controller, twice as many tasks are required than would otherwise be the case. (Such a scheme is used in the ICL 2900 system where each task has two execution record stacks, one for the task and one for the operating system.)

A single regime can still control multiple tasks if it can relax and be more permissive. The regime is not necessarily interested in every move made by its tasks—only in errors and other unusual situations. Tasks can therefore do what they like, by themselves, in private, as long as the regime finds out about any *events* in which it is interested. A regime cannot necessarily trust any of its tasks to report events but it can trust the machines which execute the tasks' programs. We saw in the previous section that a regime sets up the initial conceptual machine in which the task executes and the conceptual machine includes the real machine. The regime knows the events which will be detected by the hardware of the machine it provides (e.g. divide by zero) and may create other, software, events which may be caused programmatically when the task uses a routine of the conceptual machine (e.g. end of file condition signalled by an I/O routine). As far as the task is concerned, software and hardware events detected by the conceptual machine should be treated uniformly for the task does not really know which are which.

If tasks were to halt whenever events occur, then their regimes could assert adequate control. The regime could look at the state of each of its tasks in turn and deal with any that were idle because of the occurrence of an event—either terminating them or telling them to continue. This is rather like continuous monitoring except that the tasks have to wait for attention from their regime. A simple example of this kind of control is with a peripheral device such as the B6700 card reader, where, if the start button is pressed the device must wait until it is told to start by the I/O controller section of the operating system which periodically checks to see if this sort of event has occurred.

This last scheme has some serious disadvantages. As well as tasks having to wait for attention, the regime has to continually check all tasks, whether or not anything eventful has actually occurred. This drawback can be avoided—if the regime can trust the task's machine to recognize an event then it can further trust the machine to report when that event occurs, i.e. to *notify* the regime of the event's occurrence.

So far we have been thinking of a task as being controlled by a single regime, but in fact a task may be influenced by all of the regimes superior to it in the task hierarchy. Responsibility for control may be passed by a regime to a lower regime fully or only in part. A task may even be allowed to deal with some events itself, or even to ignore them. Thus each task (or the subservient side of a regime) must somehow maintain a list which associates with each event the regime which should be notified and whether to continue or to stop when that event occurs. This *event list* may alter as the task executes and so must have its history embedded in the task's execution record.

When a regime is informed of the occurrence of some event it must, sooner or later, take some action to deal with the event. If a regime is controlling many tasks it must expect to be notified of many events at once. The regime, being sequential, can only handle one event at a time, hence it must maintain a list of events of which it has been told yet which have not been dealt with. When a task causes an event its machine should insert an entry into the *caused-event list* of the appropriate regime.

To summarize the control situation at this stage: a regime R wishes to be informed of the occurrence of an event E in the subsidiary task T. E inserts into the event list of T an order that it (R) is to be informed when E occurs. When the machine of T notices that E has occurred, it links this information into the caused-event list of R. The machine of R notices that E has been caused and takes whatever action is appropriate.

(*b*) *Interrupts.* Control based on monitoring as described above is adequate but involves regimes in checking their "caused-event" list every now and then. Either a regime makes frequent checks or its tasks may have to wait a long time before the regime notices that an event has occurred—both situations are inefficient. This deficiency is eliminated if the checking for event occurrence is performed by the conceptual machine which executes the regime, rather than directly by the regime's programs. The machine takes many steps for each instruction it interprets and the overhead involved in checking is not, proportionally, so large—in fact, if the conceptual machine is real then the checking could be done in parallel. When the machine notices the event's occurrence it can notify the regime, but notification in this case is very fast because the machine can cause the regime to change its course of execution by automatically switching to a subroutine which has been designed to deal with the event.

Such an action, the automatic invocation of a subroutine on the occurrence of an event, is called an *interrupt,* the subroutine being called an *interrupt routine*. In the manner just outlined, an interrupt may be used to notify a regime of the occurrence of an event in a subsidiary task (even in itself). In such a case, whether or not the interrupt occurs, and what the interrupt does, are for the regime to determine. However, the event list of a task must specify the interrupt routines, as well as the regimes to be interrupted.

At the other extreme though, the same interrupt mechanism may be turned around and used by a regime to command, or force, a task to take a particular course of action which is not dependent on the occurrence of an event in the task. The task has no choice as to the action it may take with a controlling interrupt—rather than caused events a task is confronted with, possibly many, interrupts to be serviced. Hence the caused-event list is replaced by an interrupt list which may be thought of as a list of routines to be executed (we will use the term "interrupt list" although in many cases there is a list of caused events available for a regime to inspect rather than a list of routines to execute).

Interrupts are clearly central to control in computers being used for both monitoring and more direct control. They are also, as we will see, used for other purposes. However, before leaving this general plane of discussion, let us consider some examples, based on the hierarchy of Fig. IV.6, of interrupts used solely for intertask control.

i. The task C_Q, which is interpreting task Q (i.e. acting as its conceptual machine), notices Q is attempting to divide by zero and notifies C_P (interpreting P) which causes P to be interrupted. P takes appropriate action, probably terminating Q.

ii. C_Q notices that Q has produced floating point underflow but the event list of Q specifies that Q be notified. Q is interrupted with a routine to recover from the error.

iii. C_Q runs into an extracode (programmed operator) in Q's program, P is interrupted, executes a routine to simulate the instruction in the execution record of Q and then allows Q to proceed (ideally the extracode routine should not execute in the execution record of Q, but in practice Q would, in fact, execute the routine).

iv. C_Q encounters a subroutine of Q which is written in micro-code—C_Q executes the subroutine (rather than Q) in the manner of an interrupt.

(c) *Details of Interrupts and Events.* The way in which interrupts are implemented in current machines is complicated by the fact that all the tasks are not executing continuously—the reader may have noticed that some of the examples just discussed are not at all like reality. The main reason for this odd treatment is to try and unify the description of hardware and software events.

We will eventually see why interrupts are different from what has been described but, for the present, let us press on and flesh out the subject with some details, particularly regarding the B6700. The description in this section will follow the course of an interrupt, from the occurrence of the event in a task through to the interruption of its regime.

Beginning with the task in which the event occurs, we have required that there be an event list detailing each event which may occur, the regime to be notified and, possibly, the interrupt routine to be used. There is no need for an actual list of events because events, both software and hardware, are recognized as exceptional conditions which arise and are explicitly tested for in program or micro-program. As for specifying which regime to notify, most computers were designed to operate with only one operating system and all hardware events are notified to *the* operating system. For software events, it is perhaps more clear that it is not always the chief operating system which is to be informed; however, with most computers, the B6700 being no exception, the operating system is informed of all software events as well. It then becomes the operating system's job to examine all interrupts it receives, both for hardware and software events, and to interrupt the intended recipient.

The B6700 MCP maintains, for each software event, a list of the tasks to be notified and interrupted; in fact, the stacks of all such tasks are linked together with pointers. For each such task and event there may be specified one interrupt routine—this may be changed dynamically but record of the old routine is lost. For hardware interrupts, the MCP only expects one task to be interrupted. The routine to be executed when the interrupt occurs is remembered by pushing onto the task's stack a word with a special tag (6) which may be recognized by the MCP software. In this way a task may contain in its stack in first in/last out order a list of routines associated with each hardware interrupt—only the topmost of these is to be executed when the hardware event occurs. For more detailed information of B6700 events and interrupts the reader is again referred to Organick's monograph [2].

In order for regimes to control tasks and for tasks to interrupt regimes there must be some connection between the processors of the system, although such connection can be quite simple. The B6700 connection is called the "scan bus"—all processors of all types in the B6700 system are connected to this bus. The bus contains address and data lines and would be adequate for any interprocessor communication. However, the B6700 processors are divided into two classes—central and I/O (of three varieties)—and the scan bus may be used only for a central processor to command or monitor an I/O processor or for an I/O processor to direct an interrupt inwards. Communication between central processor tasks is by a different technique that uses an extra connection between the processors by which one processor can interrupt *all* others (there can be a maximum of two others). This "processor to processor" interrupt is generated when one processor executes the instruction HEYU! (The B7700 does not use HEYU but has another instruction which allows one processor to interrupt any other specific processor.)

Now consider the plight of the regime which is on the receiving end of interrupts, the organization of its interrupt list and the order in which interrupts are handled. One simple scheme is to treat the interrupt list as a queue with interrupts entered at one end and removed for execution from the other in first in/first out order. Another scheme is for the regime to be interrupted by a new interrupt immediately, even if it is already executing an interrupt routine—this gives first in/last out order. Both of these schemes are inadequate, the first because some events must be dealt with more urgently than others, the second because it is not guaranteed that the "first in" event will ever get serviced at all.

Most computers are designed with only hardware events in mind and implement a compromise between the two schemes above. Usually, the interrupts are split among a number of priority classes, each class being associated with just one interrupt routine. An event may not cause an interrupt if the regime is executing the interrupt routine for an equal or higher priority event, but it will always interrupt otherwise (the routine of equal priority would have to be interrupted by itself—this is usually disallowed because subroutines may not be recursive). The list of unserviced interrupts is maintained by hardware—information as to the interrupts which are waiting is available and is supplied on interrogation. This is necessary because the one routine of each class must distinguish between interrupts of the same priority.

Priority classes with different levels of importance are really only necessary when some interrupts must be serviced in real time. If all interrupts can wait then it is quite adequate to have only one hardware interrupt routine. Because none of the B6700 interrupts are time-critical, there is only the one interrupt routine (located at display-relative address $(0,3)$), but the interrupt list is quite complicated. The hardware interrupts are divided into two varieties—*internal* and *external*—which are treated differently. The internal interrupts always cause a call on the interrupt routine and are therefore maintained in the regime's execution record in a first in/last out fashion (the interrupt routine, as with all routines, may be used recursively). The external interrupts may be treated in this way as well but they may also be "masked out" by using the instruction DEXI (disable external interrupts) in which case a simple list of unserviced interrupts is maintained by the system hardware. External interrupts can be enabled by executing the instruction EEXI (enable external interrupts). The masking of external interrupts is associated with the *control state* of the processor (discussed in Section IV.5.1) in that entry to or exit into a control state procedure causes external interrupts to be masked (control state is specified by a bit in each PCW or RCW)—the interrupt subroutine normally causes entry to control state.

The B6700 interrupt procedure knows what event it is dealing with because it is automatically provided with two parameters P1 and P2 which initially define the interrupt, though in some cases the cause must be refined further. The types of interrupt defined by the parameters P1 and P2 are listed in Table IV.1. We will discuss most of these in the sequel, indeed we have already mentioned in this section the processor to processor interrupts, I/O processor interrupts and the "programmed operator" (extracode) interrupts.

For software events and their interrupts, the B6700 MCP maintains for each task a genuine list of caused events and their interrupt routines which are therefore dealt with in the FIFO order. Note that a B6700 routine may have a list of pending interrupts maintained in three places, in the actual list of software interrupts, in the execution record for partially serviced internal interrupts and in system hardware for disabled external interrupts.

A last topic for this section is the mechanism by which the B6700 MCP causes an event in one task to give rise to the corresponding interrupt in another. For software events the process is quite straightforward. When the event occurs, the MCP goes through the list of tasks in the event list and, for each, links the interrupt routine into the task's software interrupt list. If necessary, the task to be interrupted is indeed interrupted by execution of the HEYU instruction.

The mechanism for hardware events is more primitive. When such an event occurs in a task, the task's stack is searched, starting at the top, until the first special tag-6 word is encountered. The routine specified by the tag-6 word is located and the task caused to execute that routine. The stack search may continue back through the stacks of regimes ancestral to the task and may take some time. It is an adequate procedure for fatal events or others which do not occur often during the life of a task but it is clearly rather inefficient for events which happen frequently.

It is appropriate here to note a small deficiency in the B6700. Most machines allow interrupts to be *masked* (i.e. to be ignored) individually. The B6700 has such a facility for external interrupts only. The effect of masking for other interrupts can be obtained by entering an interrupt routine which does nothing. However, this involves the searching process and is quite slow; in fact, numerical routines which cause frequent underflows which are to be ignored execute many times slower than the same routines when not causing underflow.

IV.3. PROCESSOR SHARING

Having now built up a conceptual model of a computer system when there are no limitations on resources, we can start to extend the model in the direction of real life where the system's resources are severely restricted. In this section we will take the first step of restricting the number of processors (the active resources) in the system and providing for their recycling—despite the rapid advance in technology processors are still too expensive to be thrown away after use by one task! The discussion at this level will still assume that passive resources are unlimited and will still be somewhat unrealistic.

IV.3.1. PROCESSOR ALLOCATION

Suppose that one regime in the computer system has a limited number of processors to share among its tasks. The regime, being the controller of its tasks, naturally has the responsibility of allocating the processors to the tasks. There are two basic allocation strategies which the regime may use.

The simplest approach to allocating processors for the regime is for the regime to limit its tasks to the number of available processors—in its most blatant form this is the old monoprocessing system with just one task. This approach is also used where a task, once initiated, must continue undisturbed until completion. I/O data transfers are often of this form, and a computer system does not usually start more I/O transfers than there are channels to accept them.

If the tasks are less demanding it is possible to take the alternative approach of initiating more tasks than there are processors to run them. This usually entails the regime maintaining a queue of tasks which need processors, i.e. are *ready* to go. The regime takes a task from the front of the ready queue, and runs it with a processor for a short time, after which it is placed back in the queue (if it has not finished) and that processor is assigned another task. Maintenance of the order in which tasks are run, i.e. their order in the ready queue, is called *scheduling*. Clever scheduling is critical for overall system performance, but for an understanding of what is going on we can think of a simple "round robin" algorithm being used—it will at least work.

We have been assuming that the regime is always active but it could be the case that it in its turn is scheduled by some higher regime. This would seem to be no problem; however, in practice, there is a complication in that a regime and its tasks use the same variety of processor. As processors are scarce they cannot be dedicated for the use of a particular regime but must be shared throughout the whole system. For this reason, allocation of processors is not usually delegated but control of this function is reserved for the overall operating system. From the point of view of the operating system, the subregimes and sub-subregimes and tasks are treated equally as regards processor scheduling—the dynamic structure of tasks becomes "flattened" into the ready queue. Because of this, many systems are designed in terms of just two kinds of activity, the operating systems and others which are called "tasks".

An apparent problem here is that it may be necessary to interrupt a regime which is not executing—a strange concept. However, we have seen that, in order to handle multiple interrupts, a list of unserviced interrupts must be maintained for each regime. An interrupt can be inserted into the interrupt list whether or not a task is executing.

Now consider how a processor is switched from executing one task to executing another. This must involve the dumping of any information held locally within the processor into the execution record of the task it is executing and the retrieving of similar information from the record of the new task. For simple processors there may be little or no information to save, e.g. an I/O channel is not given a new task until it has completed the last. In this case the processor has only to be given the location of its new program and execution record: the B6700 is not unusual in having an "initiate I/O" command with which a main processor may order an I/O processor to start on a new task. The same imperative technique may be used when there is information to be saved; for example with the CDC6600 a controlling processor may issue an "exchange jump" command to the main processor which causes it to dump all its registers to a save area and pick up a new lot [4].

Alternatively, the switching can be broken into stages, a command interrupt to get the processor's attention and to cause it to execute an instruction sequence to save, switch and reload local registers. The B6700 uses this second technique for switching main processors. For the B6700, switching is greatly facilitated by the way in which the current stack of display registers is held within the execution record as well as in fast registers; there is therefore little saving to be done on a context switch. In fact, once execution is inside an interrupt routine, the last RCW/MSCW pointed to by the F register completely defines the interrupted task, i.e. one pointer per task is all that is needed. To change to a new execution record requires merely that the F pointer be changed to a new RCW/MSCW. This does not change the program or the S register but an immediate EXIT instruction would reset these.

With the B6700, because each task has a single stack, the system identifies tasks by their stacks rather than by the last RCW in the record. Within the stack area of a non-executing task the pointer to the actual stack top is held in a special word—a "top of stack control word" (TSCW)—placed in the same location in all stacks (at the base of the stack). The TSCW, as illustrated in Fig. IV.8(a), includes all the status information of an RCW and encodes values of

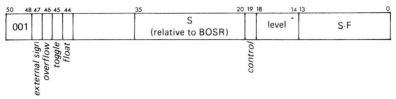

a) Top of stack control word (TSCW)

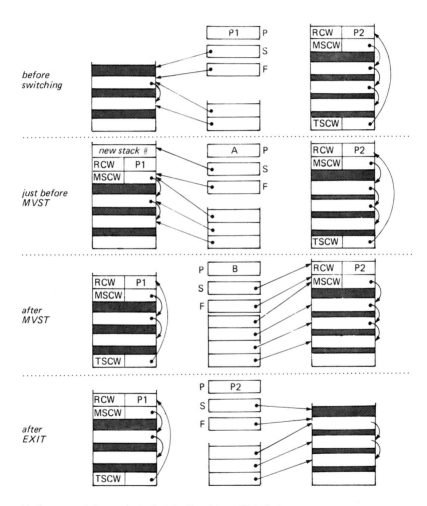

b) Sequence of changes (note that the D-registers will, in fact, point into stacks other than those being switched)

FIG. IV.8. Switching a processor between tasks in the B6700 system.

the S and F registers on switching. To switch the processor, the operating system calls a routine consisting of the following sequence:

$$\begin{array}{lll} & \text{VALC} & \text{new stack number} \\ \text{A:} & \text{MVST} & \\ \text{B:} & \text{EXIT} & \end{array}$$

The "move to stack" operator, MVST, causes a TSCW to be saved in the current task, new values of S, F and status flags to be obtained from the stack whose number was on top of the current stack, and the display registers to be reset. The EXIT operator continues the process by resetting the display registers and changing to the instruction address where the new task left off. This is illustrated in Fig. IV.8(b). Note that the TSCW contains much redundant information—on switching, the value of S is always one more than F, and the status flags are immediately changed again by EXIT. There is also no need for MVST to reset the display registers (except to handle possible interrupts between MVST and EXIT). In fact, it would have been more reasonable for MVST to have included the EXIT operator's action.

IV.3.2.   PROCESSOR SHARING BY INTERRUPT

An interrupt, as we have seen, involves a task in the "sudden" execution of a subroutine on the occurrence of some event. One naturally considers the interrupt routine as executing in the execution record of its task. However, there is no reason why the interrupt should not be serviced in some other task, as long as it leaves no trace of its temporary usurpation of that task's execution record.

It is quite usual for a computer to make use of this technique. For example, in a small computer a time-critical I/O interrupt may involve only a very small amount of work such as storing away an incoming character and directing the peripheral to read on. Rather than switching to the task which controls that device, less overhead will arise if some active task services the interrupt completely, whether or not the active task has anything to do with the I/O operation. This scheme, where "one task does another's chores", has been referred to as "backscratching".

Sharing processors by the use of interrupts is only partially motivated by savings in not having to switch tasks. We just saw that, for a machine with a well organized execution record, there is not much more overhead in switching tasks than there is in any sudden change of locality, as for example a subroutine call. To be sure, when switching tasks, an operating system must do a lot more, such as updating statistics as to the resource usage of the tasks. However, to be really fair, this should be done as well when an interrupt belonging to another task is performed, though it is perhaps defensible to ignore this. (If the backscratching principle is followed completely, one task may get charged for another's work, but it should all even out in the long run—the "swings and roundabouts" effect.) It is most likely that the real reason that interrupts are serviced directly, without task switching, is a hangover from monoprocessing; when the processor is interrupted it must be the business of the single task.

Be that as it may, there is one very good reason for not switching tasks on interrupt. A regime may be controlling many parallel tasks all of which can cause interrupts. The regime, if executed by a conventional processor, will only be able to deal with one interrupt at a time. If the regime's interrupts are instead serviced in the execution records of its tasks, then many interrupts may be handled simultaneously, without having to create execution records for individual controllers. Further, when some interrupts occur, such as errors, the task which causes them must idle until the regime has dealt with the situation. It is then quite natural to handle the interrupt in the task which causes the event rather than in the regime which should really deal with the event.

If this device is taken to extremes, then a regime may not exist as a task at all, but may instead control entirely by using interrupt routines executed by its tasks. This is accepted implicitly for regimes such as run-time support packages which provide a conceptual machine but which exert little control, if any. It has also become accepted that this is a convenient way to treat operating systems because they must control so many parallel activities. When this step is taken, the operating system does really take on a spiritual aspect; it does not exist as a mortal task (except perhaps as interprocessor synchronizing and interrupt switching hardware), yet its routines are part of the conceptual machine of every task. The operating system, in effect, controls by sending ordinary tasks into a state of transcendence where they are at one with the operating system itself.

The B6700 treats its operating system from this extreme position. The unique hardware interrupt routine may, of course, be executing in many tasks simultaneously. Although it receives all interrupts, the operating system may redirect software interrupts to be executed in other regimes or it may find and initiate routines for hardware interrupts embedded in the interrupted regime's execution record as outlined on p. 124. It is conceivable that subsystems in the B6700 could control mainly by interrupts serviced in their subject task's stacks but, as redirection of hardware interrupts is a time consuming process, most subsystems exist as tasks themselves and handle their own interrupts in their own stacks. All subsystems are constrained to accept the way the operating system controls tasks and schedules processors.

A couple of troublesome points arise from this extreme point of view. The first is that, if the operating system does not exist as a task, then the situation could arise when there are no tasks in the system at all. There would be nothing to interrupt and the whole system could never get going again! The simple solution is to always ensure that there is at least one task alive or alternatively, but ghoulishly, for the operating system to keep the last dead task available from which to initiate further activities. The B6700 MCP uses a combination of both techniques.

A second, more serious, problem could be that an interrupt can signify that the task's execution record is completely ruined and cannot be used by any processor. One interrupt of this form is that which occurs when a stack is full. The B6700 overcomes this by secretly allocating a few words extra at the top of each stack so that the interrupt routine to handle the "stack overflow" condition may execute without causing damage to other tasks. The ICL 2900 services such interrupts in the second of the two stacks it has for each task and the B7700 is modified so that stack overflow causes an automatic switch to a special home task for each processor, then if that overflows, to another special task and new interrupt routine. Neither of these changes has much to offer for they do not solve the problem in general but delay it one or two stages (in theory, though they work in practice, but so does the 6700's trick).

The B6700 then is like most computers in that hardware interrupts are not necessarily serviced in the execution record of the task for which they were intended. A hardware event may be internal, i.e. arise in the central processor, or external in an I/O processor device. For an external interrupt a processor is interrupted at random; however, if all processors have disabled external interrupts then the interrupt is saved until it can be serviced. Internal interrupts do always interrupt the processor in which they occur.

Software events, however, are directed to the interrupt queue of the task to which they belong—they are serviced when that task next becomes active. If the task to be interrupted is active when the event occurs, then execution of the HEYU operator causes the task to be usurped by the MCP's hardware interrupt routine which ensures that the task will execute the interrupt routine associated with the event when the hardware interrupt routine itself exits.

Now that we know where they are serviced, we can take a brief look at some of the B6700 interrupts in Table IV.1. Of the external interrupts, as we are leaving I/O to Chapter V the only interrupt we have to discuss is "interval timer". There has to be some method of stopping tasks which are in infinite loops and of sharing processors among equal priority tasks in fairly uniform time slices. The usual approach is to fit each processor with a clock and make it interrupt the operating system when it has used its slice. The B6700 interval timer may be initialized and activated to the 11-bit value on top of the stack by executing the instruction SINT—set interval timer. The interval timer counts down every 512 μsec and causes an external interrupt when it reaches 0.

TABLE IV.1

B6700 hardware interrupts.

(a) External
Processor to processor
  Interval timer
  Stack overflow
I/O processor
  I/O finish
    Data communications processor
    General adapter
    Change of peripheral status

(b) Internal
Alarm
  Stack overflow
  Loop
  Memory parity
  I/O processor parity
  Invalid address
  Stack underflow
  Invalid program word
Operator dependent
  A. System
    Bottom of stack
    Presence bit
    Segmented array
  B. Unexpected errors
    Memory protect
    Invalid operand
    Invalid index
    Sequence error
  C. Expected errors
    Divide by zero
    Exponent overflow
    Exponent underflow
    Integer overflow
    Programmed operator

However, the timer is "turned off" by any external interrupt and must then be reinitialized.

The B6700 internal interrupts are divided into the two classes "alarm" and "operator dependent". The alarm interrupts are all very serious errors usually indicating a hardware or system software failure. When these occur the task which caused them is terminated and a dump produced—often the MCP cannot recover from these errors and must be reinitialized; sometimes the hardware may have to be reconfigured or repaired. *Stack overflow* is caused when the stack becomes full, i.e. when the top of stack pointer (S) is increased beyond the limit of stack (LOS). *Loop* is when a single instruction executes for more than 2 sec—caused, for example, by executing a non-assigned operation code. *Memory parity* is obvious. *I/O processor parity* is in fact a parity error on the scan bus (a memory parity error in I/O data transfers causes an external I/O interrupt). *Invalid address* is caused when a processor refers to a memory module which does not respond (usually because it isn't there). *Stack underflow* occurs if S (top of stack pointer) becomes less than F—a compiler can mistakenly produce code to do this. *An invalid program word* is one whose tag is not 3. This is a redundant check, for code can only be accessed via segment descriptors anyway; however, the same interrupt is given for some invalid op-codes.

The operator-dependent interrupts may or may not be serious but they are always caused by a specific instruction, or rather by the part of the central processor which executes those instructions (the "operator families"). For these interrupts the return control word of the interrupt routine is usually adjusted (*"backed up"*) so that the return address points to the instruction which caused the interrupt and not to that following (if this has been done the P1 parameter which defines the interrupt has bit 24 set). We have divided these interrupts into three classes in Table IV.1 though this distinction is not made by the hardware or by Burroughs' documentation.

The system interrupts are expected by the operating system and are used for control purposes. *Presence bit* and *segmented array* are for virtual memory and will be discussed in the next section. *Bottom of stack* is caused when a task tries to exit from a procedure using an MSCW placed one above the TSCW in the base of the stack. This could be used to signify the end of a task—in fact it is never used at all—a task always exits normally to a procedure of the operating system which then winds it up.

The unexpected errors are quite serious and usually cause termination of a task—they are all things which a correct program should not do and their detection protects the whole system from an erroneous program. Tags are used to detect most of these. *Memory protect* is caused when an attempt is made to store into a word with a protected tag (1,3,5,7) or to use a descriptor which has a read-only bit set. The address in question is passed to the interrupt routine as parameter P2. *Invalid operand* is caused when an instruction finds that the tag of its operand indicates that it is of the wrong type. *Invalid index* occurs when a descriptor is indexed by a negative index or by one which is greater than the maximum value included in the descriptor. This can occur in the indexing operators and in many others. A *sequence error* is very serious as it indicates that an instruction found that a display register was pointing to something other than an MSCW.

The expected errors are the ones which are most likely to be handled by the

task which caused them. Their meaning is obvious from their names—
"programmed operator" is caused by some unassigned op-codes which are
intended to be emulated by the operating system (called "extracodes" by
others).

IV.3.3. SLEEPING TASKS

Although our model at this stage allows for the fact that tasks are not
executing all the time, every task does get a slice of time on a processor every so
often. Even if a task has nothing to do it must still execute. It could "twiddle its
thumbs" by going into a tight loop until something happens, for example, as
in the "lock" macroinstruction described on p. 118. Alternatively, if the task is
waiting for an interrupt it could execute a long "pause" type of instruction—
the B6700 has an instruction of this form called "idle until interrupt" (IDLE).

It is perhaps illogical for a waiting task to use a processor at all and it is
certainly wasteful if processors are expensive and the wait is of considerable
duration. To overcome this problem one can regard tasks as being able to
enter an "asleep" state where they will not be assigned a processor until they
are awakened. If a task wishes to sleep it can signify its desire to the regime
which allocates its processor. The task is placed into an "unready" list where it
will remain until either the regime notices that the task has been notified of an
event or the regime decides on some other basis to order the task to awake.
The task can be awakened merely by inserting it into the ready queue. Note
that the interrupt mechanism works just as before because an interrupt can be
linked into a task's interrupt list whether the notified task is actively executing,
waiting to execute or is just sleeping.

The lock type of synchronization mechanism is, as just pointed out,
inefficient if one task must wait for a long time for another to make the lock
available. This inefficiency may be eliminated by the task, which would
otherwise wait for the lock, going to sleep instead and the action of unlocking
causing the task's awakening. The mutual exclusion effect, provided for locks
by the hardware (considered as belonging to a controlling regime), is provided
by software of a controlling regime which puts tasks to sleep and awakens
them. The invocation of controlling software for "sleep waiting" and
causation of "unlock" events become the synchronizing primitives themselves.

We have been using "event" with its ordinary English meaning. However,
the unlocking type of events are so important that the term *event* is restricted
to this meaning in many systems. This is particularly true where, as in the
B6700, the underlying model of an operating system is that of a set of
cooperating sequential tasks rather than of a task hierarchy. The B6700 event
mechanism is well discussed in Organick's monograph; there is not too much
point in going into the matter here.

IV.4.   VIRTUAL MEMORY

In this section we will remove our last unrealistic assumption and investigate the case of memory resources in computer systems being limited. The restrictions on memory that we will now discuss are somewhat different from those that apply to processors. There is a fixed total of processors in any one computer system but, as long as there are trees left to be turned into punched cards, there is no limit to a computer's memory capacity. The trouble is, instead, that the memory which is available may be of the wrong type.

Programs naturally require different types of memory for different purposes. The memory needed by programs ranges from the fast, dynamically altering, immediate memory of small units of information, to the slow, static, large units of long term storage. The actual memory of computers consists of a variety of devices having a similar range of properties to the memory requirements of programs. One of the functions of operating systems, in cooperation with compilers and other systems programs, is the conversion or *mapping* of the symbolic names used in programs into addresses of actual memory. One of the main problems involved in this mapping is that the real memory is restricted in its capacity at each level whereas the collective requirements of programs are not restricted.

With processors, the technique used to mask out their shortage was to deal instead with unlimited numbers of tasks and to assign processors to tasks with some scheduling algorithm. Similarly, the shortage of memory of the correct type is disguised by the introduction of so-called *virtual memory* which programs may use in effectively unlimited quantities. In order to satisfy the requirements of a task for memory of one type, slower memory of a more plentiful type may have to be substituted and the faster memory allocated to the task only when most needed. The problems of mapping the programmer's virtual memory to actual memory and of managing the allocation of memory levels of different types are critical to performance—much has been written on the topic [7].

In this section, rather than elaborating at length on the operating system's role in memory management, we will concentrate on the less discussed aspect of the implications of virtual memory on hardware. First we will look at the form of memory seen by programmers; the next section will meld the relative addressing of Chapter II with virtual memory, and the last section will consider the mapping problem briefly.

IV.4.1.   THE STRUCTURE OF VIRTUAL MEMORY

High level language programs use only one kind of name—objects are referred to symbolically within statements of the language. There is no sense in which use of one name is slower or faster than another—the name of a file may appear in an input statement, that of a variable in an assignment statement, and both statements appear to execute in "unit statement time" (programmers sometimes get into trouble by unwittingly using "slow" names too frequently). Although they are used in the same way, different names are known by the programmer to have different life spans in the system. Most memory seems to the programmer to be used in one of two extreme ways—for permanent, long term storage or for temporary storage while performing some algorithm.

The "long term" storage is that which the programmer expects to remain permanently cataloged within the system, although it includes, by extension, external permanent items, such as card decks, which are kept track of by the programmer himself. Long term storage is characteristically used in large chunks such as files or the records within files, although access to individual items is sometimes required. The files consist of data, source programs and compiled object programs ready to be executed by a processor. The long term files may be thought of as residing on slow storage devices (and normally do). The system catalog or directory of files may be organized as a record structure such that any file may be addressed numerically. However, it is usual for such names to always remain symbolic because the time taken to convert a name to an actual address is small compared to the time needed to access a file.

With regard to short term memory, consider first the requirements for memory from within a task. We noted in Chapter II that storage could be accessed through an execution record which, for most purposes, could be regarded as a set of stacks or even compressed into a single stack. The execution record points to data areas which, as we saw in Chapter III, can be organized as a tree structure. Because a stack is easily embedded in a linear array, it is a small step to regard the whole memory used within a task as one structure.

As we have seen in this chapter, tasks relate externally to form a structure which exhibits the levels of control in the system. This can be viewed as the framework of a large structure, which has the memory structure of each task as its nodes. Thus, the whole short term memory is a record structure, in fact, of a similar form to long term memory. It differs from long term memory in that it may be thought of as residing in fast media with access being to individual items (though sometimes handled in large chunks). One last synthesis is to regard the whole virtual memory as one glorious giant combined structure sprouting from a common trunk in the operating system. This general concept is illustrated in Fig. IV.9.

Although a general structure like that we have outlined is the ideal behind all computer systems, the structure which is actually implemented must be modified to be more viable with current hardware. To start with, items are

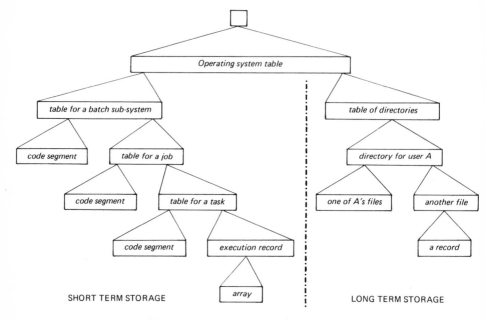

FIG. IV.9. General virtual storage structure.

moved within the structure to reflect their access needs rather than life span. Data which is used frequently, such as permanent operating system tables, need to be placed in the "short term fast" rather than the "long term slow" memory, and, similarly, some relatively short term items such as temporary files are placed in the "long term slow" memory. The short term names have to be transformed to numeric indices before they can be used, although the ability to use full or partly symbolic names may be retained as a software function.

The virtual address of any memory location in the whole system may be given by a full compound name. The name will be composed of alpha-numeric symbols for long term storage, e.g. USERCODE/CU002JAMES/ FRED/DAGG, and numeric indices for short term storage, e.g. 16.31.5.162.9.8 standing for say "job.task.subtask.execution record. array.element".

Even with such a rearrangement, most computer systems severely restrict the use and form of virtual addresses. In the simplest systems there is just one linear array, which may be the actual memory or perhaps could be mapped into the real memory by use of a single base register. The norm nowadays in larger computers is to provide three levels of virtual addressing, usually of form "task number.segment number.item". The segments are regarded as being rather large, corresponding to the size of external records. Any other structure beyond three levels, both between tasks and within tasks, has to be handled by some subterfuge or other, usually entirely by software.

There is a good reason for restricting the length of virtual addresses and that is the problem of their size. The size of an address which is constant, as for example in a program, is no great trouble, but when space must be allowed for storing a variable sized address, as in an execution record, then some restriction must be imposed. If the restricted size is too small then programs will be severely limited in what they can address, but if the size is too large then an excessive amount of space will be wasted on each address. Rather than a fixed, system-wide address size a more flexible solution would be to have a size limit of local extent, e.g. for each array, with a mechanism for extending the size if the limit is exceeded.

Our example machine, the B6700, recognizes part of the abstract virtual memory structure in its hardware but other parts must be maintained by software. The data structures rooted in a task's execution record stack may be nested to an arbitrary depth; however, as we have seen, all stacks are pointed to by data descriptors from a single array called the stack vector. The stack vector is itself pointed to by a data descriptor at relative location $D[0]+2$ in the level-zero stack of the operating system. As this stack is pointed to by a descriptor in the stack vector, there is some question as to whether the origin of the whole structure is at $D[0]+2$ or in the stack vector—both points of view can be helpful.

Be that as it may, the virtual addresses used by the system treat the memory structure as starting at $D[0]+2$ (see Fig. IV.10). These virtual addresses (SIRW's)—see Fig. IV.4—are restricted to being three-level names which refer to items within stacks. The "stack number" is the index of the stack descriptor in the stack vector. The other fields give an MSCW displacement within the stack and further displacement above that, i.e. the execution records are regarded as many "arrays" packed together (as we saw in Chapter II). Because addresses of items which lie in segments other than stacks cannot be expressed directly to the machine they must be evaluated programmatically.

IV.4.2. RELATIVE ADDRESSES AND SHARED SEGMENTS

We have now defined virtual addresses but, as we saw in Chapter II, the addresses used in programs are mainly relative, identifying a base or display register and a displacement relative to the base address. The relative form of address is required because the full address is not known when the program is compiled either because the program is recursive or, with a multiprogramming system, because the final allocation of storage is left until the program

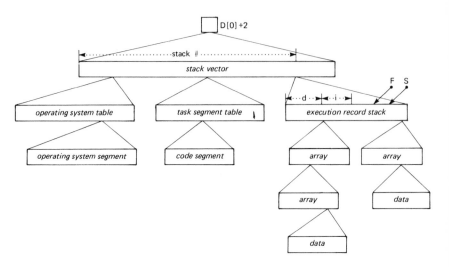

FIG. IV.10. B6700 virtual storage structure (with SIRW addressing illustrated).

is executed. We can continue to use relative addresses; however, we must consider the display registers to contain virtual addresses. This emphasizes the secondary value of relative addresses, that they may be much shorter than full virtual addresses.

With relative addressing based on display registers a task may be given access to its initial environment. Other display registers will be used by the task to point into its stack or other data segments. Typical uses of display registers are illustrated in Fig. IV.11.

Although most addresses are given relative to base or display registers, full virtual addresses are also required. Strangely enough most computers do not allow full virtual addresses to appear as constants in programs. There are many locations which remain fixed in virtual memory and it is a pity their addresses cannot be used directly. When such addresses are required they must be given using one stage of indirection through a location addressed relatively. In the case of the B6700, for example, subroutine libraries called *installation intrinsics* may be provided as a stack used as a symbol table. If a subroutine is at location l in stack s it cannot be used by the simple sequence

load   SIRW (s,l); ENTR

Instead, the SIRW has to be inserted in the *current* D[1] stack of each task which needs it say at $(1,M_t)$ and the procedure used by

NAMC $(1,M_t)$
ENTR

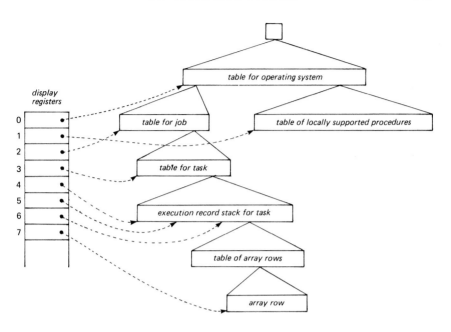

FIG. IV.11. Possible uses of base/display registers.

Such restrictions on the use of full virtual addresses do have some foundation. There are many full addresses which refer to sensitive information and one way of protecting such data is to prohibit low security tasks from creating virtual addresses and require that such addresses be supplied indirectly by a trusted higher authority. This does not really rule out compilers embedding virtual addresses directly in programs, if the compilers are regarded as trustworthy. However, the variable size of virtual addresses is a bother for compilers and the mechanism for indirect accessing of virtual addresses is a necessity in any case—hence, virtual addresses in programs seem to cause more problems than they are worth.

We have been referring to "full virtual" and "display relative" addresses as if they were the only forms; however, these are merely the extremes. It is possible to envisage addresses which start off with a register number and are followed by a compound virtual address. Such an intermediate address could be used indirectly, or even used as a base address, the only restriction being that when the address is used any base register must contain valid values, i.e. any address referring to a base register can only be used in the environment for which it was created.

The process of indexing takes on a new form when considered entirely in terms of virtual addresses. In Chapter III we considered descriptors to contain a real base address (and will think it again soon) but when an address is virtual, the base address is also virtual; in fact, it is obtained by appending zero to the address of the descriptor. This means that a descriptor may be indexed by merely appending the index to the descriptor's address. Of course, there is the limit value in the descriptor to check the index against but this check could be left until the address is used and finally converted to its real equivalent.

So far we have been dealing with virtual memory as it applies to one task. When there is more than one task the immediate question of interest is how data areas are shared, because, if tasks are to communicate at all, they must address some common area. In fact, most sharing may be performed by using the display or base registers which convey the initial environment to a task as illustrated in Fig. IV.11. Any routines, etc. which a parent regime wishes to provide may be addressed by any offspring tasks using identical relative addresses. Other addresses of shared items may be passed to a task as a parameter (i.e. some location is initialized to an address) and then used indirectly. Alternatively, tasks may use symbolic addresses, perhaps different in each task, which a higher regime can convert to common full virtual addresses in the event of their being used.

One worry when using the address of a location belonging to another task is that it may vanish while it is being used. Presumably, if a regime is providing a shared item for its family of tasks then it can trust itself not to confuse its tasks by losing the item. However, if two equals are sharing an area belonging to one of them, then the loss of a shared area becomes an event which the controlling regime must know about and deal with when it happens. Although a task may create virtual segments at its will, it cannot be given such freedom in destroying them, although, in fact, when real memory is involved both actions have to be carefully controlled.

It is often desirable to identify a section of a segment rather than an entire segment or a single item. This could be done by using a descriptor, the base address of which does not end in zero but with some other digit (or by using a limit or length which is less than that of the whole area). Of course, only such *relative descriptors* need to have a base address at all because ordinary descriptors are, in effect, their own bases. It is really an address in a *relative descriptor* form which should be placed into a display register that is used to point into a stack (note that the display register should therefore include a limit). An alternative method of specifying the base address of a relative descriptor is to identify a descriptor further up the virtual memory structure from the relative descriptor. (See Fig. IV.12 for an example of the use of relative descriptors [8].)

With the B6700, complete segments are shared by accessing their descriptors with display relative addresses. Code segment descriptors may only

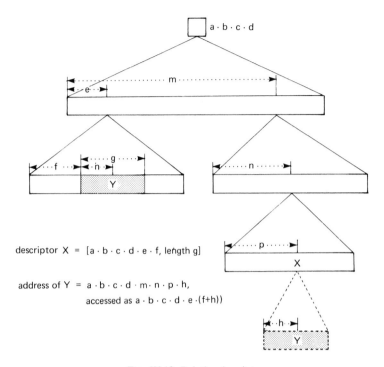

FIG. IV.12. Relative descriptors.

occur in D[0] and D[1] stacks, and such stacks are shared as a whole. The D[0] "stack", the operating system table, is shared by all tasks. Other tasks are defined by a D[2] execution record stack (a D[1] stack for operating system stacks) which uses code given by a D[1] table "stack" (an operating system task uses only D[0] programs). Thus, logically speaking, D[1] stacks are subsidiary to D[2] stacks, yet, for addressing purposes, the D[2] stack is subsidiary to D[1]. This is illustrated in Fig. IV.13 where a four processor system is executing four tasks simultaneously. Task d has a subtask c sharing its programs, and c has spawned another subtask b, which shares its program with a completely independent task a.

IV.4.3. MAPPING VIRTUAL MEMORY TO ACTUAL MEMORY

Once a virtual memory structure has been created it is a quite straightforward

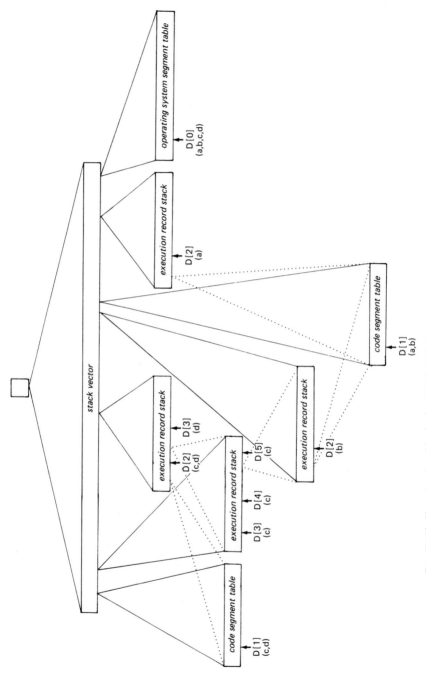

Fig. IV.13. Shared code tables in the B6700 (with four active tasks using four processors a,b,c,d).

process to site the structure in a computer's actual memory. The memory provided by a computer is usually in the form of a number of arrays of equisized locations. The size of the locations in each array and the number in each varies; the main high speed memory having the smallest locations of word, or perhaps byte size, disk memory being accessed by longer "records"—to mention but two types. Whatever the type of memory, a virtual memory segment can be placed in it as a subarray. The descriptor of that segment can have as a base address the real address of the segment, replacing, as promised, the redundant virtual address. Each segment then lies in real memory and its descriptor says exactly where it is.

As we mentioned at the start of this discussion on virtual memory, the main complication encountered when mapping virtual to actual is that there may not be enough actual memory of the type appropriate to the use which is being made of a segment. Hence, some segments are held in memory devices where they cannot be used and these must therefore be moved before they are used. This applies particularly to main high speed memory where most of the data and programs used by an executing program must reside, but it also applies to files on tape and cards which must be brought to disk memory before they can be used effectively. For the tape–disk change it is normal for the user to load the file programmatically (some systems do maintain tape catalogs and do it for you) but for the backing–main memory change it is usual nowadays for the change to be made automatically by the operating system (some old systems leave this to the programmer—then called *overlaying*).

The solution then to the shortage of short term main memory is to use a section of long term storage to hold segments which cannot fit into the main memory. Such segments are addressed numerically rather than symbolically as is usual for such storage. A reference made by a processor directly to a segment held in the secondary memory is recognized by the machine which then causes an interrupt to the level of the operating system which is, or which directs, a special memory management task called the *memory manager*. The memory manager transfers the segment from backing to real memory and alters the descriptor to reflect this change. The task which used the address may then proceed because the segment is now in the correct type of memory. Note that, although the real base address in a descriptor may change as a task executes, the virtual address represented by the descriptor remains exactly the same.

Who would want the job of a memory manager? It has to run around all day trying to fit virtual pegs into real holes and making sure that all the holes are being used to the best advantage. If the virtual segments are too large then there may be no hole in which to place them; if they are too small then there are too many to deal with and the spare spaces get even smaller. To help the memory manager, facilities can be added to hardware which enable small segments to be grouped together into larger segments and conversely to break large segments down into smaller pieces, both without altering the virtual memory structure seen by a user.

Segments can be grouped together by using, behind the programmer's back, the relative descriptor mechanism introduced in the last section. However, the usual method is to insist that smaller segments be combined into large segments as a separate, usually prior, process (though this does alter the virtual structure). Most computers do not help with this inner segmentation so it is sometimes overlooked at the overall system level that large physical segments often contain many logical segments.

Breaking large segments into smaller pieces is accomplished by what has come to be called *paging*. The large virtual segment of size s is split into equi-sized chunks, called *pages,* say of size p. An intermediate segment of descriptors of the pages is placed "between" the segment descriptor and the pages, the intermediate segments having s/p members. The base of the segment descriptor points to this page table. An index i applied to the segment descriptor is split into two sections—i/p and i mod p—the first of which is used to index the segment descriptor to find a page descriptor which is indexed by the second value. This is illustrated in Fig. IV.14. Note that if p is a power of the number base (usually 2) an index may be split without division.

The term "paged virtual memory" is usually reserved for systems which go one step further in aiding the memory manager by requiring that *all* segments be broken into pages of the same size and that all segments are multiples of the page size in length. If the real memory is similarly broken into slots of that size (sometimes called *page frames),* then there is no problem in finding a slot for a page. It seems simple (and indeed it is) but it really ignores the problem of

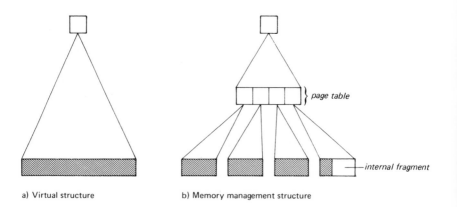

a) Virtual structure   b) Memory management structure

FIG. IV.14. Paging a large segment.

virtual segments naturally having varying sizes. A conventional paging system then is saving the memory manager some work but the buck is being passed to some other program. It should be noted that complete paging is an option which is always available to a system which is designed to handle segments of varying sizes but which also allows segments to be paged if necessary.

When the memory manager has to transfer a segment from secondary to main memory, and there are no suitable empty slots, it may need to transfer some other segments in the reverse direction to make space available. It is important that the manager does not throw out too many segments which are in active use (part of what is called the *working* set—see Coffman and Denning [9]). To help the manager make the correct choice, some systems automatically accumulate statistics in each descriptor about the use which has been made of its segment, such as how much it has been used or when last used (usually just whether or not it has been used). This information does allow fairly accurate prediction but it is unfortunate that such information is about the past—what really is required is information about the future use of segments. Until computers get crystal balls the top of "replacement strategies" will remain an interesting area of discussion [10].

The use of virtual addresses involves other problems. Whenever virtual addresses are used they must be converted into real addresses by the computer. This involves tracing through the memory structure from the top and takes one memory reference for each stage of the trip. This is an unacceptable overhead and provision must be made to reduce it, on average.

The conventional scheme of virtual memory is to have two levels of segmentation and one level of paging below that. Because the addresses of the highest level segment tables are normally held locally to a processor, any reference to memory takes two extra references—one for the segment table and one for the page table below it. Two extra references are not too bad but even these can be bypassed in the majority of cases by using a fast associative or set associative memory in each processor to link virtual with real addresses. Because there is such a great deal of locality of reference in most programs such an associative memory can be very effective [11]; it can also be extended to include the contents of the addressed location as a slave or cache memory.

Another method of reducing the address conversion overhead is provided by the display or base registers which we use already to provide relative addressing and to reduce the length of addresses. Display registers contain the initial parts of the most frequently used virtual addresses. If we associate with each virtual display address the corresponding real address then, in fact, most real addresses can be calculated with no significant overhead. This, in fact, takes us back to the way display registers were used in Chapter II.

It should be pointed out that if real addresses are kept locally in a processor then provision must be made for changing these whenever a virtual segment is moved in real memory. In what has been discussed so far, all addresses in execution records have been virtual and we have assumed that the virtual address of an object never alters during the object's lifetime. However, one simple way of reducing address conversion overheads is to allow the real addresses of items to find their way into execution records. In this case, however, the caveat above applies to execution records as well; whenever a virtual segment is moved all relevant execution records must be searched to change real addresses. Whether or not this overhead is acceptable depends, of course, on how often segments are moved.

The B6700 is a fascinating, if complicated, example of the general concepts of virtual memory. We have seen that it provides a much more general virtual memory structure than other computers. This is mapped directly to main or disk memory; a special flag in each descriptor—the *presence bit*—is on if the base address is to main memory (really that bit could be considered as part of the address). When an attempt is made to use a disk address, a "presence bit interrupt" occurs and the interrupt routine is passed the absent address as the second parameter P2. The memory manager shifts the segment in question into main memory and updates its descriptor. The interrupt routine finishes and the main program continues—the P1 parameter indicates whether the P2 parameter is to be updated and left on top of the stack. The P1 parameter also indicates that in some cases the MSCW should be altered to cause the VALC operator which invoked accidental entry to be re-entered and continue to "track down" a value.

The main memory of the B6700 is maintained by the MCP as linked lists of in-use and available areas. The memory manager has to search the available list to find an area of adequate size when it wishes to bring a segment in from the disk. To help speed up this search an instruction called "linked list lookup" (LLLU) is provided. LLLU starts with three items on top of the stack; the second is the descriptor of an array in which the linked list lies (the operating system uses a descriptor pointing to all of main memory), the first item is the index in the array of the first list element and the third item is the value being searched for. Each linked list word is considered to contain two fields—a 28-bit value (which for the memory list represents the size of an area) and a 20-bit pointer to the next link word. LLLU scans through the list until it finds either a link of zero indicating the end of the list or a link word with a value greater or equal to that being searched for. In the former case − 1 is left on top of the stack, in the latter case the index of the link word *before* the one containing the required value is left on top of the stack— this is so that the word located may be de-linked from the list. This is illustrated in Fig. IV.15.

The B6700 virtual addresses—the SIRW's—are restricted to the first three levels of the virtual memory structure. Whenever an SIRW is used it takes a

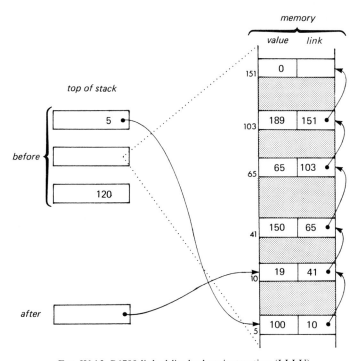

Fig. IV.15. B6700 linked list lookup instruction (LLLU).

full two extra memory references to locate the value in question—one to get the descriptor at $D[0] + 2$ which points to the stack vector, another to obtain the descriptor of the stack. These two references are bypassed, however, if the SIRW refers to the current stack, the number and base of which are held local to the processor. The hardware allows for stacks being in secondary memory and always checks for this when an SIRW is evaluated. The hardware implements a complicated scheme for ensuring that presence bit interrupts caused by absent stacks (or the stack vector) can restart the interrupted task correctly—in fact, this feature is never used because stacks are never moved to secondary memory.

The B6700 allows data segments to be paged though this is confusingly called "segmentation". The indexing operators consider a segmented array to be broken into 256-*word* sections but both the type and length of the data items (given by the descriptor) are taken into account when splitting the index. There is no mechanism for reducing memory references when accessing a "segmented" array. The "segmented array interrupt" caused by string processing instructions allows string scanning operations to be programmatically restarted when they run off the end of a page.

The B6700 display registers contain only real addresses although the corresponding links embedded in the execution record are virtual, in the form of a stack number and a displacement. There is no special mechanism whereby the displays can be updated automatically if a stack is moved, but causing each processor to be interrupted by an HEYU would update the display.

Because virtual addresses are restricted to three levels but the structure isn't, the only way array elements outside of stacks can be addressed is by real addresses. Execution records must be searched when the real addresses alter—this is accepted and is aided by the hardware in a number of ways. To start with, only the base addresses of descriptors are real—an indexed descriptor is in the form of "base + index"—the index is not added to the base address until the indexed descriptor is used. Secondly there is only one descriptor of an absent segment on secondary storage; this is called the *"mom"* and is always pointed to by link words associated with the segment. Other descriptors, indexed or otherwise, are marked, using a special bit, as copies. These, rather than containing the base disk address, contain the actual main memory address of the *mom* descriptor. When a copy of an absent descriptor is brought into a stack (e.g. by NXLN or LOAD) a copy descriptor is created automatically by the hardware. Both *mom* and copies of absent descriptors are marked as absent and attempts to use them cause "presence bit" interrupts.

The memory manager's job is then somewhat easier. An address into a segment can be identified by its base field. When a segment is removed such descriptors must be searched for, marked absent and converted to copies pointing to the *mom*. The *mom* contains the segment's real address—whenever the segment is moved again only the *mom* need be altered. When a presence bit interrupt occurs the absent segment is returned to memory and only the base address of the *mom* descriptor updated. Further presence bit interrupts will occur when copies of the now present descriptor are used but these are much easier to deal with (and one would have thought that they could have been handled in hardware).

The time consuming task of searching stacks for descriptors is facilitated by a special instruction "masked search for equal"—SRCH. This instruction expects to find the top three items of the current stack containing an indexed descriptor into the array to be searched, a mask defining the field to be searched for, and the value which is sought. The descriptor is expected to be indexed but an unindexed descriptor is acceptable and is converted to indexed form with an index of "length − 1". SRCH scans down the array looking for the appropriate value (the mask and value include the tag field). If the value is found its index is left on the stack—otherwise − 1 is left to indicate failure.

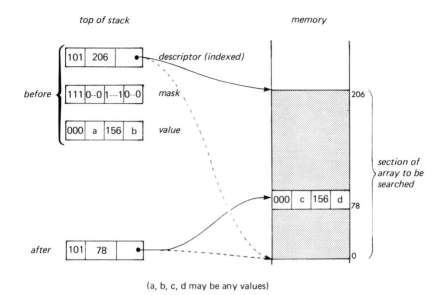

FIG. IV.16. B6700 masked search for equal instruction (SRCH).

SRCH is illustrated in Fig. IV.16. Note that both SRCH and LLLU may be (and are) used for other purposes both by the operating system and user programs.

Virtual memory segments may be created by any task. Because all B6700 programming is in higher level languages, compilers are trusted to produce new descriptors marked as absent and with a base of zero. The memory manager interprets such a descriptor as being new and allocates a new area when it is first used. Compilers are also trusted to call an operating system recovery procedure "block exit" when cutting back a stack which may contain descriptors (of memory and of files). The operating system recovers the resources based in the stacks of deceased tasks.

When a task is initiated in the B6700 only the D[1] segment table is required to be present. Each code and data area is made present as it is used. Grouping virtual segments into actual segments is not allowed for in the B6700 hardware (except by storage areas being included in stacks). This means that, as most programs use many little segments, it takes them some time, many disk accesses and presence bit interrupts to get going properly. This is perhaps satisfactory in a general multiprogramming environment but makes real time interactive work a bit slow. For this reason, the B6700 operating system combines the segments of some interactive jobs into a swapping area which is moved in and out of disk as a whole. Because a task using the swapping area is not run while the area is absent, the operating system does not have to alter the segment descriptors within the area or within the stack when the area is swapped out.

We have reached the point of almost full development of our description of the B6700 central processor. The full descriptions of some of the instructions can now be understood. We will refer the reader to the B6700 manual [12] for details but as an example we have included, as Fig. IV.17, the full description of the VALC operator given in "algorithmic English".

IV.5. PROTECTION

Multiprogramming, where there are many tasks sharing a computer system's resources, emphasizes the vulnerability of simple computers. The various tasks in the system will, in the main, be executing without knowledge of other tasks and should not be affected by the others. Such will be the case if all tasks are well behaved but, realistically, there will always be some which, by error, or design, will have a deleterious effect on their fellows. It is clear that in order to be at all viable, a multiprogramming system needs a *protection mechanism* for ensuring that tasks do not harm other tasks, the operating system or, for that matter, themselves.

The topic of protection in computers has become entwined with the related subjects of security and privacy—"protection" is often used in the sense of protecting one's own data from the prying eyes of others. Security should have an important impact on computer architecture, in future, but it is not a subject which was addressed in the B6700, and we will therefore not discuss it here. Be that as it may, before a system can be secure it must at least implement a protection mechanism because otherwise nothing is safe. The B6700 does provide protection, in the limited sense, to a degree exceeding most of its contemporaries and is worthy of discussion [13].

The main aim of protection is to confine any effects of a task to those resources that the task has been assigned by its controlling regimes. Any resource which is used has to be referred to by some name or other. If we consider such names as being part of the virtual address hierarchy, then we can consider the function of protection to be the restriction of the use of addresses by tasks. For some addresses the restriction needs be total but for others only certain kinds of use need be restricted, e.g. storing into a memory location could be prohibited though reading is allowed. Protection of a task from itself may involve further restrictions, for example, division by zero could be disallowed as indicative of error.

VALC starting with the address couple (level,index):

Chase display-relative addresses until other than an IRW is found, i.e.
repeatedly,
get the word addressed by D[level] + index and
if that word is an IRW then distribute it to (level,index)

Chase full virtual addresses until other than an SIRW is found, i.e.
repeatedly,
if the last word obtained is an SIRW
then distribute it to, say, (stack-no.,disp.,index);
if the stack-no. isn't that of the current stack
then find the base address of that stack, i.e.
get the stack-vector descriptor from D[0] +2,
check the stack-no. against the length field of the stack-vector and cause
an 'invalid index' interrupt if it is greater, but if it's OK
get the descriptor of that stack and extract the base address;
get the word addressed by base+disp.+index using BOSR or the address just
found as the base.

If the last word found is a PCW
then enter the thunk procedure *(so called accidental entry)*, i.e. -
construct a RCW (with V-bit set) and distribute the PCW and segment descriptor,
place a MSCW in the stack below the RCW,
update the display registers starting with the MSCW given by the last D[level]
or base of stack + disp, which will:-
complete the VALC *(execution continues with the next instruction i.e. inside
the thunk)*.

Chase data descriptors until other than a data descriptor is found, i.e.
repeatedly,
if the last word found is a data descriptor then
if the array isn't present then cause a 'presence bit' interrupt;
if the data descriptor isn't indexed then
automatically index it,i.e.
get the top word of the stack as an index but
if this isn't an operand then cause an 'invalid operand' interrupt,
integerize the index,
check the index and cause an 'invalid index' interrupt if it is negative or
greater than the length of the descriptor,
convert the descriptor to indexed form;
if the descriptor *(now indexed)* is 'segmented'
then perform 'paging' i.e.
split the index,
fetch the segment descriptor and
index that;
get the word addressed by the descriptor.

If the last word found is a single precision operand or an indexed string descriptor
then leave that word on top of the stack,but

if the last word found is a double precision operand or was ultimately pointed to by
a double precision descriptor then fetch the second word as well, or

if the last word found is an SIW then convert it into an operand.

For the above three cases finish the VALC normally, but if the last word found is
anything else then cause an 'invalid operand' interrupt!

FIG. IV.17. The complete B6700 VALC instruction.

The only way to restrict a task so that it cannot make destructive mistakes is to make its machine smarter, i.e. by using intelligent instructions which check for many error situations which could arise. Complex processors provide fewer chances for error than simpler architectures because a more restrictive model is imposed. For example, a processor using descriptors may check an index to ensure that it is within range, whereas a simple processor where indexing is addition only has no basis for such a check. Information held in descriptors or provided by tags enables instructions to check that the items they are dealing with are the correct type. Another example mentioned previously is that tasks may be stopped from creating sensitive addresses before they have any chance to try and use them.

With the B6700, much protection is provided by its rather intelligent instructions. Experience has shown that compared with more conventional machines, most program errors are detected and located much more quickly. Common errors such as exceeding of array bounds are caught as a matter of course. Others, such as use of uninitialized variables, may be detected if a compiler arranges for it (by initializing the variables to a word with a nonsense tag).

Most of the examples just discussed are attempts to be positive and prevent protection violations from arising. No matter how thorough such prevention may be there is always the chance that some unsafe act may occur. To ensure complete protection it is necessary to implement more negative protection enforcement.

IV.5.1.   RINGS OF PROTECTION

Programs have natural levels of requirement for errorlessness which correspond to their permanence, importance and extent of use. It is expected that a new program will contain errors; it is most annoying when they are found in a compiler; but it is a disaster if a central part of an operating system fails. Few programs will even really be error free, it is just that those which are most critical will receive more attention and will become more trustworthy. Levels of trust also underlie the protection provided by intelligent instructions. The micro-routines which implement instructions are very frequently used and tested. However, they can contain errors, especially if the processor is a new design. The same trust is seen with the interpreters which are sometimes used to insulate a system from new programs and to provide intelligence missing from the hardware.

Some protection schemes recognize these natural levels of trustworthiness by providing each task with a trust index in some range, e.g. 0–15. The most trusted level, say zero, is only assigned to tasks of the operating system which are allowed to do anything—these should be kept as few as possible. The levels of trust naturally follow the hierarchy of tasks, but rather than being associated permanently with tasks, trust levels apply to programs, for any task must be allowed to use a routine supplied by a regime which would normally be more trustworthy than the task. In particular, the level of trust may be altered for the duration of a single instruction. Furthermore, the level of trust may vary among the routines local to a task—following the principle of trusting as little as possible.

In a similar manner to levels of trust, levels or *rings of protection* [14] can also be associated with all items resident in the system memory. The level of protection is a property like any other and could be part of the descriptor of an area, or, in the case of items in an array having differing levels of protection by the use of tags. Protection is now ensured by comparison of level of trust with ring of protection. A task executing a program of trust level n cannot alter a memory location of ring m if m < n. No matter what an untrusted procedure does, it can never harm areas or items protected from it.

Levels of protection do have to be associated with logical rather than physical areas of memory. An example is a stack which may contain areas of local storage for many procedures of different levels of protection. Further, a stack contains items such as block markers which can only be altered by certain instructions—such as subroutine exit, and other items of record maintained by an operating system. Although we have been talking in terms of protecting items of memory from being *altered,* the same mechanism can help provide other aspects of security. Some systems provide separate levels of read protection and execution, i.e. some areas may not even be read by untrusted tasks and some subroutines may not be executed. There are also interesting problems encountered with protection ring schemes when procedures are passed parameters which come from a different protection ring than the procedure itself.

The B6700 provides two levels of both trust and protection. A program may execute in *control* or *normal* state and an area may be read-only or an individual word may be protected by an odd tag. However, these are not related—protected areas and words are still protected in control state. Of the sensitive operating system instructions listed in Table IV.2, only $1\frac{1}{2}$ are confined to control state ("set interval timer" and the "initiate I/O" and "set interrupt mask" functions of "scan out"). It is hard to see why these are treated specially because there are so many other devastating instructions which are allowed in normal state. For example, the overwrites, STAG, and two others we have not discussed yet which may be used to access the scratch pad memory used by the hardware algorithms—"read processor register" (RPRR—replaces the top of stack with the register of that number) and "set processor register" (SPRR—destructively stores the top of stack into the

TABLE IV.2

B6700 instructions used by an operating system.

OVRD — *overwrite destructive*	} *store regardless of tags*
OVRN — *overwrite non-destructive*	
EEXI — *enable external interrupts*	
DEXI — *disable external interrupts*	
WHOI — *read processor identification number*	
HEYU — *cause processor-to-processor interrupt*	
MVST — *move to new stack*	
STAG — *set tag field*	
RTAG — *read tag field*	
LLLU — *linked list lookup*	
SRCH — *masked search for equal*	
RDLK — *read with lock*	
RPRR — *read from processor register*	
SPRR — *store into processor register*	
SINT — *set interval timer*	
SCNI — *scan in*	} *I/O instructions*
SCNO — *scan out*	

register the number of which is next to top). Control state is really just used to disable external interrupts on procedure entry or return. In the B7700, however, there are some extra control instructions and when these are used they cause a "privileged operator" interrupt (in the B6700 an "invalid operator" is given if the sensitive instructions are executed in normal state).

Though not in the hardware, the B6700 does have a full two-level protection scheme. All programming is performed in high level language and the compilers are trusted to produce address couples or SIRW's which point within the bounds of a stack. The compilers are aided by the two types of store instruction—overwrites will only be generated in carefully considered situations. Once the compilers settle down then this form of protection is fairly secure; however, testing a new compiler is impossible during normal operation for it is so easy for bad code to "bomb" the system. Too much has to be trusted in the B6700, for, to be realistic, all compilers and operating systems contain bugs which cause occasional crashes.

IV.6. NOTES

1. For example, Shaw, A. C. (1974), Hansen, P. B. (1973) and Tsichritzis, D. C. and Bernstein, P. A. (1974).
2. Organick, E. I. (1973).
3. The term *task* is preferred here solely because of the confusing similarity of *processors* and *processes* when spoken with a sloppy colonial accent.
4. Thornton, J. E. (1970).
5. The term *virtual machine* is a more often used equivalent of *conceptual machine*. Unfortunately, *virtual machine,* because of its association with an IBM operating system, has taken on a more restricted meaning, namely that of a conceptual machine identical to the real machine on which it is implemented. *Conceptual machine* should avoid this confusing association.
6. For a discussion of the mutual exclusion problem see one of the texts mentioned in Note 1 above.
7. A general discussion of memory management is given by Hoare, C. A. R. and McKeag, R. M. (1972).
8. Self-relative descriptors were introduced (as *relative codewords*) in the Basic Language Machine—see Iliffe, J. K. (1968).
9. The working set concept is discussed in Coftman, E. G. Jr. and Denning, P. J. (1973).
10. For replacement strategies see Belady, L. A. and Kuehner, C. J. (1969).
11. There seems to be no general reference on the use of associative memories to bypass virtual address translation. The reader is referred to specific instances— MULTICS as discussed in Organick, E. I. (1972) and the IBM System/370 "Table Lookaside Buffer" in IBM (1974).
12. Burroughs (1969).
13. See Shankar, K. S. (1977) for a discussion of computer security.
14. Rings of protection are described in Schroeder, M. D. and Saltzer, J. H. (1972).

V. Input/Output

In this chapter we complete our discussion of computer architecture proper with consideration of a topic that we have so far managed to avoid, namely input/output.

The characteristic of I/O that is immediately apparent at any level on which it is approached, and which is why it is worth avoiding, is its complexity of detail. This is largely because of the variety of physical characteristics of the peripheral devices being controlled. For example, a peripheral device may or may not require real time control, the unit of data transferred between device and computer may be a single bit or a complete record, the character codes may vary, the procedures for controlling devices may differ, and the rate of data transfer may range from 10 characters per second to in excess of 1 000 000 characters per second. This diversity can only be appreciated by studying a real example in detail. Happily, we do not have space for such a study here and must refer the reader to other texts [1]. Our discussion will be confined mainly to processors of the central complex—I/O processors, data communications front-ends and other specialized controllers.

A second factor contributing to I/O's complexity is the prevalence of real time control. Most I/O devices involve mechanical motion of some kind, that, because of its inertia, must be controlled on its own terms. For example, a magnetic tape must be set in motion before being read, and, once reading has started, it must be continued for a whole block of data. Each character must be read as it passes the read head and must be stored away before the next character is read. Now, central computers are fast and can respond in real time; however, it may be very inconvenient for them to do so if they must save a large context when embarking on even a small new task like reading a character from an I/O device. It is need for real time control that, we will see, mandates the use of special purpose processors to assist with I/O.

In the next section below we will discuss, in a general manner, how computers impose some order on the I/O chaos. The second section goes into the organization of the I/O side of the B6700 and B7700 in some detail, and the last section treats some aspects of availability that are well illustrated by the B6700.

V.1.   The Hierarchy of I/O Processors

Because I/O operations are infrequent in comparison to the rate of execution of other CPU instructions, the hardware/software tradeoff for I/O is heavily biased in favor of performing as much as possible in software [2]. The need for flexibility in use of new peripherals also makes it unwise to bury details of I/O device control in CPU hardware [3]. On the other hand, the I/O device controllers themselves should not be excessively sophisticated when the CPU can provide any necessary algorithmic manipulation [4].

Such considerations tend to cause computer I/O systems to have the following characteristics:

I/O is controlled in terms of the physical organization of data on peripherals;

I/O data and control structures are restricted to very simple standard forms.

It is the purpose and effect of the restrictions that I/O demands heavy involvement of CPU software. The form of the restrictions and the amount of CPU software supervision required varies with the power of the computer.

Mini-computers tend to restrict the unit of I/O transfer to 1 character whereas the large computers deal with whole records of data in one I/O operation. Mini-computers also have simple I/O control protocols involving much hand shaking whereas larger machines may specify a complete control sequence with one I/O instruction.

V.1.1.   LEVELS OF I/O TASKS AND THEIR PROCESSORS

For computers of the class of the B6700/B7700 that we are discussing, the imposed uniform I/O data structure is a *record* comprising a sequence of characters, each of which is composed of bits. The basic I/O operation is thus the execution of a conceptually simple algorithm, the input version of which is shown in a structured form in Fig. V.1, where a record of "length" characters is obtained and stored at a character address "base". As shown in Fig. V.1 there are three main levels in the algorithm (marked I, II and III), though not all of these may be necessary; for example, level III is unnecessary if a peripheral deals with characters in parallel rather than as a stream of bits. In Chapter IV we traced the hierarchy of tasks down to the top level of the I/O algorithm, but now we can further develop the hierarchy down into the nether regions of I/O.

The I/O algorithm could well be executed in its entirety by a general purpose processor, but consider what processing power is really required by each level of the algorithm. At level I all that is required of a processor is that it can access main memory, add and subtract 1, and test for zero. The next level is even simpler, the processor having only to recognize when it has received a

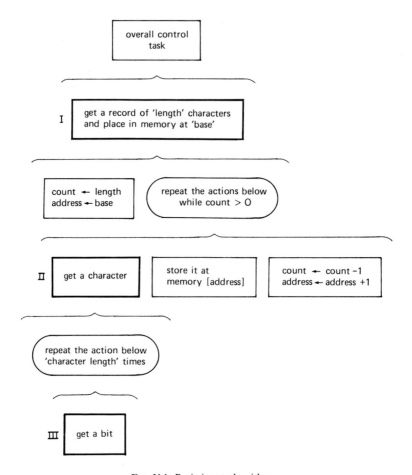

FIG. V.1. Basic input algorithm.

characters worth of bits. For these two levels a general purpose processor's power would be wasted. The last level III is even more simple in concept but it is very special, in fact, so special that digital control may be inappropriate.

We can conclude that a general purpose processor is unnecessary in order to perform the lower levels of I/O, but would one be reasonable?

To make our discussion simple assume that we are dealing with records of 1000 characters, each character being 10 bits long; furthermore, that each bit is produced by the device in 100 nsec (a reasonable rate for a disk). On this basis the level II algorithm for getting a character will have to deal with 1 bit every 100 nsec, the level I algorithm with 1 character every μsec, while the task making use of the input data only has to handle a record every msec or so.

Although unsuited, a general processor could possibly be used for the level I algorithm but at level II the data must be dealt with so quickly and frequently that a special quickly reacting processor is needed to do the job.

These considerations show that general purpose processors are neither necessary nor sufficient for I/O and suggest that a range of processors be used instead, the processors having properties suited to the different levels of the I/O algorithm. The special purpose I/O processors will show properties corresponding to their level—a progression from generality to speciality, from logical complexity to simplicity, from large contexts to small contexts, from non-real time to fast real time operation, and from large units of data to small units. A single I/O task will be split into subtasks at the levels shown in the algorithm, with each subtask having its own special processor. The tasks and processors are illustrated in Fig. V.2 (note that, for completeness, two levels of CPU task are also shown).

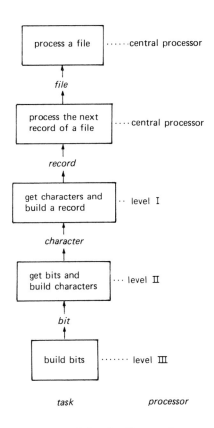

FIG. V.2. Levels of input task.

The processors used at level I are often called *data channels,* much of a misnomer but for history's sake [5]. At the level of assembly of bits into character there is no widely used name, but this level of task is often part of the function of a *peripheral controller.* Only devices that deal with bit streams need a distinct third level of I/O processor; there is no common nomenclature. In order to avoid confusion we will use the neutral terms level I, level II and level III processor when referring to the processor that performs the data transfer operations. As we shall see soon, the data transfer processors must often perform more complicated operations than those illustrated in Fig. V.1, particularly with regard to controlling processors lower down the hierarchy.

V.1.2.   SHARING AND ALLOCATION OF DATA TRANSFER PROCESSORS

The extent to which processors and controllers are shared, and the manner in which they are shared, both vary with the level of the I/O task being performed. Let us assume for the following discussion that there are actually three levels of processor used for I/O below the level of the CPU. All of the processors are system resources like any other and their allocation is thus the responsibility of the overall operating system.

A physical record is the smallest unit of information which may be obtained from an I/O device in one operation. The size of a record depends on the physical properties of the device—it may be fixed as for a card reader or variable by characters as for paper tape or variable by larger blocks as with disk records. Whatever its size may be, the transfer of a record involves a sequence of character transfers each of which may need to be handled in real time. The imposed common I/O organization must allow for transfer of records from very fast devices, hence all levels of I/O task must be in existence for at least the duration of one record transfer.

The lowest, level III tasks are each dedicated to a particular peripheral device (by our definition) and, in fact, may be identified with the device controllers themselves. Level III processors must be allocated to level III I/O tasks for at least the transfer of one complete record; they cannot be shared within this period. Furthermore, some devices are such that, although a record is the smallest item which may be obtained in one access, the records are grouped into larger files which must be dealt with as a whole, e.g. decks of cards. For these devices, allocation must be for the duration of the processing of an entire file.

At the next level, the level II processors must be allocated to level II tasks for one complete record transfer. They may, however, be shared in between record transfers even if the peripheral devices are transferring complete files. Each level II processor may, therefore, be connected to a number of devices though the level II processor will only be used by one record transfer task at a time and will therefore deal with only one device at a time [6].

At level I the flow of information becomes less continuous. Although a level I processor can, like a level II processor, be dedicated to the transfer of a complete record (sometimes then called a *selector channel*), it would, with slow devices, spend most of its time doing nothing. It is therefore more usual to share each level I processor among several data transfer tasks.

It is possible at level I to not have special I/O processors at all but to share a central processor which, of course, has the necessary simple arithmetic powers to execute level I tasks. This may be done using micro-code (sometimes called "process or hesitation" or "processor cycle stealing") or by using ordinary control tasks. In this latter case, the processor could be shared by scheduling but, because the I/O task must respond in real time, this would normally imply that the processor be dedicated to executing its I/O tasks.

It is more usual to share the central processor by interrupts in which case the switching of tasks is fast enough for real time response. If different peripherals are being controlled simultaneously, one finds that their "time criticalness" varies—it may be essential for the interrupt for one device to be serviced completely within 50 μsec while another could wait for up to 50 msec. For this reason the devices, or rather the interrupts they can cause, are often divided into levels of priority in the manner discussed in Section IV.2.3.

This priority interrupt scheme is sometimes used by larger computers, but not for sharing the central processors among channel tasks. With a large computer there will be so much I/O data being transferred that the central processor would be mainly devoted to I/O control. The algorithmic powers of the processor would be wasted; hence, it is usual for larger computers to indeed have special level I processors which are shared among the level I tasks.

We saw that level II and III processors are allocated by the operating system but only in between record (or file) transfers. Their allocation is therefore not a real time task and can be easily handled by some minion of the operating system executed by a central processor. However, when level I processors are shared, the allocation must be on a character-by-character basis. If a central task were to perform the allocation, there would be no advantage in having a special channel processor, because the allocation task would gobble just as much central processor time as if the CPU executed the transfer itself. We find instead that a special, more simple processor is devoted to the task of allocating the level I processor.

The level I allocation task is unvarying and its program is thus hard, or at least firm, wired. In fact, as illustrated in Fig. V.3, level I data transfer tasks and the allocation task are usually executed in the same processor, called an *I/O processor*.

It is hard to distinguish between the level I processor and its allocator; the

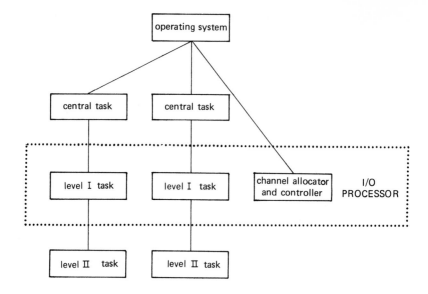

FIG. V.3. Control of channel tasks.

matter is further complicated by other controlling responsibilities also being executed by the I/O processor. In some cases the sharing of the level I processor is termed *multiplexing* because a data bus is often shared along with the channel processor.

The level I processor allocation task is subservient to nothing but the operating system and one must therefore regard an I/O processor as being on an equal footing with central processors. The level I tasks are definitely subservient to individual central tasks, however. This has led to some confusion of concepts. It has become usual to make all level I tasks directly subservient to the operating system, as a result of which all I/O operations have to be initiated by an operating system task. It is unusual, if not unknown, for a level I task to direct an I/O-complete interrupt to a specific central task. However, in some computers there are two interrupts caused by normal completion of a level I task, the I/O-complete interrupt and a channel-available interrupt—both are directed to the operating system but the former is expected to be redirected to some other task.

One effect of the sharing of processors used for I/O data transfer is that the higher the level of task the fewer the processors that are needed. In a simple system one finds the various processors connected in a hierarchy which reflects their allocation method. Figure V.4 shows the I/O control organization of a

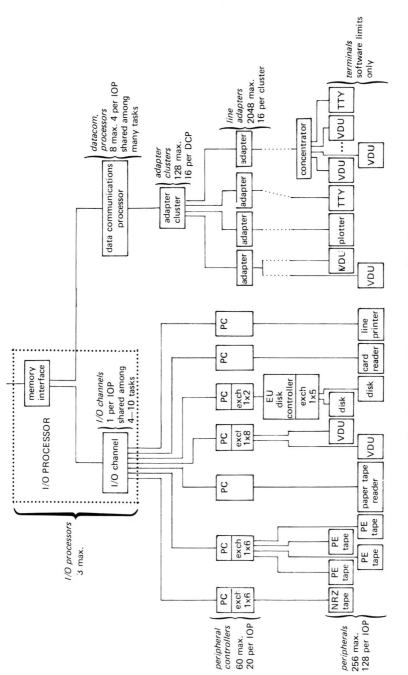

FIG. V.4. The I/O processor hierarchy of a small B6700 system.

small B6700 system. (The I/O organization is, as we will see in Section V.3, often much more complicated than a simple hierarchy.) We will consider the details of the B6700 later but for now a few remarks on the function and allocation of the processors to assist in the comprehension of Fig. V.4.

To start with there are two main types of I/O processor in B6700 systems—the I/O processor itself (IOP), which is used for controlling on-site peripherals, and the data communications processor (DCP). Logically these are independent although the DCP is physically dependent on the IOP in a number of ways, one being that it shares the IOP's memory interface. This use of different processors exhibits a trend that could be taken further than the two types of the B6700; the ICL 2900 has four different I/O processors, for example.

The B6700 I/O processor is sometimes referred to as a multiplexor. It allocates the level I processor part of itself, and the I/O data bus, to level I tasks on the basis of needs indicated by the level II processors called peripheral controllers. There can be up to 10 level I tasks in existence at any one time, the maximum being a purchasable option. The peripheral controllers receive characters from devices but not usually in the form of a bit stream. In the case of disks there is a device controller (called an EU—electronics unit) that may be shared among five disks. However, for most devices the hierarchy may be considered as ending at the peripheral controller with character-sized units of data. Note the inclusion of *exchanges* in the hierarchy as these are, from one point of view, also processors which receive commands to select a path.

The data communications processor is designed to deal with data communications devices operating at speeds up to 9600 baud and, as this is slower than the transfer rate for most peripheral devices, the DCP can handle more level I tasks than the I/O processor. Each DCP can deal with 256 lines, each line with possibly many terminals. The DCP has active, at any time, one overall allocation task, one control task for each line being used (which "calls" a program for a record transfer from one station on the line), and some other control tasks, amounting in all to possibly hundreds of tasks sharing the one processor. The programs executed by the DCP are changeable micro-code.

The "adapter cluster" is a highly specialized processor which performs the level II task of building characters from bits as well as performing other control functions. The level II processor of the cluster is multiplexed between 16 lines. The level III processor is the "line adapter" which senses the line and receives or transmits bits. As shown, though, the data communications hierarchy may be extended into the remote network.

V.1.3.   CONTROL OF I/O TASKS AND PROCESSORS

So far in our treatment of I/O we have considered only the data transfer function of I/O tasks, their processors, and how the processors are allocated. Now we must complete this general discussion by looking at how the tasks and processors are controlled. We dealt with control of tasks in Section IV.2.3 where we saw that control could be maintained if a regime could initiate and terminate tasks and monitor their progress as they executed. For central tasks we noted that an interrupt mechanism is the main means of ensuring control; interrupts are directed both "down" to cause tasks to obey a certain program and "up" to get the attention of a regime in order to notify it of the occurrence of an event. I/O tasks, unlike most central tasks, are working within real time constraints and it is not too surprising to find that they need a more special means of control.

In our discussion of control we talked rather loosely about a regime being able to look at what its tasks are doing. We were assuming that the regime could examine the execution records of its tasks while they were executing. That is fine if the execution record is held in a memory common to both the task and the regime. However, part of the execution record may be held in a memory which the regime cannot get at directly. This happens temporarily in central tasks when they are executing, because some important items such as the current instruction address are kept as the local context in a processor. For I/O tasks this hidden information becomes a greater problem for it is usual, because the execution record is quite simple, to keep all of the execution record (apart from the data being transmitted) in a special memory.

As was noted in the previous section the I/O task hierarchy is often complicated by the manner in which the processors are allocated, there being a special I/O task which allocates the level I processor among a group of level I tasks. The level I processor allocator is often executed by a part of a special I/O processor and it is directly subservient to the operating system (or to one of the operating system tasks). The allocator has access to the execution records of the level I tasks, hence it has also become usual for all control of level I tasks to be made via the channel allocator, which may therefore be termed a *controller* as well. When a central task needs to initiate, terminate or monitor one of its level I tasks, it must request the operating system to order the controller section of the I/O processor to do the job.

Operations that are to be executed by the level I controller are most often represented as CPU instructions that are executed synchronously, i.e. they appear to the programmer to be executed by the CPU. Typical commands would be to start, stop or interrogate the status of a level I task. An instruction to start a level I task must also specify a program for the level I processor. Such a program is usually very simple and is often included in, or implied by, the I/O instruction. When there is actually a program its individual steps are commonly called *commands*.

Even if a level I program has just one step, such as "read a record", this will probably involve the level I task in sending more than one instruction on down to the level II processor. These instructions to peripherals, by common use called *orders*, may be, for example, to condition a peripheral to receive information, to transmit information or to wind up an operation. A very simple device at the lowest level may have to be specifically ordered to transmit every character of a record.

One important feature to consider when comparing I/O systems of different computers is how and when they become specific to the characteristics of particular peripherals. It seems to be accepted that the I/O features provided by a high level conceptual machine should be independent, as much as possible, of the device; for example, it should be possible to switch output from a printer to a disk or remote teletype merely by somehow changing the device name in the file definition. At the lowest level of the processor hierarchy the level III or II processor has to be specific to the device. At the levels in between, flexibility is traded off with complexity. For example, the level I program's commands may include orders to a lower level controller in their exact form, or, alternatively, the level I processor may know of the device's characteristics and generate the necessary orders. In the first situation (often found in smaller computers) the level I program must be complicated and detailed but it is easy to deal with a new device. The alternative makes the program simple but it may be hard to include a new device for that would require modification to the level I processor. A compromise is to have an I/O channel with a changeable micro-program.

The other aspect of control, i.e. how a regime is notified of its task's need for attention, also varies over the I/O hierarchy. At the lowest level the device controllers are devoted to their devices and continuously monitor them for interesting events; similarly, level II processors are devoted to a device for a complete record transfer. At a higher level, the level I tasks are devoted to a single peripheral for one operation but the level I processors are shared. If the tasks are multiplexed using a round-robin algorithm then the effect of continuous monitoring is obtained, but if they are otherwise scheduled a level II processor must be able to notify the level I allocator in the event of its needing attention. At the highest level (level I to CPU) the call for attention is most likely not time-critical and an ordinary interrupt is quite adequate.

The ability of tasks to control and to be controlled is dependent on their being able to communicate. Communication of both data and commands may be via a passive stored memory, or, if the task being communicated with is active, via an active interprocessor connection. There will be different tradeoffs between the two means of communication at different levels in the I/O processor hierarchy (and, of course, from computer to computer).

Between central tasks, as they may not be executing, most communication is via a memory, the only necessary interprocessor connection being a simple interrupt signal. Between central and I/O tasks the same technique could be used (typified by the B7700—see below), but more usually there is a compromise where part of an I/O command is sent directly to an I/O processor (as in the B6700 as we shall see) and part is in memory.

V.2   B6700/B7700 I/O PROCESSORS

The B6700 serves as a fine example of the I/O side of a computer for its I/O architecture is much more conventional than the architecture of its CPU. We will discuss, in the first four subsections below, the B6700 I/O organization and its three types of I/O processor. The last subsection is devoted to the B7700 I/O processor which is quite different from that of the B6700 and much more unusual.

V.2.1.   B6700 I/O CONTROL

As well as central processors (CPU's), a B6700 system may include three types of I/O processor. The main I/O processor is called the *I/O processor* itself—we will use the name IOP to distinguish it from the general term. The other I/O processors are the data communications processor (DCP) and the disk file optimizer (DFO). We will consider each I/O processor and its subsidiaries individually but let us first see how the processors communicate with each other.

The I/O processors all execute continuous scheduling and allocation tasks independently of the central processor's control. They also execute specific control commands at the request of the operating system in the central processors. Provision is therefore made for transmission of control signals outward and for this purpose the *scan bus* interconnection is used.

Only the central processors may send commands via the scan bus. The bus is allocated to the CPU's in a round-robin fashion using a flying bit in a special interprocessor connection loop called the *scan interlock*. Only the CPU in possession of the interlock bit may use the bus and when it has finished it must pass the bit on to the next processor.

Central processors have two I/O instructions for controlling the I/O processors, the *scan-in* (SCNI) and *scan-out* (SCNO) instructions. For both instructions the top of the stack should contain an operand called a *scan command word* (see Fig. V.5(a)), the right-most 20 bits of which are placed on the scan bus as a processor number and an instruction for that processor. The scan bus has 80 lines, one of which is set to distinguish between scan-in and scan-out. If the operation is scan-out, the CPU places the 51-bit word from the next to top of stack onto the bus and this is accepted by the

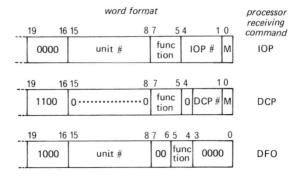

a) scan command words (M= all processors respond)

b) interrupt literal for external interrupts

c) priority of external interrupts

FIG. V.5. B6700 interprocessor communication details.

addressed processor (and both words deleted from the stack). If the operation is scan-in, then the addressed processor places a data word on the bus and this replaces the top of stack. What the data words are and what further action is taken is dependent on the type of the I/O processor. Note how scan-in is like LOAD and scan-out like STOD—i.e. interprocessor communication is very like referring to memory, though the two actions are not unified [7].

Notification of interrupts is not quite so clean. One would expect either that there would be just one I/O interrupt, the cause to be distinguished by further interrogation, or one interrupt for each processor. In fact, there are two different external interrupts, one from each of two IOP's designated A and B, presumably because in the original design of the B6700 there were but two IOP's. The external interrupt lines are physically part of the scan bus but logically they are separate as they may be turned on by the IOP's at any time rather than only in response to a CPU scan instruction. DCP's, DFO's, and any IOP's in excess of the basic two, must communicate their interrupt via one of the IOP's A or B. The central processor which is interrupted must scan-in from the IOP an "interrupt literal" which defines the interrupt and tells what processor caused it. This scan-in is performed automatically as part of the interrupt process and the "interrupt literal" becomes the P1 parameter to the main hardware interrupt subroutine. There are further connections between central processors to ensure that only one is interrupted for any external interrupt.

The various command buses are shown for a medium sized B6700 system in Fig. V.6. In addition to the I/O buses just discussed, the processor-to-processor, or HEYU, connection (discussed in Chapter IV) is also shown. Note that the DFO has no interrupt signal line because it does not cause any interrupts.

Transfer of data between the I/O processors and main memory also involves a design compromise. Because the interface necessary to deal with memory is complex and expensive the capability of communicating directly with memory is reserved for the processors that require a high memory bandwidth—the CPU's and IOP's. Each DCP accesses memory via an IOP (see Fig. V.4), there being four subsidiary memory ports provided by each IOP. Provision is made for devices, other than DCP's, that require direct memory access to be connected to memory via an IOP but this is not often used. DFO's do not need to communicate with main memory at all.

V.2.2. B6700 I/O PROCESSOR

The B6700 IOP performs the functions of any I/O processor:

it controls and monitors its I/O hierarchy, receives commands from the operating system, and directs interrupts toward the operating system;

it executes tasks that transfer data between the main memory and peripheral devices;

it allocates its level I processor among competing tasks.

The IOP is hardwired and all the above activities go on in parallel, not existing as conventional programs. Let us try and keep the three activities separate for the purposes of discussion, though it will become clear that they are inextricably entwined.

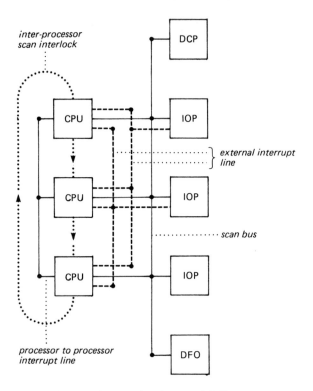

FIG. V.6. Command connections between B6700 processors.

1. *Control in the IOP*

Here we run through the control aspects of the IOP. Our discussion will touch on the components of the IOP as illustrated in Fig. V.7.

As can be seen in the list of interrupt types in Fig. V.5(a) only one type of I/O interrupt arises within the IOP, the other interrupts being passed via the IOP from some other processor or controller. The internal interrupt is "I/O finish" and indicates that a channel task has completed either normally or in error. The I/O finish interrupt literal contains no information to further refine its cause—such information must be obtained by the operating system interrogating the IOP identified in the right-most four bits of the interrupt literal.

The IOP may be set up to monitor selected peripherals for a "change of status". Each peripheral that is being monitored is connected by a special direct line to a word in the IOP called the *status change vector* (of up to 32 bits). If the peripheral does change status the bit in the status change vector is set to 1

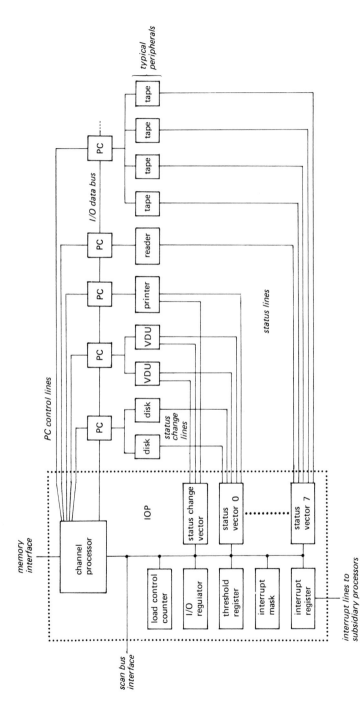

Fig. V.7. B6700 I/O processor—bus and control line structure.

and the IOP notifies a CPU of a *status change* interrupt. The operating system must interrogate the status change vector in order to identify the device that changed status. This facility is used only for printers' and operators' visual display units to indicate end of paper motion or cursor movement respectively.

The IOP receives interrupt signals from other processors and remembers their occurrence in a 10-bit *interrupt register*. The operating system may wish to instruct the IOP to ignore certain interrupts. Hence, corresponding to the interrupt register, the IOP maintains a 10-bit *interrupt mask* which is such that if a bit in the mask is 1 then the corresponding interrupt is ignored. If an unmasked bit in the interrupt register is ever 1 a CPU is interrupted and informed of the source of the interruption—the bit in the interrupt register being cleared. As shown in Fig. V.5 there are, in fact, only five such interrupts defined, from up to four DCP's and another IOP.

As well as the special "status change" control lines the IOP has a standard form of connection with all peripherals and peripheral controllers (PC's). Each peripheral is connected by one *status* line to the IOP in order to indicate whether or not the peripheral is busy. Each peripheral device is assigned a *unit number* in the range 0–255 and the status line from the peripheral is wired into the corresponding position in one of the eight *status vectors* of 32 bits each. These status vectors may also be interrogated by the operating system.

Each IOP may be connected to a maximum of only 20 peripheral controllers but some PC's may be used to control many peripherals, the allocation of peripherals to PC's being permanent. Although each PC is assigned an identifying number, called a *channel number*, I/O operations refer to the unit number of a peripheral rather than the PC channel number. The IOP is therefore *wired* to map unit numbers to PC channel numbers (in a fairly easy to alter manner); also wired in is knowledge of the type of the device handled by each PC (each PC only handles devices of one type).

The peripheral controllers share a common 16-bit data bus but each has its own special 4-wire control connection to the IOP. The four control lines are used:

i. by the PC to signal the IOP when it is ready to transfer data;

ii. by the IOP to order the PC to transfer data;

iii. by the IOP to order the PC to accept the number of a unit with which to perform an I/O operation;

iv. by the PC to indicate its busy status to the IOP.

Apart from the above control signals, the PC's receive orders as characters on the data bus.

The IOP is used to keep time in the whole system. It contains a "*time of day clock*", generates clock pulses, and initiates clear and load signals.

For the dynamic reconfiguration option (to be discussed in Section V.3.2) the IOP contains a "*load control counter*" which counts the number of times (from 1 to 7) the IOP has initiated a system load.

A last pair of registers of interest is the combination of *I/O regulator* and *threshold register*. The I/O regulator is set to a value reflecting the current amount of I/O traffic on the I/O data bus; it is incremented by 1 for each tape I/O and 2 for each disk I/O data transfer. The threshold register contains a value in the same range as the I/O regulator (1–15). The IOP will not initiate a new channel task that would make the I/O regulator exceed the threshold register, for if it did the I/O data bus might become overloaded.

TABLE V.1

B6700 I/O processor scan commands.

(a) Scan-in

    read time of day clock
    read interrupt mask   ⎫
    read interrupt register ⎬ variants
    read I/O regulator
    read load control counter
    interrogate peripheral status
    read interrupt literal
    interrogate peripheral unit type
    interrogate I/O path
    access request result descriptor

(b) Scan-out

    set time of day clock
    set interrupt mask
    set threshold register
    set load control counter ⎫
    step load control counter ⎬ variants
    initiate I/O

The scan-out and scan-in commands listed in Table V.1 may now be described. The scan-in commands always result in the transfer of one word from the IOP to the CPU from which the scan was initiated. The scan-in functions "read time of day clock", "read interrupt mask/register", "read I/O regulator", "read load control counter" and "interrogate peripheral status" are pure transfers of information from a register within the IOP (the last command must specify which of the eight status vectors or the status change vector is to be read). Three scan-ins involve the IOP in a small amount of calculation. "Read interrupt literal" returns an *interrupt literal* which indicates the highest priority interrupt as yet unserviced (see Fig. V.5(c)). Only unmasked interrupts figure in the interrupt literal. "Interrogate peripheral unit type" sends to the CPU an 8-bit value which indicates the type of the specified peripheral (or zero indicating that a peripheral of that number is not attached to the IOP). "Interrogate I/O path" returns true if the controller of the peripheral in question is not busy and if there is space for another channel task, and false otherwise. The last scan-in operation is "access request result descriptor"—this command is given by the operating system in response to an "I/O finish" interrupt. The IOP purges the completed task and sends the operating system a "result descriptor" word which indicates the state of the task when it finished.

As mentioned earlier, some of the scan-in operations may be directed to all IOP's. In this case the CPU hardware sends a scan-in to each IOP in turn and combines the resulting data. The result from "interrogate I/O path" will indicate which IOP's, if any, have a path to the peripheral and the result from "interrogate peripheral status" will be the "or" of the vector words from each IOP. "Read time of day clock" is sent to IOP A by default and "interrogate unit type" will return the first non-zero value, if any, received from any IOP.

There are fewer scan-out commands. "Set time of day clock", "set threshold register", "set load control counter" and "set interrupt mask" transfer the scan data word to the specified register. "Step load control counter" increments the said register by 1. The other command is to "initiate I/O" but we will discuss this in the following description of the level I tasks.

2.   Level I Tasks

A level I task is initiated by the controlling section of the IOP in response to an "initiate I/O" scan-out. The scan-out instruction specifies the location of a "channel command" which is best regarded as a set of parameters supplied to a hardwired program built into the channel processor (the parameter bits are listed in Table V.2).

An I/O command consists of two words, an IOCW (control word) and an IOCE (control extension), residing in the B6700 main memory. A full level I program is usually given by one command but commands may be chained together to form a list of operations to be performed as one channel sequence. The data area associated with a particular command may be physically contiguous with the command or may be located somewhere else in memory. The ability to chain commands is a late addition to the B6700 repertoire; in fact, single commands are all that are used by the B6700 MCP [8] though remotely located data areas (also a late feature) are used. A simple command and a chained sequence of commands are both illustrated in Fig. V.8.

The level I processor executing a level I task may be thought of as in Fig.

TABLE V.2

Standard option bits of B6700 I/O control words and result descriptors (i.e. those not particular to a device).

(a) Control words
IOCW

47 chained command	—	*this command is chained to the next*
46 remote data area	—	*buffer area is not contiguous with command*
45 software attention	—	*set corresponding bit in result descriptor*
44 read/write	—	*input or output operation*
43 memory inhibit	—	*no main memory transfer*
42 translate	—	*translate into (input) or from (output) EBCDIC*
41 frame size	—	*6-bit or 8-bit data*
40 memory protect	—	*ignore data area tag protection*
39 backward	—	*backwards operation for tapes*
38 test	—	*test device to get result descriptor (no I/O)*

37 tag } — {
36 options }

1. *store double precision tags*
2. *store single precision tags*
3. *store program tags*
4. *transfer tags unchanged*

IOCE (if bits 47 or 46 are on in the IOCW)

25 ascii	—	*translate into (output) or from (input) ASCII*
23 interrupt	—	*cause "I/O complete interrupt" after this command (if chained)*

(b) Result descriptors

16 memory protect error	—	*attempted to store data into a word with protected tag*
6 memory parity error	—	*main memory parity error*
5 memory address error	—	*memory did not respond (not operational)*
4 descriptor error	—	*error in form of area descriptor*
3 not ready	—	*peripheral went not-ready*
2 control busy	—	*no PC available to control peripheral*
1 software attention	—	*set if required by the command*
0 exception	—	*other device-specific error*

V.9. It has a word interface (48 bits) with main memory and a 2-character temporary connection (16 bits) directly via a data bus to one of the 20 peripheral controllers. Each peripheral controller is also connected to the level I processor by four control lines. The main functional parts are a word data buffer register and a translate network, but there are also other registers and control circuits, some of which are illustrated.

A single command, started directly by "scan-out", or by chaining from a preceding command, provides the IOP with the peripheral unit number for this operation, the command address, and the length of the I/O transfer in

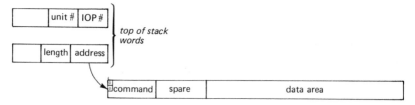

a) simple single-step I/O sequence

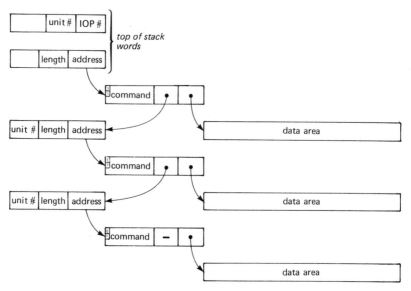

b) chained I/O sequence with remote commands

FIG. V.8. Form of B6700 I/O sequences.

characters (actually in words + extra characters). The IOP uses the unit number to find the channel number (i.e. the number of the PC of the peripheral) and conditions any exchanges not built into the peripheral controller to open the data path to the peripheral. The channel number, the command address and length of data transfer are also loaded into registers and the level I task is started.

Now the level I processor proceeds to read the first and the second words of the command from memory. The command is used to generate an order for a peripheral controller. The order consists of a one-byte opcode, e.g. read/write,

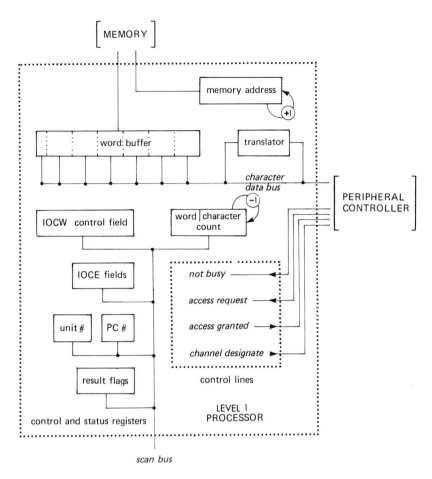

FIG. V.9. Idealized B6700 level I processor.

etc., and up to 5 further bytes to refine the order (including a disk address for a disk PC).

Once the peripheral controller has been given its order, the level I task waits for a signal from the PC that it is ready to transmit data. When the PC signals, the level I processor transfers the character (or two characters), translating it if necessary. When the processor has dealt with a complete word of 6 or 8 characters (of 8 or 6 bits respectively), it stores them in, or fetches a new word from, main memory.

This process continues until a complete record has been moved, or until the operation is complete in some other way, e.g. an error occurs. The channel task then replaces its length register with a device-dependent *result descriptor* formed from conditions within the channel processor and from a final result byte sent by the peripheral controller. The channel number register is changed to 11111 (or 11011 for a chained operation for which an interrupt was requested) to show that it is finished. The control section of the IOP notices this and, if appropriate, causes an I/O finish interrupt.

The final stage in the life of a level I I/O task is that the operating system scans in the result descriptor. A descriptor gives the address of the last character transferred, a 17-bit error field, and the unit number of the device involved. The channel task is purged and its resources reallocated.

For a chained operation an I/O finish interrupt is generated after a single step in the level I program, if the appropriate command bit was on, and the task idles until the operating system scans in the result descriptor. When it continues, the level I task stores in the second word of the command the address of the last character transferred and changes a bit in the command to indicate that this has been done. It then finds the next command and processes that. The final command, when finished, causes final interrupt and the operating system is given, not a result descriptor, but a *result pointer* which is of the same form as a result descriptor but points to the last IOCW instead of the last character transferred.

The standard parts of result descriptors are listed in Table V.2.

3.   *IOP Allocation*

For each level I task the contents of the various registers just described are held in one large word of an associative memory addressed by the channel number. The number of channel tasks which can be executed simultaneously is thus limited to between 4 and 10 depending on how much associative memory is installed. Whenever a PC indicates to the channel controller, by turning on its "access request" line, that it wishes to transfer data, the associative memory is addressed by the number of that channel, the memory word distributed, the request dealt with, and the results stored back in the memory. In the case of multiple requests, priority is given to the channel with the lowest number; thus the channel number assignments are usually made in order of decreasing urgency for data transfers.

The associative memory also needs to be read when an I/O operation is initiated but this use has a lower priority than that for a data transfer. Initiation of an I/O operation and reading of a result descriptor are separate hardwired programs and can thus carry on in parallel with data transfers, the only conflict being over use of the associative memory. An unused memory word has an address of 00000, one that contains a result descriptor 11111, and in between steps of a chained sequence the address is set to 11011 if an interrupt was called for at that stage. A scan-in to obtain a result descriptor will obtain the first word with an address of either 11111 or 11011. The IOP can tell if any particular PC may be accessed because, if so, its number is not in an associative memory address field.

V.2.3. B6700 DATA COMMUNICATIONS PROCESSOR

The B6700 data communications processor offers a total contrast to the system's main I/O processor. In almost all details the two devices are quite different, although both processors serve much the same purpose.

There isn't really anything significantly different about data communications which requires such special treatment. The console visual display units of the B6700, for example, are basically data communications terminals yet they are controlled by an IOP. Conversely, the B6700 DCP is often used to interface slow on-site peripherals such as plotters. Rather than there being a clear difference between the requirements of local and remote peripherals they can only be distinguished by the *extremes* in the way they are used.

Most data communications terminals are designed to be connected to a computer via a single transmission line. It is accepted that transmission errors will be quite frequent. In order to correct these errors, and to maintain control on a single line, the controller at the computer end and the terminal itself are often expected to follow quite complicated control strategies called line *protocols*.

In contrast, local peripherals are usually connected to a computer by multiple control and data lines. Transmission errors are not expected to happen very often and recovery from such errors, e.g. retrying an operation, is usually left to operating system software. The control strategy for local peripherals is therefore usually simpler than that for data communications devices.

Line protocols and control strategies could well be hardwired. However, any data communications processor must be flexible, and be capable of handling new devices and protocols. Manufacturers of computers have tried to insist (not always successfully) that they provide all the local peripherals to their main-frames. They have never been able to do that with data communications devices both because the connection to the computer is so tenuous and because data communications devices were in common use well before the time of computers. One finds then that data communications networks include different devices produced by different manufacturers, some of which were not even conceived of when the computer was produced and some which predate the computer by many years. This diversity and need for flexibility make it desirable that a data communications processor be programmable rather than hardwired.

As well as by its variety, a data communications network is distinguished by the multiplicity of its devices connected to the computer, in most cases many more than the number of local peripherals. Furthermore, every data communications line attached to the computer needs to be monitored continuously while a service is being offered. However, to offset its demands, data communications has another important feature, that data transmission rates are slow. The maximum rate is often limited to less than 1000 characters per second (9600 baud for example) and, in many networks, the average rate over all lines is much less. Even if a fast terminal is being used, it is not a serious fault if the controlling processor occasionally fails to keep up with the speed of transmission, for the protocols allow recovery from such errors by retransmission. This makes it feasible to use a comparatively slow microprogrammed I/O processor to control data communications—the B6700 DCP being a case in point.

V.2.3.1.   *Control in the DCP*
The B6700 DCP may be summed up as a conventional vertically micro-programmed processor. It is connected to, and controls, the very specialized *adapter clusters,* but the DCP itself is almost completely non-specialized. Unlike the IOP, which is concrete in its purpose, the DCP is a *tabla rasa* needing a program to determine its use. It is the program of the DCP which must be compared with the IOP. Although it is not our purpose here to discuss software, we must, of necessity, digress a little and discuss the B6700 I/O software before looking at the DCP hardware.

The local and remote sides of the B6700 I/O system were developed independently. However, there has always been an integration of local and remote logical files which, at the programming language level, may be used quite interchangeably. Below this level the two sides immediately diverge in their appearance to the user, but despite their differences, both local and remote I/O have the same logical structure to a much lower level.

For local I/O, operations concerning a particular device are initially placed in a queue unique to that device. When the operating system, in the guise of a procedure called STARTIO, determines that the device is free, it moves the command to a *channel queue* from where it is dealt with when there is space for the operation available in an IOP. Each I/O operation is defined by an *I/O control block* (IOCB) which consists of queue links, and a few words of information ending with the I/O control words (usually with the data buffer immediately appended).

For remote I/O, operations for a station are placed initially in a queue unique to that station. When the operating system, in the guise of a special permanent task called the *data communications controller* (DCC—one for each DCP), determines that the station is free, the operation is moved to a *request queue* from where it is dealt with. An operation in this case is called a *message* and is a few words of control information again followed, if appropriate, by a buffer area.

At this stage of description the only real difference between central and remote I/O is that the latter's queues are set up by a permanent task. The DCC is permanent because, while data communications is active, any station may start sending a message. Of course, the same is true of on-site peripherals—a start button may be pressed at any time. However, for on-site I/O this condition is checked for periodically by the operating system and no information is transferred until necessary. Incidentally, sudden initiation of input of either type will cause the creation of a task to handle the traffic, a message control system (MCS) for data communications to interpret the message and for local I/O a task called "control card" to read in and schedule a job (if from a card reader) or "controller" to interpret messages from a system control console.

From here on down, the two sides of the I/O system are handled differently even if the overall effect is the same. For local I/O, the operating system (procedure INITIATEIO) removes I/O operations from the channel queue and tells the IOP what to do by using an "initiate I/O" scan-out command. On an "I/O finish" interrupt the operating system will perform a "scan-in" to read the result descriptor and will then notify the task that originally requested the operation.

For data communications the request queue is handled by a routine executed by the DCP. Most commands to the DCP are given to it in its request queue. The DCP in turn places results such as input messages and status indicators into another queue called the *result queue*. This is dealt with by the DCC, which notifies the task that originally requested the operation.

Because most commands to the DCP are included as messages in the request queue, the central processor needs only limited hardware powers for directly controlling a DCP. The DCP's are connected to the scan bus but there are only 3 scan-out commands. These are:

i. "Initialize" which sends to the DCP the location in main memory of its program.
ii. "Halt" which stops the DCP.
iii. "Set attention needed" which sets a flag in the DCP and is used by the DCC to notify an idling DCP that something has been placed in its request queue.

In the other direction, the DCP needs to interrupt the operating system (indirectly via an IOP) to notify the DCC that something has been placed in a previously empty result queue. Apart from these four control functions all communication between the processors is done by software via the request and result queues.

The programs executed by the DCP are generated from a description of the data communications network written in a special language called *network definition language* (NDL). Each DCP thus has its own micro-program especially tailored to the network it controls. The controlling programs for the DCP are much the same from system to system but make use, when executing, of installation-specific tables and procedures generated from the NDL.

The DCP has access to the computer's main memory and also, as a usual option, may be equipped with its own fast local memory. When the DCP receives an "initialize" scan-out command, it is also supplied with the starting address of a program in main memory. If the DCP has local memory, it then transfers its program over, and whether using local or main memory, starts operating. The DCP executes the one fixed set of programs until it is reinitialized.

Unlike the IOP which executes its control, data transfer and scheduling, tasks in parallel, in a DCP only one task may be active. We may think of there being a task in overall control allocating the DCP between itself and other tasks. Tasks are set up to deal with operations from the request queue and there may be tasks active for control by handling data from each line and station (level I tasks). Thus, although there is no actual parallelism, the DCP performs the same types of tasks as the IOP in a multiprogrammed, time-sliced fashion.

The allocation of the DCP processor to competing tasks is of interest. Level II tasks in the adapter clusters raise flags to tell the controlling task in the DCP when they need attention but there is no interrupt of the task currently being executed. Instead, each DCP task is trusted to return back to the controlling task every so often in order that the processor can, if necessary, be allocated to a more needy task. In this way all time-critical tasks can be serviced in real time. A flag waving for more than 500 μsec is noted by the hardware and is regarded as system failure. This seldom happens because all the programs are well tested, being written for a cooperative purpose, and the time-critical parts for dealing with clusters are rather short.

The way that the DCP is switched between tasks is reminiscent of the IOP. The DCP has a small scratchpad memory of eight 48-bit words which is the context of the task being executed. When tasks are changed, one block of information is rolled out of the scratchpad memory and another lot rolled in. One word of the scratchpad is used to build up/break down 48-bit words to/from characters—just as in the IOP.

So far we have been discussing software but have slipped some hardware details in as well; we have mentioned the scan-out commands, instruction counter, scratchpad memory and an instruction to interrupt the MCP. There is not much else of interest in the DCP! Like all practical micro-programmed machines the instruction set is bewildering in its detail but each instruction, once determined, is very simple. There are instructions to move data over various buses between registers and the scratchpad, instructions to read data from main memory, and a few instructions to perform simple 8-bit arithmetic and logical operations. Some of the more interesting features are:

i. an instruction equivalent to "read with lock" for synchronizing access to main memory queues;

ii. a set of registers CC, CA, CI (cluster command, address, information) for interfacing with adapter clusters;

iii. instructions to read, write and interrogate adapter clusters;

iv. two flags CAN and SAN (cluster and system attention needed) which can be tested by the DCP, in lieu of interrupts;

v. an instruction to idle until a CAN or SAN setting occurs;

vi. a translate instruction for converting ASCII characters to EBCDIC;

vii. a number of interrupts arising on fault conditions—the interrupts are simple forced branches to one of many fixed, low-address locations.

V.2.3.2.   The Adapter Cluster
Each of the 8 possible data communications processors in a B6700 system can control up to 16 adapter clusters each of which can handle 16 data communications lines (each line is thus identified by a DCP #, cluster #, adapter #, triplet). Whereas the DCP is a completely non-specific processor, the adapter cluster has been carefully tailored to fulfil its purpose. In fact, the adapter cluster is much more like the IOP than the DCP as it is hardwired and executes controlling, allocation, and level II data transfer tasks in parallel.

The allocation section of the cluster then shares its data transfer mechanism among 16 level II data transfer tasks. Similar to the IOP, the execution record of each task is stored packed into a 56-bit word of small fast local memory and while a task is being executed its record is distributed to the high speed registers of the cluster. Every 200 nsec the next record is read from the local memory, the data transfer task is given one execution step, and the record written back. This goes on continuously treating all data transfer tasks equally in a round-robin fashion. The cluster thus allocates its line processor by pure multiplexing and gives the effect of 16 data transfer tasks executing in parallel, each performing one step every 3·2 μsec. This is in contrast to the IOP allocation mechanism where the data transfer mechanism is allocated on the basis of priority and need. All commands from the DCP to the adapter are specific to a particular line. Consequently, it is reasonable to ignore the allocation and overall control parts of the cluster and believe that there are actually 16 level II data transfer processors in each cluster. An outline of one of these conceptual cluster processors is given in Fig. V.10.

The cluster is a versatile piece of equipment. It is designed to control standard data communication lines and modems, handling all the grubby details of timing, synchronizing, etc., so that the DCP can concern itself with data in character form and the logical, rather than physical, control of the line. The algorithm followed by each data transfer task is determined by the current contents of some of the registers in its cluster processor, and the DCP controls each processor by loading its registers, which are thus rather like parameters to a built-in procedure.

The DCP has four instructions for handling the clusters (apart from the instructions which deal with the masking of cluster signals). Each instruction expects the register CA to have been already loaded with the name of a cluster

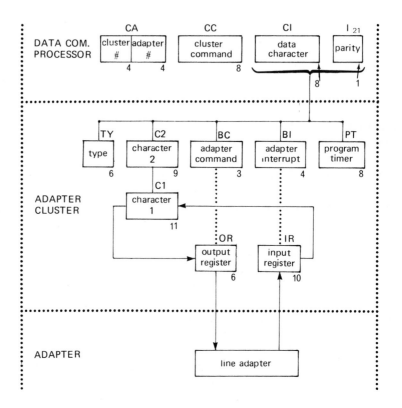

FIG. V.10. B6700 "line processor" (much simplified).

data transfer task in the form of a (cluster number, adapter number) pair, register CC to contain or receive control information, and CI to be used for a character of data (extended to another register I_{21} for a parity bit). One instruction "adapter write" transfers CI to the cluster processor registers selected by CC. Another instruction "adapter interrogate" reads into CI the register selected by CC. The other two instructions are non-specific reads which only transfer a data character from the cluster to CI when a task needs attention. These read instructions are "adapter read *if* needed", which also branches if a read is performed, and "adapter read *when* needed", which idles until attention is required.

One of the cluster processor registers (TY) specifies the type of the line being controlled. The one cluster can deal with tasks using automatic calling units, voice response devices, touch tone devices, synchronous lines of four standard types, and 15 varieties of synchronous line.

Each cluster processor includes a program timer which may be set by the DCP to time-out after a certain period. Three bits of the timer define its "tick time" and the other five its duration. By this means a time-out can be arranged to occur as soon as $1 \times 6 \cdot 4$ μsec has elapsed or may be left for as long as $30 \times 13 \cdot 421$ sec.

The main controlling parameter to the cluster processor is the 3-bit BC register. This may be set by the DCP to cause the cluster processor to transmit or receive a character, to idle, or to cause a break condition in the line. The BC register and others are de-coded to provide control signals for the adapter which is the level III processor in the hierarchy. The state of the adapter being controlled is maintained in the 5-bit BI register which, like the other registers, may be read by the DCP.

The last important register as far as the DCP is concerned is the character buffer C2 in which the DCP reads or writes the next character being transput. The cluster, when it needs, shifts the C2 character to/from the C1 register. C1 is a shift register used by the cluster for assembling single bits into characters or disassembling them into bits.

There are four events which can arise in a cluster data transfer task and cause the cluster processor to signal the DCP that it needs attention. When the DCP executes a cluster read in response to the call for attention, the cause is encoded and transferred to its register CC. The events are "data present", "control", "byte request" and "program timer". "Program timer", of course, signifies a time-out. "Byte request" indicates that C2 is empty when transmitting and "data present" that it is full when receiving. The "control" event indicates some change in status of the line—about 30 different conditions are recognized and may be distinguished by the contents of BC/BI which are transferred to C1 on the adapter read.

Finally to get down to the level of the line adapter. The cluster communicates to an adapter via a 6-bit output register and a 12-bit input register. What these are used for varies with the type and function of the adapter. Most adapters handle a bit of data at a time and, apart from one line each way for data, most of the lines between the adapter and cluster are used for control signals. The most usual adapters are for modem or direct connect lines.

V.2.4.   B6700 DISK FILE OPTIMIZER

The algorithms involved in controlling peripheral devices can be quite complex. In the past, with control logic being expensive, it was a sensible tradeoff to keep the hardwired peripheral controllers simple and perform as much control as possible from higher up the I/O processor hierarchy, even to the extent of controlling from the CPU. Nowadays control logic, in the form of micro-processors, is relatively inexpensive and it is more reasonable to make the control functions of the peripheral controller more complex and reduce the control burden on the more central processors. Once a peripheral controller contains a micro-processor it is reasonable to perform new control functions that were previously not feasible.

Disk storage controllers provide a good example. The control logic is necessarily complex for it must match a data address with the stage of rotation of the disk itself and initiate transfers at the appropriate time. It must also perform extensive error checking and correction in order to attain high storage densities. With micro-programmed control, in addition to the above functions, it becomes possible to perform a certain amount of content addressing—the controller can scan a given track for the occurrence of a desired key [10]. It is even possible to leave complete data access methods up to the controller and to make the disk fully associative.

Whether disks are conventionally or associatively addressed, they suffer from the delay of latency—the, on average, half revolution time which must elapse before information becomes available. In a multiprogramming system, the effective latency can be much reduced by, instead of performing disk accesses in the order in which they are generated, doing them in such an order that the next access performed requires the least delay. For this to be possible, the "re-orderer" must know the physical stage of rotation of the disks. As the disk controller already has that information, if it could handle multiple requests it could optimize the order in which they are performed. If disks, because of special requirements such as their speed, are handled by a special I/O processor, then it is quite logical to let the I/O processor perform the optimizing. Another possibility is to have the optimization performed by a lobe of the operating system executing in a central processor.

Disk access optimization could be performed by the operating system if it could interrogate each disk unit to find its rotational position in the same manner as any other I/O control operation. For this to be completely effective the operating system would have to be able to interrogate all disk controllers at all times. That is not possible if an I/O channel is unavailable or the controller is busy performing some other task; hence, if it is to perform disk access optimization the operating system must have a special direct connection to all relevant disk controllers. (It is feasible to perform disk optimization though with excessive overhead if the operating system remembers the last access made to each disk unit and, knowing the time that has elapsed since then, calculates its current position.)

With the B6700, in order to fit in with the I/O processor and fixed head disk controllers already in production, optimization had to be performed by the operating system. To provide the rotational position information, the basic disk controllers (called EU's—electronics units) are connected to a common bus. At any time, one of the EU's can be addressed and told to place onto the bus the rotational position (*shaft position*) of one of its disk file storage units (DFS—one EU may control up to five of them).

Rather than the CPU addressing the EU's directly, the whole task of optimizing disk accesses is left to a special hardwired processor called the disk file optimizer (DFO). The DFO is connected to the central processors via the scan bus, and to the EU's by the other bus just mentioned. In essence, the DFO accepts from the operating system information on disk access requests, it keeps track of these, and, when requested by the operating system, indicates which request will involve the least delay.

As seen in Fig. V.11, each DFO can communicate with two groups (A and B) each of up to 10 disk controllers (up to 100 disk storage units in all). Each group also shares up to four peripheral controllers through an exchange (only one PC is shown in Fig. V.11). The DFO maintains a stack of up to 32 control words (illustrated in Fig. V.12(a)), each of which describes a disk access. Each control word contains the DFO number, the shaft position required for the access and a reference value (link) for the operating system (usually the address of the corresponding IOCW). For each of the two groups of EU's, the DFO maintains a register giving the current least latency (*delta* A and B) and a pointer to the control word having that latency. The DFO continuously scans its stack of control words comparing desired with actual shaft positions. If the difference is less than the current delta but greater than a threshold value (chosen to give the operating system time to initiate an actual I/O operation), and the EU is not busy, then the appropriate delta is updated. In this way, the DFO always knows the best next disk access to perform for both of its two groups of disks.

The DFO accepts two scan-out commands (see Fig. V.12(b)). One is to clear its stack of control words and the other is to accept another control word from the scan bus. The control word (see Fig. V.12(c)) contains a BCD disk address;

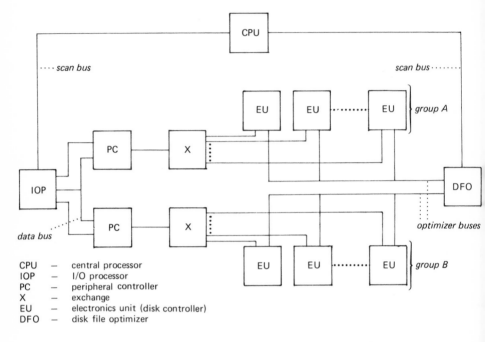

CPU — central processor
IOP — I/O processor
PC — peripheral controller
X — exchange
EU — electronics unit (disk controller)
DFO — disk file optimizer

FIG. V.11. Bus connections for a B6700 Disk File Optimizer.

this is converted to a shaft position by the DFO before insertion into its stack.

There are also three scan-in commands. One, the usual, is to supply the operating system with the optimal control word, which is then replaced in the optimizer stack by the top word in the stack (some stack!). Another scan-in is to read the top control word—successive applications of this command are used to gently empty the stack. The last scan-in, "status", returns a word giving the unit numbers of the exchanges and the actual capacity of the DFO stack.

The DFO is unusual in that it cannot interrupt or signal the operating system. Instead, when it notices a strange event, it tells the operating system when it is next requested to supply a control word. The control word as returned on the scan bus has a status field which may be used to indicate that an event has been noticed (see Fig. V.12(c)).

Finally, note that there may be two DFO's in any one B6700 system. Normally these look after separate groups of EU's but the two may be connected so that both have access to the same set of 40 EU's, some *directly* and some *indirectly*. The scan address recognized by a DFO may be the

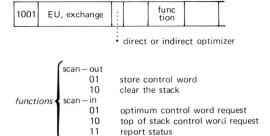

a)   control word in an optimizer stack

$$\boxed{1001}\ \boxed{\text{EU, exchange}}\ \vdots\ \boxed{}\ \boxed{\substack{\text{func}\\\text{tion}}}\ \boxed{}$$

⋮ direct or indirect optimizer

functions {
	scan − out	
	01	store control word
	10	clear the stack
	scan − in	
	01	optimum control word request
	10	top of stack control word request
	11	report status

b)   scan command words

$$\boxed{\qquad\text{link}\qquad}\ \boxed{}\ \boxed{\qquad\text{address}\qquad}$$

scan data to DFO

$$\boxed{\text{status}}\ \boxed{}\ \boxed{\quad\text{link}\quad}\ \boxed{\qquad\qquad}\ \vdots$$

scan data from DFO   ⋮ attention

status condition bits {
no access to OEX	—	EU not there or busted
SU not available	—	DFS didn't respond
OS parity error	—	error in DFO stack
disk address error	—	error in disk address/shaft position conversion
optimized control word	—	⎫
TOS control word	—	⎬ normal results
stack empty	—	no control words in stack
control word not available	—	all exchanges busy for required device

c)   scan data words

FIG. V.12. B6700 Disk File Optimizer details.

number of any one of its EU's—a special bit in the address is used to direct a scan request to the direct or indirect optimizer in the case of an EU optimized by both DFO's.

V.2.5.   B7700 I/O MODULE

The B6700 and its big brother the B7700 are for the most part two implementations of exactly the same architecture, the B7700 merely being designed to be faster. There are a few differences of detail, some of which we have already met, but the major architectural differences between the B6700 and the B7700 lie in the area of I/O. With the B7700, the I/O processor is not like that of the B6700 but is a much "higher level" processor called the I/O module (IOM).

The peripherals and other processors in the I/O hierarchy (PC, DCP and DFO) are the same for both the B6700 and B7700. The I/O system software is also the same down to the level of placing I/O requests in device queues. The essential difference between the IOP and IOM is that, in the B7700, the lowest operating system I/O functions (finding available channel paths, controlling the DFO and starting I/O operations) are handed over to the IOM rather than being executed by a CPU (CPM with the B7700). The B6700 IOP functions are also performed by the B7700 IOM. Thus, both systems do almost exactly the same operations but the division of labor among processors is changed.

That the IOM is really executing operating system algorithms is emphasized in the B7700 by the equal rank given to the IOM and CPM. Each processor, IOM or CPM, in a B7700 system is connected by an interrupt path to every other processor and any processor may direct an interrupt to any of the others (although the IOM and CPM do handle interrupts differently). The IOM is controlled (like the DCP) through queues in memory. There is only one interrupt accepted by the IOM and this causes it, when it is ready, to obtain a command from a fixed location in main memory. This command location (called a *home address*) is a fixed address initially but the address may be altered by the operating system.

As there is no scan bus for a CPM to control its DCP's this function is also left to the IOM (there is still a scan-in operation executable on a CPM but it may only be used to read the "time of day" clock built into the CPM of the B7700, rather than in the IOP as in the B6700). The IOM has *pseudo-scan buses* which it uses to send commands to the DCP and DFO in the formats that they expect.

We will now run through the commands that the IOM can be given at its home address (these are listed in Table V.3). The "DFO/DCP scan-out" and the "DFO scan-in" tell the DFO to send on the command to the appropriate processor. The IOM, when the system is loaded, is initially inhibited from performing any I/O operation. In this state, the operating system must

TABLE V.3

B7700 I/O Module commands.

DFO/DCP scan-out
DFO scan-in
synchronous I/O
activate IOM
inhibit IOM
set channel busy   } variants
set channel reserved
reset channel busy   } variants
reset channel reserved
load DFO flags
interrogate peripheral status
load unit table address
load I/O queue header table address
load status queue header address
start I/O

---

completely control I/O just as in the B6700—for this purpose the "synchronous I/O" command is used to force the IOM to initiate a single I/O operation. The IOM can be given control of I/O by using "activate IOM" and may be re-inhibited by "inhibit IOM". For purposes of maintaining and partitioning a large system, the IOM can be instructed to ignore any PC by using "set channel busy/reserved"—a process which can be reversed by the "reset channel busy/reserved" commands. Selected DFO's can be similarly ignored by use of the "load DFO flags" command. The "interrogate peripheral status" command is similar to that of the B6700 IOP; in this case the selected status vector is placed in the word next to the home address word (rather than on the CPU stack)—the same location is used for DFO scan-in data. The status change vector now includes indication of a DCP interrupt because there is no interrupt literal.

The four "load" commands alter the four addresses held local to the IOM (see Fig. V.13); these define the home address, the I/O system description, the current I/O queues, and the I/O results. The I/O system description and I/O queues are shared by all IOM's but each has its own home address and result queue (see Fig. V.13).

The configuration of the I/O system is defined by the unit table, in which there is one word for each peripheral in the system. The B7700 IOM is more transparent to the details of the peripherals than is the B6700 IOP and each unit table word contains information which would be built into the IOP. For example, each unit table word includes the channel address of the PC which controls the device (in some cases, where a device may be controlled by more

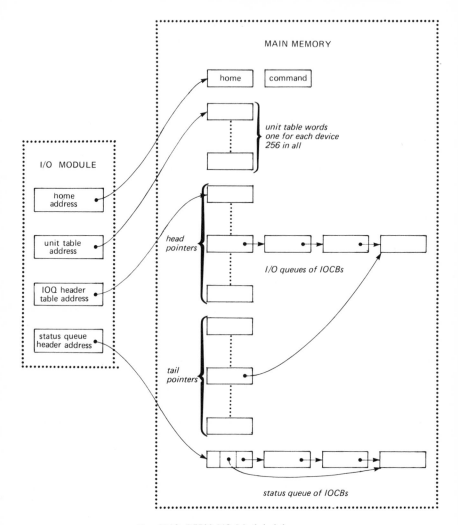

FIG. V.13. B7700 I/O Module job map.

than one PC, the range of channel addresses). If the PC which controls one device may also control others (the usual situation), the unit table words for all devices controlled by the PC are linked together (each has a pointer to the unit of lowest number, and a pointer to that of next highest number, except for the last in a group which is indicated by a special bit). Another bit in the unit table word can be used to tell the IOM that a disk I/O operation is to be optimized using the DFO's. The IOM may also alter the unit table to reflect information to the CPM—one bit is used to indicate that the unit is in use and a field is set to indicate which PC is being used (if the device may use one of a number of PC's).

While the unit table is, apart from a few status bits, static between reconfigurations of the system, the queues of I/O requests or commands for each device are very dynamic and are organized as linked lists. A request is defined by an I/O command block, as in the B6700, but of a different form. For each peripheral unit, there is one queue of IOCB's, the head pointer being at address "IOQ head table address" + "unit number", a tail pointer being at "IOQ head table address × 256" + "unit number", where "IOQ head table address" is the content of that register in the IOM. When the head pointer is zero, the queue has no entries.

The I/O unit queues contain the I/O operations which have not yet been dealt with by an IOM. IOCB's are placed at the tail of a queue by the operating system in a CPM but removed from the head of the queue and initiated by the IOM. The operating system only interrupts an IOM with a "start I/O" command (the last of Table V.3) if it inserts an IOCB into an empty queue (and the device is not busy), otherwise the IOCB is just linked onto the tail of the queue. The IOM, once started on a queue, initiates the queued commands one at a time until the queue is empty. As both an IOM and a CPM could try to access an I/O queue simultaneously, a lock bit is available in the corresponding unit table word and this always is "read with lock" before the queue is altered. It is possible, if more than one path exists to a device, for two or more IOM's to deal with the same queue.

The B7700 IOM is so designed that it can deal with all its peripheral controllers simultaneously; there can be as many "level I" tasks active as there are PC's—up to 28, in fact. (The B6700 IOP can handle 20 PC's but only 10 at once and even then it may not have the capacity to deal with 10 fast peripherals.) With the IOM, when a task finishes and consequently a PC, channel processor and device all become available, they may immediately be re-used if there is a relevant IOCB queued. The IOM will check the queue of the device for any entries, but if there are none, it will also go through the queues of every other device connected to the PC before letting the PC idle.

A disk unit which is having its requests optimized is treated specially. When a space is available in a DFO stack, the IOCB is de-linked from the queue and a DFO control word scanned out to a DFO. The control word contains the memory address of the IOCB so that the IOCB is not lost. When a PC for a disk becomes available, the IOM scans in a control word from the DFO and starts an I/O operation.

An IOCB contains six words preceding and contiguous to an I/O buffer area. These words are called "I/O linkage", "sidelink", "buffer descriptor",

"I/O control", "channel designate" and "result descriptor". The "I/O linkage" word contains the address of the next IOCB in the queue (or zero if it is the last) and also a bit indicating that the operating system should be interrupted when the operation is completed. The "sidelink" word can contain the address of an IOCB for a different device—when this operation is initiated the sidelink IOCB is placed into the appropriate queue (presumably this allows some temporal ordering of I/O operations for different peripherals). The "I/O control" word contains control information for the channel processor in the form of 12 bits of options much as in the B6700 IOP commands. The rest of I/O control is not used but orders for the device are placed in the next word—the "channel designate" word in *exactly* the form to be transmitted to the PC (not generated by the IOM which is transparent to such matters). The "buffer descriptor" word points to the data area which can thus be located remotely from the IOCB, but by convention it is adjacent. The "result descriptor" word is provided for the IOM to insert the result descriptor when the I/O operation is completed.

The result or *status* queue for each IOM is given by the "status queue header address" held local to the IOM. This points to the "status queue header word" which contains the head and tail addresses of the result queue. The IOM links an IOCB into the tail of the result queue when the operation it describes has been completed. The operating system removes the head of the queue, looks at the result descriptor and takes appropriate action (the SQH word also contains a lock bit). The IOM can cause two interrupts, "change of status" and "error". When an ordinary IOCB is linked into the queue an interrupt is not given if the queue is not empty, the "change of status" interrupt is given if the IOCB was placed into an empty queue or the IOCB link word demands that an interrupt be caused. The status interrupt is also given when the status change vector alters or when a DCP directs an attention signal to the operating system—these genuine status changes are distinguished by another bit in the SQH word—if it is on, then the operating system interrogates the status vector to see "what's up".

An ordinary device error does not cause an error interrupt but an error result descriptor is inserted into the unit IOCB which is then linked into the status queue. The IOM sets a bit in the unit table word to remind itself not to initiate further operations for that device until so directed by the operating system. The error interrupts are caused when a non-device-specific error occurs in the IOM. To handle these situations, the system maintains a queue of 10 dummy IOCB's for the mythical device number zero. When an error occurs, one of these is de-linked from the unit zero queue and placed in the status queue with an appropriate error result descriptor. The operating system is given an error interrupt and it finds a description of the error in the tail IOCB. Although the IOM does direct interrupts to the operating system, unlike the B6700, these are given to a specific CPM, the number of which is also in the status queue header.

The B7700 IOM is organized into much more clearly distinguished parts than the B6700 IOP (see Fig. V.14). One section called, for some obscure reason, the *translator,* receives the interrupts from a CPM, de-codes the home address commands and initiates channel operations. As well as a separate *memory interface unit,* the IOM has four data transfer sections. The first of

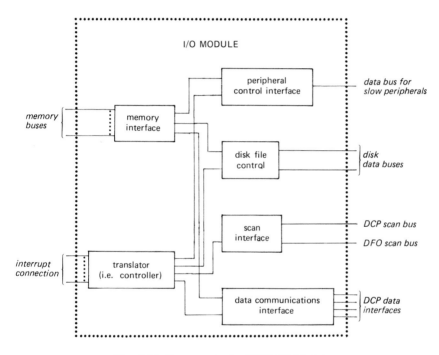

Fig. V.14. Components of a B7700 I/O Module.

these, the *peripheral control interface,* is very like the B6700 IOP channel controller; it allocates one "level I" processor and data bus to up to 20 tasks but only handles slow peripherals. The fast disk peripherals are handled by the *disk file interface*—this allocates two "level I" processors and data buses to eight tasks, providing double word data buffering for each task. Data traffic to/from up to four DCP's is passed through a *data communications interface* and scan commands for DCP's and DFO's are handled by a *scan interface.*

V.3. AVAILABILITY

Optimistically, most of our discussion up to this point has been made assuming that computers always operate correctly. Although we tend to brush aside such dismal details, things being as they are, the rate of occurrence of errors, and the computer system's behavior in the face of error, are of considerable practical importance. This is particularly true with systems supporting large data communications networks because all on-line users may be affected by any failure of the system.

Computer system attributes with regard to errors can make a quite complex topic, hard to pin down because it has both hardware and software aspects. However, systems may be roughly characterized under the following headings.

Reliability measures the system's failure rate. Failures may be caused by hardware or software and are of varying degrees of seriousness, running from failures that merely affect one user to those that crash the entire system. Hardware reliability is a function of hardware technology, care in design, extent of testing, and the provision in hardware for automatic correction of errors (error correcting codes, checks on arithmetic with automatic re-execution). Software reliability depends on care in design and de-bugging, extent of use and testing—"high level" hardware (for example, array bounds checking) as in the B6700 improves matters by catching errors early (even if they do no apparent harm). Software is used to improve hardware reliability by, for example, re-trying I/O operations or allowing check-pointing of program execution with later re-execution if necessary. Such use merges with the next topic.

Recovery from errors with minimal disruption to users is always a laudable goal. Excellence in recovery is sometimes referred to as a "fail-soft" characteristic. This is largely a software function but hardware architecture assists by catching errors early, specifying a cause of failure precisely, and allowing alternative access paths to data needed for recovery [10]. This last characteristic impinges on the next topic.

Availability measures the proportion of time a system may be used when it is needed. Any system or subsystem may be characterized at any time as being simply available or unavailable for use. However, there are degrees of availability, depending on how the performance of the system is degraded by the unavailability of non-critical components. High levels of availability may only be obtained from unreliable systems (into which class computers, alas, fall) by replication of critical components.

V.3.1. REPLICATION OF COMPONENTS

Information stored on I/O devices, such as disks, is only highly available if it is duplicated, either on another device of the same type, or backed up on a secondary, slower device—such duplication is a software function not of concern here. For our purposes, a system can be considered to have desirable high availability characteristics if no failure in any piece of hardware will cause the system to be entirely unavailable or lose the ability to access critical peripherals (other than the peripheral device itself failing).

The most direct approach to attaining high availability is to use *loosely coupled* multiprocessing, where two, otherwise independent, systems share peripheral controllers (and thereby peripherals) or front-end data communications processors. If one of the two systems fails, the other is still available to continue operation, albeit at a lower level of performance, while the failed system is repaired. If the hardware is reasonably reliable, and repairs are effected with dispatch, the odds are slim on the two systems being failed at the same time.

Loosely coupled systems are in wide use but do have some disadvantages. One disadvantage involves performance. Loosely coupled systems are not able to share work as readily as tightly coupled MP systems ("tightly coupled" being a common term for the type of multiprocessing we met in Chapter IV); furthermore, they run up overhead when the two operating systems contend for the use of their shared peripherals. Another disadvantage is that if any critical component of either system fails, that entire system is unavailable although most of its components are quite usable. This is more of a disadvantage to recovery than to performance because, even if all usable components are made available, the system is likely unbalanced (e.g. if one CPU fails it does not improve performance to have both IOP's available rather than just one).

The opposite extreme to loose coupling is illustrated by the B6700 approach, as illustrated in Fig. V.15. This is only a selected part of a larger system with just enough modules shown to illustrate a few points. (All unmarked paths are data paths except the IOP–PC connection which represents a direct path for control but a bus for data.) Any unit in the system of Fig. V.15 could be removed and the system would still be usable, indeed any one of each unit could be removed and the remainder would constitute a usable system.

The different peripherals of the I/O network (no longer a simple hierarchy) have differing availability characteristics. One card reader will be unavailable if the reader, its PC, or the IOP fails. A tape unit can become unavailable if it fails itself or an exchange fails, but alternate paths are available if a PC or IOP is busted. With the disks we reach the highest level of availability where the only

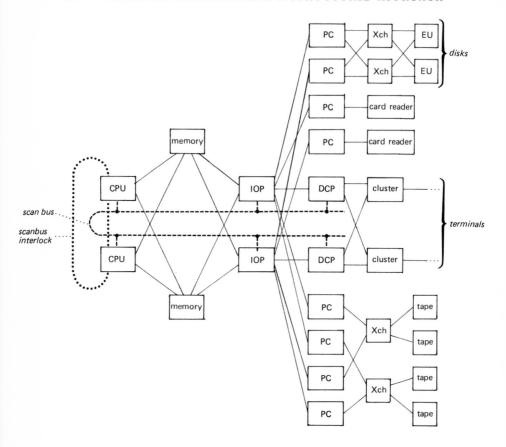

FIG. V.15. B6700 system with complete duplication.

single device, failure of which would deny the disk to the system, is the EU (disk controller—effectively the device itself). Note, in passing, that both disks and tapes may be accessed using more than one path—this improves performance by levelling the loads on IOP's as well as improving availability.

With multiple units of each type and multiple paths between them, the potential for high availability is there but the realization of this may not happen. System software can recognize and isolate some faulty components but not all; some will have to be dealt with externally by operator or engineer.

The B6700 operating system can collapse either aware that something has gone wrong or unaware of the fault (e.g. in a loop). In one case, the human operator is told of the fault; in the other, he recognizes it by the system's autistic behavior. At any rate, in both cases, the system is eventually re-loaded by performing what is called a *halt/load* or *warm start*. When it is re-loaded the operating system checks all the system memory and constructs links around any faulty modules. It also determines the system configuration and notices which devices are not there or not working.

In the above situations the software automatically partitions out a usable system; however, there are many faults from which the software cannot automatically recover. A halt load requires the use of the CPU with address 1, the IOP named A and the memory module that includes address 0. If any of these units are not available, then the system cannot get started unless other devices are given these critical names. Another problem is the scan bus interlock which contains a flying bit. If one CUP is not working then the bit will not necessarily be passed on by that CPU; hence the busted CPU must be bypassed. The same applies to IOP's which, if faulty, could make the scan bus unusable.

If a system with replicated components is to be reliable, there must be some way of quickly changing the configuration to remove faulty modules. Let us see how this is done with the B6700.

V.3.2. THE B6700 RECONFIGURATION SYSTEMS

An ordinary B6700 system may be reconfigured by a field engineer but only after some delay. To enable less specialized personnel to do reconfiguration, there is a B6700 option called the *Controlled Reconfiguration System*. This uses switches and interchangeable plugboards to allow fast changes of CPU, IOP and memory module addresses and routing of scan and scan interlock lines. As well as allowing faulty components to be removed, a controlled reconfiguration system can be split into two completely independent systems. This facility can be used, for example, to test experimental software on one system while providing a regular service on the other. It is expected that each half has an independent power supply and so can be switched off if necessary.

As the peripheral devices are all shared among the whole system, provision must be made to assign them to one side or the other. How this is done depends on the form of the connection. Some different methods are illustrated in Fig. V.16 for the system of Fig. V.15 (with unused connections removed). In the example, card readers are no trouble as each is connected to only one IOP. The adapter clusters only need to be switched by software to the appropriate DCP. The tape units are assigned by merely turning off two of the PC's which are then ignored by the simplex systems. The disk reconfiguration involves disabling one "port" of each PC and EU.

The time taken to reconfigure a system is only a matter of minutes (once the device at fault is determined). This may still be unacceptable and as a further alternative a faster *Dynamic Reconfiguration System* is available. This has the

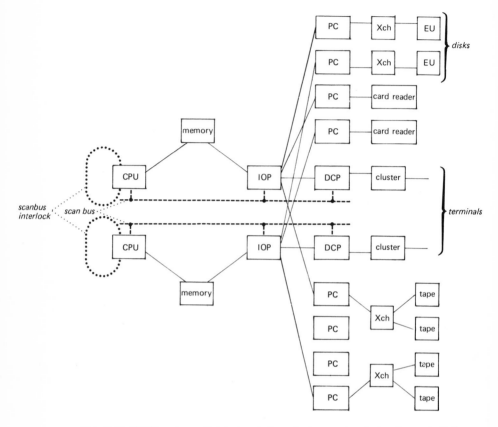

FIG. V.16. B6700 system split into two independent computers (using the controlled reconfiguration system).

same splittable features of the "controlled" system but also allows automatic selection of new configurations.

A dynamic reconfiguration setup is illustrated in Fig. V.16. The modules of the system are organized into *groups,* each with its own independent power supply. A group is usually a complete subsystem in itself. Groups are combined together as logical *teams* which are complete independent systems. There may be two teams, although parts of the hardware make provision for four groups which can be configured into up to four arbitrary teams.

Each group contains a *Redesignation Emergency Unit* (REU). This monitors its own group, and any other REU's in its team (to which it is connected), for signs of what is called *distress.* These omens indicate a crash and include:

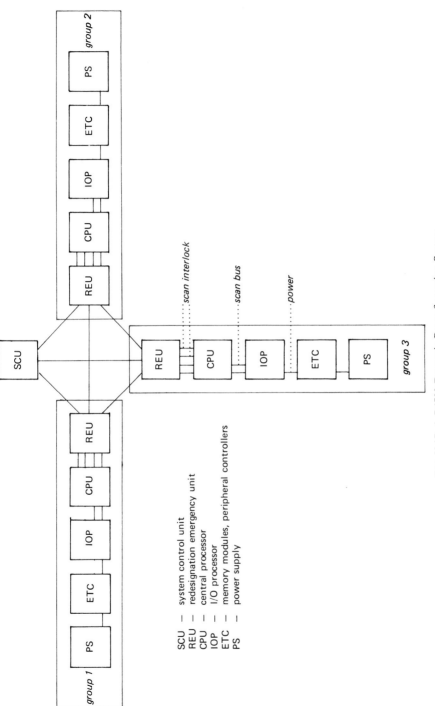

SCU — system control unit
REU — redesignation emergency unit
CPU — central processor
IOP — I/O processor
ETC — memory modules, peripheral controllers
PS — power supply

FIG. V.17. A B6700 Dynamic Reconfiguration System.

i. power failure in another group of that team;
ii. no CPU executing for the last 30 sec;
iii. a halt/load did not take place after 1 sec;
iv. a lost scan interlock bit;
v. a CPU in a recursive loop.

Another distress situation is the load control counter in IOP-A becoming seven—indicating that the operating system has tried seven times to recover from a fault but has failed.

When the reconfiguration emergency unit recognizes trouble, it notifies the *System Control Unit* (SCU). This device contains all the reconfiguration panels for controlled reconfiguration but, for dynamic reconfiguration, the SCU uses a 15-word plugboard read-only memory to define possible system configurations. When it is notified of a failure, the SCU reads the next configuration from its memory and sends that information back to the REU's. The REU's set up and check the new configuration and try another halt/load.

This process continues until a configuration is found which halt/loads successfully. Successive configurations change unit addresses or drop units or whole groups in a systematic order. When one configuration works, it is a safe assumption that a defective unit has been isolated—this can then be repaired off-line. If nothing works then there are two fall back configurations wired into the REU's—these may also be used if the SCU fails.

The example in Fig. V.17 shows a current maximum configuration but the dynamic reconfiguration system is designed to work with four groups. The Redesignation Emergency Units may be connected together, as shown in Fig. V.18, in a full 4-node graph. When a new configuration is required, the system control unit sends to each REU information as to what team it belongs to. The REU's independently contact others in their team and, by turning off some connections, set up (among other things) a circuit for the scan interlock bit—some example configurations are illustrated in Fig. V.17. The REU's check for impossible configurations such as there being no IOP-A in a team—such errors are also regarded as a case of distress.

V.5 NOTES

1. See, for example, Bartee, T. C. (1960 and later editions).
2. The tradeoffs have varied with time. Early computers, particularly those with no interrupt structures, tended to have expensive, sophisticated controllers and appear simple to CPU software. In machines of the B6700 time frame the device controllers tended to be simple with reliance on central control but, nowadays, with inexpensive micro-processors the control again tends to be distributed, though in micro-processor firmware rather than being hardwired.

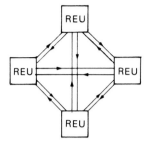

a) permanent connections between REUs

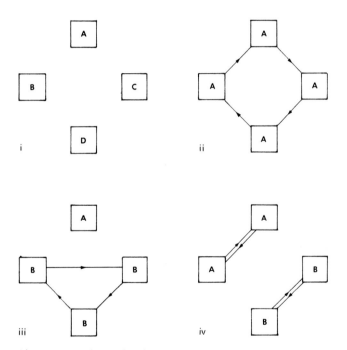

b) some example scan interlock connections

FIG. V.18. B6700 Redesignation Emergency Unit configurations.

3. Note that the B6700 is unusual in, in fact, wiring details of I/O devices into its I/O processor.
4. True for hardwired controllers. With devices that have micro-coded controllers it is not so unreasonable to move CPU function to the device, particularly activities (such as searching keys in a file) that are improved by real time control. The advent of inexpensive micro-processors is accelerating this trend.
5. The I/O path is certainly a channel for data flow and the name "data channel" or just "channel" reflects this view. Actually the term "subchannel" is often used for the level I data transfer processor or task, with "channel" being the processor that multiplexes the subchannels.
6. Although not usual, it is quite possible for a peripheral controller to be designed so that it can actually be transferring two records from different devices simultaneously. For our discussion we could consider such a processor as being a number of conceptual level II processors.
7. As is the case in some small computers, such as the DEC PDP 11.
8. As of 1975.
9. Exemplified by the IBM 3033 disk and its successors; see Ahearn, G. R., Dishon, Y. and Snively, R. N. (1972).
10. Hardware, if appropriately designed, can greatly assist in recovery from software failures. For an architecture designed for this purpose see Randell, B. (1975).

VI. High Performance

It is somewhat anomalous to leave until last the discussion of architectural features included in computers in order to make them faster. The very first computers incorporated devices specifically to make programs run more quickly [1], and since then there has been much more effort put into making computers faster than into any other aspect of their architecture (and much more written about it than anything else [2]).

The reason for our late discussion of performance is primarily that it involves a lower level of architecture. The previously discussed aspects— algorithms, data structures, operating systems and input/output—have to be understood by systems programmers in order for a computer to be used; such is not the case for most of the aspects of architecture that we will discuss that have been introduced to enhance performance. Furthermore, if a new architecture is being considered, its overall design, including its suitability for languages and operating systems, may contribute more to work performed than excessive attention to detail in the speed of execution of programs.

Be that as it may, there are a number of architectural tricks that are pervasive in computers in which high performance is a design goal. Section VI.2 below deals with such techniques used in computer memory and Section VI.3 with processors. Section VI.1 discusses performance improvement in general.

VI.1. PERFORMANCE IMPROVEMENT

There has always been a limited, but well-funded, market for a computer that can apply more power to a single problem than can easily be attained from the technology of the time. Correspondingly, there has been a succession of computers with interesting architectures designed to fill this need. We will not discuss such machines here, for they do not fall within the general purpose category—besides, because of their novelty, they have been well documented elsewhere [3].

In the commercial, general purpose, computing market, radical changes in computer architecture, to improve performance or for any other reason, have not been feasible for many years. The requirement that new machines not obsolete customer investment in software has restricted changes to being extensions of old architectures or, in the case of changes to improve performance, to being made at a lower level that is not visible to the system's programmer. Because the route to improving throughput by conceptual changes that fix recognized faults in an architecture has become blocked, methods for improving performance behind the architecture's "back" have assumed a great practical importance; it is such methods that this chapter discusses.

It is never a good policy for a performance-improving extension of an old architecture or of a new architecture to be visible to the programmer. As technology changes, what was once a help may become a hindrance kept only for compatibility with the past. An illustration of a feature which does not obey the rule is the set of general registers found in conventional machines. The general registers are thought of as a fast local memory and the systems and applications programmers have to go out of their way to make sure that the registers are used efficiently, although with small machines the registers may not be fast, and with large machines there is much more fast storage to be used than that supplied by the registers.

Contrast this with the B6700 stack speed-up mechanism which provides fast registers without altering the stack as seen by the programmer. Even if, as is ideal, speed-up features are not visible to the programmer, they are still subject to abuse. Unfortunately, if the programmer knows about the feature then it is always possible for him to make it work better by bending his program to suit its characteristics. This can be discouraged by ensuring that the speed-up device works so well without the programmer's knowledge that the returns to be obtained by tailoring programs are not worth the trouble.

Our main example for this chapter, the Burroughs B7700, a fast version of the B6700, illustrates the general points just discussed. The B7700 does have a few extra instructions but these are, in the main, minor improvements which do not obsolete old programs. The really big visible difference is the B7700 I/O module, but it will if necessary work like a B6700 I/O processor and when its full power is being used it mainly shifts the execution of part of the operating system from one processor to another. The other speed-up features work well without any alteration to programs [4].

When considered from a general viewpoint there are basically very few methods of making a computer faster without radically altering its architecture. A computer system consists of many interdependent units and if it is analyzed while working some units may be found that are causing more delay than others. If the system is too slow, then the first step towards its improvement is to locate these bottlenecks and, by some ruse or other, remove them. Of course, a particular design may be nearly perfectly balanced with no obvious single bottleneck (or with every part a bottleneck if viewed obtusely) but, because technology improves at varying rates for different devices, such is rarely the case for long.

A bottleneck caused by a particular device may be eliminated in a number of obvious ways:

    i. use a faster device;
    ii. do something else productive while waiting;
    iii. do not use the device so much;
    iv. use more than one device;
    v. use economical combinations of fast and slow devices.

The one significant new feature with these speed-up techniques is the use of parallelism [5]. In the next two sections we will see all the different approaches above being put into use, usually in combination with one another. The discussion will be oriented towards the B7700, which is a good example of most speed-up techniques, though we will have to refer to some other machines for a few features which the B7700 lacks.

VI.2.   THE MEMORY BOTTLENECK

The combined needs for storage of all users of a multiprogramming system at any time can be very large indeed. As we noted in Chapter IV it is always possible to provide storage of sufficient capacity, but, unfortunately, it is not feasible to provide sufficient storage with the most desirable properties. Storage that may be accessed quickly enough not to hold up the processors is too expensive and insufficiently dense to be provided in large amounts. Storage of sufficient capacity, e.g. disk storage, is too slow to be addressed directly by a processor. Consequently, most computers are provided with a main memory that is a compromise, being too small and too slow (often of access time about an order of magnitude slower than the processor cycle time).

We have already discussed the problem of main memory being too small. To recap briefly: Most data and code in active use is held in a large backing store, and whenever a task needs to deal with information thereon the operating system takes over and makes the information present, the task is put to sleep while it is waiting and the processor is used to perform some other task rather than remaining idle. If we were to regress to regarding the backing store as *the* main memory then this technique may be viewed as the use of a fast device to bypass a slow one, but, because the access times of main memory and backing store are so different (about four orders of magnitude), it is more usual to consider the backing store as solving the main storage capacity problem [6].

At the boundary between a processor and main fast storage there is less of a variation in speed; however, the discrepancy is still so great that much of a processor's time may be spent waiting for memory accesses. The multiprogramming technique outlined above, which here takes on the form of intermingling the execution of instructions of several programs, has been proposed but not yet implemented in any computer [7], one reason being that the expense of the storage within the processor for maintaining multiple program contexts has so far been too great. The difference in speed of operation of processor and main storage has to be overcome for a processor executing a single program. Solutions again lie in the use of very small high speed memories local to the processor and accessible at the processor's own rate of operation.

The delay caused by main memory is worsened with virtual memory where a number of memory references to descriptors may be required in order to track down the address of each virtual location. On the other hand, the problem is alleviated to a certain extent by carefully designing the processor so that the only references made to main memory are those which are absolutely necessary, i.e. the processor is provided with local memory (sometimes called *scratchpad* memory) which it uses for temporary specialized purposes. We have seen the examples of display or base registers used for shortening addresses. Instructions such as the B6700 VALC operator (illustrated in Fig. IV.15) reduce the number of memory references because they stand in place of complete subroutines, i.e. they may be viewed as micro-routines residing permanently in local memory—the use of micro-code to assist the operating system is another example of the same mechanism.

Even if the processor's implicit references to main storage are eliminated entirely, the program's explicit references must still be made. The obvious solution to overcoming the bottleneck of the program's references is to provide a small fast local memory for the programmer to load and use instead—such a local memory usually taking the form of a set of general registers. The use of such a local memory is contrary to our principle of keeping speed-improving devices invisible to the programmer, and, as we warned, may not optimize the use of the system as a whole. The programmer may, for example, not make the correct choice regarding what should be kept locally, but the whole local memory will have to be swapped when a processor changes contexts, thus unnecessarily increasing overhead. Local memory will be used optimally if it is used to contain locations that are actually referred frequently, not those that a programmer says will be used frequently.

The best use of local memory is then for it to be invisible to the programmer and for it to contain the most frequently referenced quantities. The ability to identify the most frequently referenced quantities depends on recognizing the patterns in which references are made. If the local memory is large and is capable of holding information from a large part of a program, or from several programs, then the predominant pattern is one of locality of reference. Large local memories that hold most recently referenced information are called *cache* memories and have become standard in large general purpose computers [8]. Unfortunately our example here, the B7700, is from an era when local memory was still rather expensive and relatively small. If the local memory is small, better use can be made of the memory if the finer patterns of its use are taken into account. The B7700 has three separate local memories designed to capitalize on the different access patterns detectable in three different circumstances in which memory is referenced, viz., for the program, transfers to and from the stack and for operands. We will discuss each B7700 mechanism in turn; although the use of special mechanisms is not currently standard, they are instructive because, as processor speed is improved relative to cache memory, the same technique as exemplified by the B7700 again comes into play to alleviate the bottleneck at the cache itself.

VI.2.1. PROGRAM BUFFER

The sequence of memory references needed to access a program follows an extremely simple underlying pattern in conventional computers. Instructions are obtained, one after another, from ascending addresses in memory. Unfortunately this sequence is broken by branch instructions, subroutine calls, and interrupts. These, particularly the branch instructions, occur rather frequently but the resulting disorder is compensated by a second pattern whereby many programs spend the bulk of their time executing tight little loops. Making use of the sequential pattern are *look ahead* devices which read program words before they are needed. The pattern of small loops is used in *look behind* devices which save instructions after they have been executed in case they are needed again.

The B7700 has a program buffer that is a fairly typical mixture of look ahead and look behind though its main emphasis is look behind. The device, much simplified, is illustrated in Fig. VI.1. The buffer consists of 32 words and thus, at an average of 3·5 instructions per word, may hold loops of over 80 instructions in length. Contained within the buffer is a copy of one section of the program being executed by the processor. The buffer is organized in a circular manner with that portion which contains the current program being between addresses BR and PWP with the corresponding main memory addresses being PLR and PUR–1. The word containing the instruction currently being executed is in the buffer at PB; there is no need to keep a

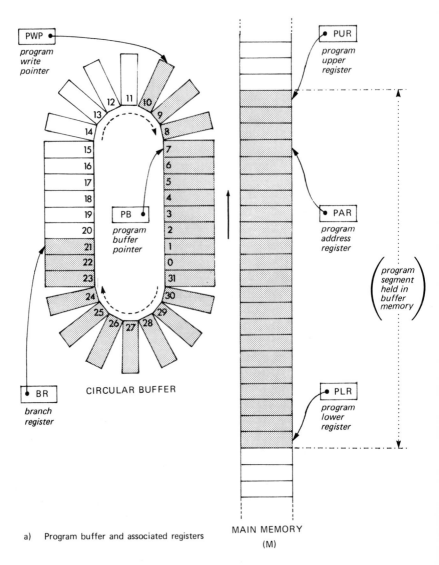

a)   Program buffer and associated registers

MAIN MEMORY
(M)

FIG. VI.1. B7700 program buffer (highly simplified).

corresponding main memory address as it is PLR + (PB–BR); however, it is pointed to by PAR when a branch is taking place.

The buffer starts empty with PB = BR = PWP = 0. PB "pushing" against PWP causes the next word to be fetched to the buffer. This continues until PWP "bumps" into BR, indicating that the buffer is full—BR is then incremented and words are lost from the buffer. In this way up to 32 words of the last program are kept in the buffer.

For a branch instruction the address of the destination word is placed in PAR. If this lies in the range [PLR, PUR] then the required word is in the buffer and may be fetched by re-setting PB appropriately and continuing. If the branch destination is outside the buffer then the buffer pointers are reset to empty the buffer and start the process of fetching and saving another part of the program.

The details of the B7700 program buffer are complicated by a couple of practical improvements. First, two program words are always read from the buffer because some instructions will lie across a word boundary. Secondly, rather than being organized on a simple word-by-word basis the buffer really consists of 4 blocks of 16 words where a block is fetched to, or deleted from, the buffer as a whole. This last feature gives the B7700 a certain degree of look ahead as up to 8 words ($8 \times 3 \cdot 5$ instructions) may be fetched before they are needed (the B6700 has a much more limited look ahead to the end of the current program word). Waiting would still be required before the first word of the next block arrived from memory, but this is taken care of by fetching a new block of two words before the last block is finished—all of which makes the buffer algorithms rather complex.

Simple look ahead schemes as in the B7700 quickly run foul of branches forward in the code. Some look ahead program buffers examine each instruction as it is fetched from memory and try to take sensible action if they encounter a branch. An unconditional branch usually causes the buffer to start fetching from the destination address but a conditional branch raises the quandary as to where the program will go. Some look ahead units give up and wait for the condition to be tested, others cover both possibilities by fetching instructions from the destination and current code stream, and others make a guess as to which way the branch will go. The guess is usually based on observed frequencies for different opcodes, although some computers attempt to remember where branches went previously as that is a good predictor of where they will go in future [9]. The B7700 makes no special allowance for branches in its 8-word look ahead, although a forward branch to within the 8 words will be serviced without going outside the buffer.

Note that, if a program can modify itself as it executes, the maintenance of a program buffer is made a lot more complicated. This adds to the many reasons for disallowing such a practice.

VI.2.2.   STACK BUFFER

The pattern of memory use for a temporary storage stack is simpler than that of a program stream, not suffering complications of the kind caused by branch instructions. We have already discussed the simple mechanism used in the B6700 where a local memory consisting of the two registers A (coupled with X) and B (coupled with Y) is used to hold the top of stack. The B7700 extends this by placing a 32-word buffer between the stack in memory and the top of stack items in its processor.

The stack buffer, again simplified, is shown in Fig. VI.2. As the stack is pushed down, words are placed into the buffer and when it is popped up they

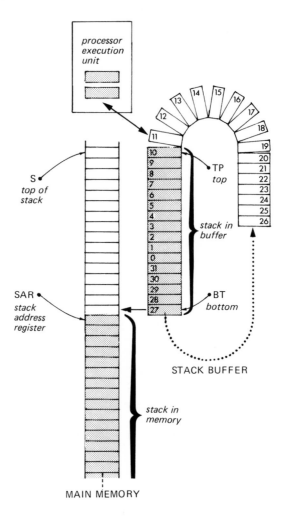

FIG. VI.2. B7700 stack buffer (simplified).

are taken from the buffer. In the case of pushing when the buffer is full the currently bottom location is written to memory and re-used at the top. In the case of popping when the buffer is empty, words are taken directly from the stack in memory—there is no attempt made to read words from the memory stack into the buffer before they are required. (Actually, words are read from memory in blocks of four, hence up to three words can be read ahead. The actual stack mechanism is more complex than just described in a manner analogous to the program buffer.)

If stacks were being used solely for temporary storage then the stack buffer would cause no problems; in fact, 32 registers would be rather excessive. However, the B6700 and B7700 use the stack for other purposes, particularly to hold more permanent information addressed relative to display registers, e.g. the parameters and local variables of procedures. These are initialized by being pushed into the stack and could well be in the stack buffer when referred to as operands. The B7700 therefore checks all memory references to see if they refer to items in the stack buffer and both fetches and stores may be made *in situ*.

Buffers containing data encounter a serious problem when multiprocessing is considered. Items in the buffer may be used and updated by more than one processor but the buffers are local to each processor. There must be some mechanism for ensuring that items held in the buffer of one processor accurately reflect the latest modifications made by other processors. Data in the stack buffer can be updated by storing, by using an address relative to a display register, or by being pushed into the buffer. The former method of modification applies to any operand buffer and the B7700 uses the same technique for both stack and operand buffer as discussed in the next section. Buffer integrity under the latter type of modification can be ensured by much more specialized mechanisms.

Two processors actively sharing a stack must be executing tasks that have a common ancestor or with one task being an ancestor of the other. If all data in the stack is pushed through to memory when the tasks are created then such information is never again popped back to the stack, or in the B7700 re-fetched to the stack buffer because there is no prefetch for popping. Hence software alone can ensure that items in the stack do not run into multiprocessing integrity problems. In the case of the B7700 the situation is complicated by the 4-word transfers that could cause up to 3 words to be fetched to the stack buffer that would possibly be copies of shared operands. The B7700 keeps careful track of such words. They are never read as operands (e.g. using VALC) from the buffer but are read from main memory. Stores into the possibly shared words are also made to main storage and the values in the stack buffer are never pushed through to main storage. Thus the possibly shared words are maintained with up-to-date values in main storage yet the values in the stack buffer are also correct in case they are not stored operands and eventually rise to the top of the stack (some optimizing compilers produce tricky code where temporary storage items pushed into the buffer are also referenced by display-relative addresses).

There are some instructions which require that the stack be entirely in main memory—MVST (move to a new stack) is the obvious example. When this instruction is encountered the buffer is unloaded back to memory before the instruction is executed. The same happens with SPRR (set processor register) which could alter the stack pointers. (Furthermore, all processors dump all buffers when RDLK is executed by any processor—see below.)

VI.2.3.   DATA BUFFER

The manner in which data is accessed exhibits two patterns. The *sequential* pattern, i.e. once an address is used there is a high probability of the next highest address being used soon, is a result of array processing, scanning of strings and files. The other pattern is *locality of reference* where there is a high probability of data just referenced being used again soon. These two patterns are somewhat contradictory but the latter is by far the most important. When the area of computation being observed is large, the sequential pattern is definitely a second order effect.

The locality of reference pattern also applies to references made for instructions and for stacks. Most computers, where large local storage is viable, combine the buffers for all three types of reference and concentrate on capitalizing on the locality of reference pattern. The most common mechanism is a "set associative cache" where the most recently referenced information is maintained. The secondary sequential pattern, incidentally also exhibited by instruction and stack references, is sometimes considered by prefetching information to the cache when the immediately preceding data is referenced. We will not go into the standard mechanism and its major variants here, suffice it to say that the mechanisms of the B7700 illustrate many of the ideas if not the details [10].

The B7700 only attempts to make use of the locality of reference pattern although it has an extremely small local memory and special hardware in the CPU for performing efficient sequential operations, vector mode and string scanning. The stack buffer already provides fast storage for the local variable to a procedure, no doubt those most likely to be referenced. The data buffer, see Fig. VI.3, or associative memory, therefore, is restricted to holding data referenced using an IRW (indirect reference word). This will preclude sequential string scanning data from being stored in the operand buffer.

The B7700 data buffer may hold up to 16 data words each of which is placed in the buffer along with its address. Along with each (address, data word) pair

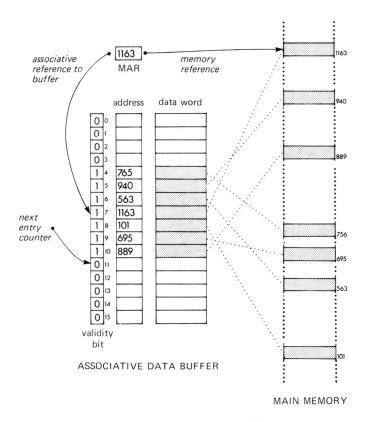

FIG. VI.3. B7700 associative data buffer.

there is a validity bit; these are all turned off initially to indicate that the buffer is empty. As accesses are made to memory a check is made by comparing the required address with all valid addresses in the buffer (an associative search) and making the reference to the buffer instead of main memory if a copy of that word is present in the buffer. A store is also made to main memory to ensure that it contains up-to-date information. If the required word is not in the buffer then the reference is made to main memory and in the case of a *fetch* the word is also entered in the buffer. This may require the deletion of something in the buffer if it is full. The B7700 simplistically chooses the item which has been in the buffer the longest, which it knows because the buffer is used in a circular fashion, rather than the more optimal choice of the least recently used item.

It can be noted at this stage how references following the sequential pattern vitiate the effect of the buffer at optimizing repeated references to the same location. Each address will be quickly pushed through the buffer; for example, with a program which passes sequentially through two arrays no entry in the buffer will remain for more than 8 cycles. This still may be a great improvement over having no buffer at all, and of course, the larger the buffer the less trouble the sequential effect will cause.

The B7700 solution to the multiprocessing integrity problem is to require use of shared areas to be signalled by execution of the synchronizing RDLK instruction. This causes all processors to be notified to empty their buffers and refer directly to main memory whence all information in the buffers will reflect the current values in main memory (and the synchronizing instruction will work correctly). Note that this solution is only viable with small buffers. More complex techniques are required if buffers are larger to avoid unnecessary purging of information [11].

A related problem when a processor has more than one buffer is that copies of the same address could get into each buffer. In the B7700, all references to data are made first to the stack buffer so that the stack buffer always contains the most up-to-date copy of a word.

VI.3.   THE PROCESSOR BOTTLENECK

If a processor makes use of buffer devices so that memory delays are so reduced that they are as infrequent as possible, then further increase in speed can only be obtained by improving the processor itself. If the technology and logical design are the best which are available then there is no other recourse than to alter the organization of the processor and to introduce parallelism. We will only dip deeply enough into this subject to outline the B7700's organization for the topic has been extensively described elsewhere.

VI.3.1.   THE PIPELINED PROCESSOR

In our description of memory buffer devices we still gave the impression that instructions were to be executed one after the other even though that was not completely the case because the fetching of instructions from main memory could be done before it was time to execute them and we considered such memory accesses as taking place in parallel with other instruction execution. Further progress requires that we recognize and accept that more than one instruction may be undergoing execution at the same time.

It so happens that most instructions go through a number of distinct steps when they are executed; the most obvious steps are:

i. fetch the instruction;
ii. fetch its operands;
iii. perform the operation;
iv. store the result away.

If these steps are performed by independent units then it is possible to process four (or more, if there are more steps) instructions at once, each at a different step in its execution. The model which springs immediately to mind is that of a production line or *pipeline* with instructions continually flowing past the devices, which execute each step.

The model, illustrated in Fig. VI.4 for the four steps listed above, shows each step executed by a separate processor with its own local memories. Instructions and data are passed down the pipeline with input queues to each processor in order to smooth the flow. Although the model is amazingly simple and easy to understand, it suffers from the defect that the real situation has a lot of complications. The worst of these is that execution steps of adjacent instructions are not necessarily independent.

There are some circumstances where the steps are completely independent. For example, in the CDC 6600 computer [12] there are 10 peripheral processors which have their instructions executed in 10 interleaved steps by one processor. The 10 instructions being executed at once are independent because they come from different programs. However, most computers

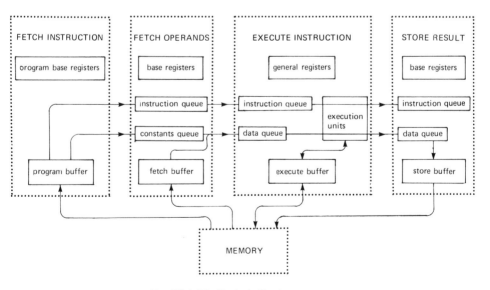

FIG. VI.4. Idealized pipelined processor.

execute only one program at once and within a single program there are usually many dependencies. Consider

$$A := B + C$$
$$D := A + E$$

where the fetch from A must be performed after the store into A, and

$$A := B + C$$
$$\text{if} \quad A > 0 \text{ then} \quad \text{go to } 1$$

where the branch cannot be made until the calculation is completed. These dependencies are overcome by imposing interlocks on the execution of instructions in the pipeline so that some instructions cannot proceed until others have finished. The control of the pipeline can be very complex.

The B7700 is pipelined and its solution to dependency problems is to arrange that all data accesses to memory take place in the program order, and to halt execution of conditional branches until the condition has been evaluated. The main change to overall pipeline organization is to introduce one unit, the *store unit*, which is responsible for all data fetches and stores. The reader is referred to Fig. VI.5 for the following discussion.

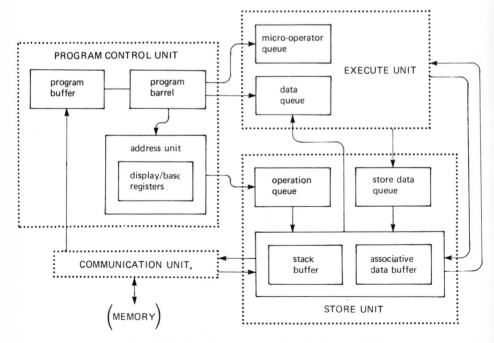

FIG. VI.5. B7700 Central Processor Module (highly simplified).

The first unit, the *program control unit,* contains the program buffer. Instructions are extracted from the program buffer and in a so-called *program barrel* are converted into sequences of smaller steps called micro-operators which are placed in the *micro-operator queue* of the execute unit. (Some adjacent instructions will be combined, e.g. NAMC, INDX becomes "LOAD and INDEX".) Relative addresses are converted into real addresses in the *address unit,* which contains display and base registers, and then placed in the *operation* queue of the *store* unit. The program control unit executes "literal call" instructions and places the constant operands in the *data queue* of the execute unit. Conditional branch instructions cause a hiatus in the issuing of micro-operators until the last instruction before the branch has been executed. The program unit can ask the execution unit to notify it when any particular micro-operator has been completed.

The store unit handles all memory data accesses. Most requests come from the program control unit but the execution unit can obtain priority for the operation queue for its own special memory references, for example, when chasing pointers in a link list look up operation. The storage unit must wait for the execution unit to provide data for a store operation. Otherwise accesses in the operation queue are performed in the specified order as quickly as possible. Data read from memory is placed into the data queue of the execute unit. This last unit receives entries from both the program control unit and the store unit. To ensure that the data items are not misordered, the program control unit reserves a place in the data queue for every data fetch and the identification of the place is carried through the operation queue enabling the store unit to place the data from memory into the correct place in the data queue.

The execution unit works on its micro-operator queue and data queue executing each micro-operator in turn. When results are to be stored they are placed in the store data queue of the store unit, the store taking place when that request reaches the end of the operation queue. The execute unit has its own temporary memory for the top of stack registers and other intermediate results.

Another complication with the pipeline model is that almost any instruction can cause an error interrupt. If a fault does occur it would be nice to know which of the instructions caused the trouble. Some machines have accepted imprecision in their interrupts which can thus only identify the approximate location of an instruction which causes a fault. The B7700 gets around this by carrying through the pipeline the address of the instruction from which each micro-operator originated. An associated problem is that partially executed instructions may have caused some effect on the environment which, according to the sequential definition of the machine, should not have happened. Some machines have attempted to unexecute instructions and others just accept this problem as well. It does not happen with the B7700 because only one instruction performs an operation at any time.

VI.4.   NOTES

1. The index registers on early computers were primarily a performance-improving device though other applications became equally important.
2. The *ACM Computing Surveys Journal* **9** (1), March 1977, special issue devoted to "Parallel Processors and Processing", contains survey papers on various types of fast computer.
3. Kuck, D. J. (1977).
4. However, it is possible to generate code that takes advantage of quantitative features of the B7700 design—the B6700/B7700 computers have selectable "B7700" options.
5. A good introduction and survey of the use of parallelism is provided by Lorin, H. (1972).
6. Some older computers, IBM 650 being the most widely used, addressed a rotational backing store as the main memory.
7. Flynn, M. J. (1972).
8. Cache memories are termed "slave stores" in British terminology (Wilkes, M. V., 1965). They first saw wide use in the IBM System/360–370 machines starting with the model 85—Conti, C. J., Gibson, D. H. and Pitkowsky, S. H. (1968).
9. Used in the Manchester University MU5—Ibbett, R. N. (1972).
10. The data buffer described here is that of early models of the B7700. Later models have a much more conventional set-associative cache containing 1024 words (6K bytes) of data.
11. Tang, C. K. (1976).
12. Thornton, J. E. (1970).

References

Abrams, P. S. (1970). An APL Machine: technical report no. 3. Stanford Laboratories SU-SEL-70-017.

Ahearn, G. R., Dishon, Y. and Snively, R. N. (1972). Design innovations of the IBM 3830 and 2835 storage control units. *IBM Journal of Research and Development* **16** (1), 11–18.

Aiken, H. H. and Hopper, G. M. (1946). The automatic sequence controlled calculator. *Electrical Engineering* **65**, 384–391, 449–454, 552–558. (Reprinted in Randell (1973), *vide infra.*)

Allen, J. (1978). "The Anatomy of LISP." McGraw-Hill, New York.

Allmark, R. H. and Lucking, J. R. (1962). Design of an arithmetic unit incorporating a nesting store. *Proceedings of the IFIP Congress, 1962*, pp. 694–698. (Reprinted in Bell and Newell (1971), *vide infra.*)

Amdahl, G. M., Blaauw, G. A. and Brooks, F. P. (1964). Architecture of the IBM System/360. *IBM Journal of Research and Development* **8** (2), 87–101.

Anderson, J. P., Hoffman, S. A., Shifman, J. and Wilkes, R. J. (1962). D825—a multiple computer system for command control. *Proceedings of the Fall Joint Computer Conference*, **22**, 86–96. (Reprinted in Bell and Newell (1971), *vide infra.*)

Barron, D. W. (1977). "An Introduction to the Study of Programming Languages." Cambridge University Press, Cambridge.

Bartee, T. C. (1960). "Digital Computer Fundamentals." McGraw-Hill, New York.

Barton, R. S. (1961). A new approach to the functional design of a digital computer. *Proceedings of the Western Joint Computer Conference, 1961*, pp. 393–396.

Barton, R. S. (1970). Ideas for computer systems organization—a personal survey. *In* "Software Engineering" (J. T. Tou, ed.). Academic Press, New York and London, pp. 7–16.

Bashe, C. J., Buchholz, W. and Rochester, N. (1954). The IBM type 702, an electronic data processing machine for business. *Journal of the Association for Computing Machinery* **1** (4), 149–169.

Bauer, W. F. (1968). Computer communications systems: patterns and prospects. *In* "Computers and Communications: Toward a Computer Utility" (F. J. Gruenberger, ed.). Prentice-Hall, Englewood Cliffs, N.J., pp. 13–36.

Belady, L. A. and Kuehner, C. J. (1969). Dynamic space sharing in computer systems. *Communications of the Association for Computing Machinery* **12** (5), 282–288.

Bell, C. G. and Newell, A. (1971). "Computer Structures." McGraw-Hill, New York.

Bell, G., Cady, R., McFarland, H., Delagi, B., O'Laughlin, J. and Noonan, R. (1970). A new architecture for minicomputers, the DEC PDP-11. *Proceedings of the Spring Joint Computer Conference*, **36**, 657–675.

Berkling, K. J. (1971). A computing machine based on tree structures. *IEEE Transactions on Computers* **20** (4), 404–418.

Bulman, D. M. (1977). Stack computers. *Computer* **10** (5), 14–16.

Burks, A. W., Goldstine, H. H., and von Neumann, J. (1946). Preliminary discussion of the logical design of electronic computing instrument. Report to the Ordnance Department, U.S. Army. (Reprinted in Bell and Newell (1971), *vide supra*.)

Burroughs (1968). "Burroughs B5500 Information Processing Systems Reference Manual," Form 1021326.

Burroughs (1969). "Burroughs B6700 Information Processing System Reference Manual," AA119114, AA190266.

Carlson, C. B. (1963). The mechanization of a push down stack. *Proceedings of the Eastern Joint Computer Conference, 1963*, p. 243.

Carlson, C. R. (1975). A survey of high level language computer architecture. In "High-Level Language Computer Architecture" (Y. Chu, ed.). Academic Press, New York and London, pp. 31–62.

Carpenter, B. E. and Doran, R. W. (1977). The other Turing machine. *Computer Journal* **20** (3), 269–279.

Chu, Y. (ed.) (1975). "High-Level Language Computer Architecture." Academic Press, New York and London.

Cleary, J. C. (1969). Process handling on Burroughs B6500. *Proceedings of the 4th Australian Computing Conference, 1969*, pp. 231–239.

Coffman, E. G. Jr. and Denning, P. J. (1973). "Operating Systems Theory." Prentice-Hall, Englewood Cliffs, N.J.

Conti, C. J., Gibson, D. H., and Pitkowsky, S. H. (1968). Structural aspects of the System 360 model 85. 1. General organization. *IBM Systems Journal* **7** (1), 2–14.

Cosserat, D. C. (1972). A capability oriented multi-processor system for real-time applications. Paper presented at an international conference on "Computer Communications," Washington, D.C., October 1972.

Davis, G. M. (1960). The English Electric KDF9 computer system. *Computer Bulletin*, **4** (12), 119–120.

Dijkstra, E. W. (1960). Recursive programming. *Numerical Mathematics* **2**, 312–318.

Doran, R. W. (1972). A computer organization with an explicitly tree-structured machine language. *Australian Computer Journal* **4**, 21–30.

Doran, R. W. (1975). The architecture of stack machines. *In* "High-Level Language Computer Architecture" (Y. Chu, ed.). Academic Press, New York and London, pp. 63–109.

Doran, R. W. (1976). The ICL2900 computer architecture. *Computer Architecture News*, September 1976, pp. 24–47.

Feustal, E. A. (1973). On the advantages of tagged architecture. *IEEE Transactions on Computers* **22** (7), 643–656.

Flynn, M. J. (1972). Toward more efficient computer optimizations. *Proceedings of the Spring Joint Computer Conference, 1972*, pp. 1211–1217.

Griswold, R. E., Poage, J. F. and Polansky, I. P. (1971). "The Snobol 4 Programming Language." Prentice-Hall, Englewood Cliffs, N.J.

Gruenberger, F. J. (ed.) (1968). "Computers and Communications: Toward a Computer Utility." Prentice-Hall, Englewood Cliffs, N.J.

Hansen, P. B. (1973). "Operating System Principles." Prentice-Hall, Englewood Cliffs, N.J.

Hauck, E. A. and Dent, B. A. (1968). Burroughs' B6500/B7500 stack mechanism. *Proceedings of the Spring Joint Computer Conference, 1968*, pp. 245–251.

Herwitz, P. S. and Pomerere, J. H. (1960). The Harvest system. *Proceedings of the Western Joint Computer Conference, 1960*, pp. 23–32.

Hoare, C. A. R. (1975). Data reliability. Paper presented at the international conference on "Reliable Software," 21–23 April 1975. IEEE Catalog No. 75 CHO 940-7C SR, pp. 528–533.

Hoare, C. A. R. and McKeag, R. M. (1972). Store management techniques. *In* "Operating Systems Techniques," APIC Studies in Data Processing No. 9 (C. A. R. Hoare and R. H. Perrot, eds). Academic Press, New York and London, pp. 117–151.

Huxtable, D. H. R. and Pinkerton, J. M. M. (1977). The hardware/software interface of the ICL2900 range of computers. *Computer Journal* **20** (4), 290–295.

Ibbett, R. N. (1972). The MU5 instruction pipeline. *Computer Journal* **15** (1), 43–50.

Ibbett, R. N. and Capon, P. C. (1978). The development of the MU5 computer system. *Communications of the Association for Computing Machinery* **21** (1), 13–24.

IBM (1974). "IBM System/370 Principles of Operation," 4th ed., Doc. GA22-7000-4.

Iliffe, J. K. (1968). "Basic Machine Principles." American Elsevier, New York.

Iliffe, J. K. and Jodeit, J. G. (1962). A dynamic storage allocation system. *Computer Journal* **5**, 200–209.

Ingerman, P. (1961). Thunks. *Communications of the Association for Computing Machinery* **4**, 55–58.

Keedy, J. L. (1977). An outline of the ICL2900 series system architecture. *Australian Computer Journal* **9** (2) 53–62.

Kilburn, T., Morris, D., Rohl, J. S. and Sumner, F. H. (1968). A system design proposal. *IFIPS Congress Proceedings, 1968*, pp. 806–811.

Knuth, D. E. (1968). "The Art of Computer Programming, Vol. 1, Fundamental Algorithms." Addison-Wesley, Reading, Mass.

Kuck, D. J. (1977). A survey of parallel machine organization and programming. *Computing Surveys* **9** (1), 29–59.

Lavington, S. H. (1975). "A History of Manchester Computers." National Computing Centre Publications, Manchester.

Lavington, S. H. (1978). The Manchester Mark I and Atlas: a historical perspective. *Communications of the Association for Computing Machinery* **21** (1), 4–12.

Leiner, A. C. (1954). System specifications for the DYSEAC. *Journal of the Association for Computing Machinery* **1**, 57.

Linsey, C. H. (1971). Making the hardware suit the language. *In* "Algol 68 Implementation" (J. E. L. Peck, ed.). North Holland, Amsterdam, pp. 347–365.

Lorin, H. (1972). "Parallelism in Hardware and Software: Real and Apparent Concurrency." Prentice-Hall, Englewood Cliffs, N.J.

Lukasiewicz, J. (1929). "Element logiki mathematycznej." Moscow. (Republished in translation as "Elements of Mathematical Logic". Pergamon Press, Oxford and New York, 1963.)

McKeeman, W. M. (1975). Stack computers. *In* "Introduction to Computer architecture" (H. S. Stone, ed.). Science Research Associates, Chicago, pp. 281–316.

Mersel, J. (1956). Program interruption on the Univac scientific computer. *Proceedings of the Western Joint Computer Conference, 1956*, pp. 52–53.

Minsky, M. L. (1967). "Computation—Finite and Infinite Machines." Prentice-Hall, Englewood Cliffs, N.J.

Organick, E. I. (1972). "The MULTICS System." MIT Press, Cambridge, Mass.

Organick, E. I. (1973). "Computer Systems Organization—the B6700/B7700 Series." Academic Press, New York and London.

Randell, B. (ed.) (1973). "The Origins of Digital Computers—Selected Papers." Springer Verlag, Berlin, Heidelberg, and New York.

Randell, B. (1975). System structure for software fault tolerance. *IEEE Transactions on Software Engineering* **SE1** (2), 220–232.

Randell, B. and Russell, L. J. (1964). "Algol 60 Implementation." Academic Press, New York and London.

Redmond, K. C. and Smith T. M. (1977). Lessons from "Project Whirlwind." *IEEE Spectrum*, October 1977, pp 50–59.

Russell, R. M. (1978). The CRAY-1 computer system. *Communications of the Association for Computing Machinery* **21** (1), 63–72.

Schroeder, M. D. and Saltzer, J. H. (1972). A hardware architecture for implementing protection rings. *Communications of the Association for Computing Machinery* **15**, 157–170.

Shankar, K. S. (1977). The total security problem: an overview. *Computer*, June 1977, pp. 55–62.

Shapiro, M. D. (1972). A SNOBOL machine: a higher-level language processor in a conventional hardware framework. *COMPCON Digest, 1972*, pp. 41–44.

Shaw, A. C. (1974). "The Logical Design of Operating Systems." Prentice-Hall, Englewood Cliffs, N.J.

Simon, H. A. (1969). "The Sciences of the Artificial." MIT Press, Cambridge, Mass.

Tang, C. K. (1976). Cache system design in the tightly coupled multiprocessor system. *Proceedings of the National Computer Conference, 1976*, pp. 749–753.

Thornton, J. E. (1970). "Design of a Computer—the Control Data 6600." Scott-Foresman, New York.

Tomasulo, R. M. (1967). An efficient algorithm for exploiting multiple arithmetic units. *IBM Journal of Research and Development* **11** (1), 25–33.

Tsichritzis, D. C. and Bernstein, P. A. (1974). "Operating Systems." Academic Press, New York and London.

Turing, A. M. (1945). Proposals for development in the Mathematics Division of an automatic computing machine (ACE). Report E882. Executive Committee. NPL. (Reprinted in April 1972 with a foreword by D. W. Davies as *NPL Report Com. Sci. 57.*)

von Neumann, J. (1945). First draft of a report on the EDVAC (30 June, 1945). Contract no. W-670-ORD-4926. Moore School of Electrical Engineering. University of Pennsylvania. (Extracts included in Randell (1973), *vide supra.*)

Wilkes, M. V. (1965). Slave memories and dynamic storage allocation. *IEEE Transactions on Electronic Computers* **14** (2), 270–271.

Wilkinson, J. H. (1954). The pilot ACE. *In* "Automatic Digital Computation. Proceedings of a Symposium held at NPL, 25–29 March 1953." HMSO, London. (Reprinted in Bell and Newell (1971), *vide supra.*)

Wilkinson, J. H. (1975). The pilot ACE at the National Physical Laboratory. *Radio*

Wilner, W. T. (1972). Burroughs' B1700 memory utilization. *Proceedings of the Eastern Joint Computer Conference, 1972*, pp. 579–586.

Wilner, W. T. (1974). Structured programs, arcadian machines and the Burroughs' B1700. *Lecture Notes in Computer Science* **7**, 139–142.

Index of B6700/B7700 Terms and Features

Note that instructions are listed by mnemonic only, the full names of instructions are given in the text. The mnemonics of string processing, decimal and vector mode instructions are not included—see Tables III.3, III.4 and III.5

General Subject Index